D1542729

STATES, MARKETS, FAMILIES

Gender, Liberalism and Social Policy
in Australia, Canada, Great Britain
and the United States

The 1990s have seen dramatic restructuring of state
social provision in the US, the UK, Canada and Australia. This important book examines the impact of
changes in social policy regimes on gender roles and
relations. Structured thematically and systematically
comparative, it analyses three key policy areas: labour
markets, income maintenance, and reproductive rights.
Largely driven by issues of equality, it considers the role
of the state as a site for gender and sexual politics at a
time when primacy is given to the market, developing
an argument about social citzenship in the process.
Three eminent scholars – Julia S. O'Connor, Ann
Shola Orloff and Sheila Shaver – make a landmark
contribution to debates about social policy and gender
relations in this era of economic restructuring and
deregulation.

Julia S. O'Connor is Director of the National Economic
and Social Council in Dublin. She is on leave of absence
from McMaster University in Canada. She is the author
of *From Women in the Welfare State to Gendering Welfare
State Regimes* (1996). **Ann Shola Orloff** is Professor of
Sociology at Northwestern University, Illinois. She is the
author of *The Politics of Pensions: A Comparative Analysis
of Britain, Canada and the United States, 1880–1940*
(1993). **Sheila Shaver** is Deputy Director of the Social
Policy Research Centre, University of New South Wales
in Sydney. Her publications include *Universality and
Selectivity in Income Support to the Aged* (1997). Each has
published widely in the field of social policy.

In memory of our parents
Sheila Allen and Batt O'Connor
Kathleen and Edgar Orloff
Margaret Gibson and Max M. Shaver

STATES, MARKETS, FAMILIES

Gender, Liberalism and Social Policy
in Australia, Canada, Great Britain and the
United States

JULIA S. O'CONNOR,
ANN SHOLA ORLOFF
and SHEILA SHAVER

CAMBRIDGE
UNIVERSITY PRESS

PUBLISHED BY THE PRESS SYNDICATE OF THE UNIVERSITY OF CAMBRIDGE
The Pitt Building, Trumpington Street, Cambridge, United Kingdom

CAMBRIDGE UNIVERSITY PRESS
The Edinburgh Building, Cambridge CB2 2RU, UK   http://www.cup.cam.ac.uk
40 West 20th Street, New York, NY 10011–4211, USA   http://www.cup.org
10 Stamford Road, Oakleigh, Melbourne 3166, Australia

© Julia S. O'Connor, Ann Shola Orloff and Sheila Shaver 1999

First published 1999

Printed in Singapore by Kin Keong Printing Co. Pte Ltd

Typeset in New Baskerville 10/12 pt

A catalogue record for this book is available from the British Library

National Library of Australia Cataloguing in Publication data
O'Connor, Julia Sila, 1947–   .
States, markets, families: gender, liberalism and social policy
in Australia, Canada, Great Britain and the United States.
Bibliography.
Includes index.
ISBN 0 521 63092 4.
ISBN 0 521 63881 X (pbk).
1. Sex role – Australia. 2. Sex role – Canada. 3. Sex role
– Great Britain. 4. Sex role – United States. 5. Family
policy – Australia. 6. Family policy – Canada. 7. Family
policy – Great Britain. 8. Family policy – United States.
9. Australia – Social policy. 10. Canada – Social policy.
11. Great Britain – Social policy – 1979–   . 12. United
States – Social policy – 1993–   . I. Orloff, Ann Shola. II. Title.
361.612

Library of Congress Cataloguing in Publication data
O'Connor, Julia S. (Julia Sila), 1947–   .
States, markets, families: gender, liberalism, and social policy
in Australia, Canada, Great Britain, and the United States/Julia
S. O'Connor, Ann Shola Orloff, and Sheila Shaver.
p.   cm.
Includes bibliographical references and index.
ISBN 0-521-63092-4 (hardcover: alk. paper).
ISBN 0-521-63881-X (pbk.: alk. paper).
1. Social policy. 2. Women – Government policy. 3. Liberalism.
4. Social planning. 5. Public welfare. I. Orloff, Ann Shola.
II. Shaver, Sheila. III. Title.
HN17.5.O258   1999
361.6′1–dc21   98–25258
                                                           CIP

ISBN 0 521 63092 4 hardback
ISBN 0 521 63881 X paperback

Contents

Tables

Acknowledgements

This project has been part of our lives for a long time. As an international collaboration, it has been particularly challenging, and the authors wish above all to thank one another for the stimulation and mutual support that has seen it through to completion.

Not least of the challenges of the project has been how three authors, spread across at least two and often three continents, might get together for the live argument about ideas, theories and methodological issues that even the miracle of email does not allow. We have very real debts to international meetings and research funding arrangements which have helped to support our work. The idea for the project was born when Ann Orloff and Sheila Shaver met at a conference on Women in the Welfare State at the University of Wisconsin in 1989, and it became a reality when Julia O'Connor joined at a meeting of the American Sociological Association a year later. The annual meetings of the International Sociological Association's Research Committee on Poverty, Social Welfare and Social Policy (RC19) served as our point of rendezvous and its members as a source of comment on and critique of our arguments in the years thereafter. The first versions of several parts of the book were first presented in this forum. Walter Korpi was President of RC19 until July 1994. His influence on comparative welfare state research is inestimable. His encouragement of this project is acknowledged with gratitude. We are pleased to acknowledge the equally generous support of Stein Ringen who took over from Walter as President of RC19 and who at an early stage in the project provided us with the space at Oxford University for a three-day meeting. We also thank Julia Adams, Edwin Amenta, Jane Collins, Robert Goodin, Jane Lewis, Rianne Mahon, Jane Millar, Jill Quadagno, Anne Showstack Sassoon, and Fiona Williams for reading part or all of the manuscript and offering suggestions, comments and corrections. Of course, we are responsible for imperfections that remain. At various times, we also received helpful advice and statistical data from Deborah Mitchell, Tim Smeeding, Lee Rainwater, Joakim Palme and Janet Gornick.

Other bodies provided support enabling Julia O'Connor and Ann Orloff to spend periods in Australia researching Australian social policy and getting to know Australian scholars. Julia O'Connor and Sheila Shaver would like to thank the International Council for Canadian Studies for a grant through its Programme for International Research Linkages enabling them to meet with a wider group of Canadian and Australian colleagues in Sydney in 1993. Ann Orloff much appreciates the opportunity to visit and teach at the Royal Melbourne Institute of Technology. Both Julia O'Connor and Ann Orloff benefited from periods at the Australian National University through fellowships provided under the Reshaping Australian Institutions program of its Research School of Social Sciences.

Of course we also have individual debts. Julia O'Connor acknowledges with gratitude the financial assistance of the Arts Research Board, McMaster University and the Canadian Social Science and Humanities Research Council (grant 410-91-0976). She acknowledges the excellent research assistance of Ruth Frater, Jim Mulvale and Aisling Byrne and the administrative support of Tracy Curran. She thanks family and friends for support and encouragement.

Ann Orloff received research support from the German Marshall Fund of the United States, the Research Committee of the Graduate School and the Women's Studies Research Center, both at the University of Wisconsin–Madison, and from a Canadian Studies Faculty Research Grant. She thanks Kathrina Zippel for excellent and efficient research assistance; Steve Halebsky, Greg Maney, Renee Monson, Matt Sloan and Alan Silver also provided help in locating library, electronic and newspaper materials. Julia Perry and Joan Corbett of the Australian Department of Social Security graciously provided very useful materials. She warmly acknowledges the support of Paul and Joanne Moskowitz.

Sheila Shaver's research was supported by the Social Policy Research Centre at the University of New South Wales throughout the life of the project. She is grateful to Marilyn McHugh, Merrin Thompson and Diana Encel for their able and generous research assistance and to Peter Saunders for his directorial support for the place of gender research in the program of the Centre. She also thanks Ellen Immergut for incisive comment on an early version of Chapter 5 and Jeremy Beckett for help and advice throughout.

We would all like to thank Kathrina Zippel for her intelligent and technically sophisticated work in formatting the final manuscript and undertaking the demanding task of collating references.

As a book, *States, Markets, Families* has been ably supported by Phillipa McGuinness of Cambridge University Press. We would also like to thank four anonymous readers for understanding what we have tried to do and providing constructive criticism of our achievement of it, and Sally Nicholls for bringing polish and consistency to our final text.

An earlier version of Chapter 5 appeared in *Critical Social Policy* (1993/94, 13 (3): 66–93) under the title 'Body rights, social rights and the liberal welfare state'.

CHAPTER 1

Gendering Theories and Comparisons of Welfare States

The 1990s will likely be remembered as a period of contentious restructuring of state social provision – one in which issues of gender are quite marked. Since the late 1970s and early 1980s, Australia, Great Britain, Canada and the United States of America have experienced a rise in the popularity of ideologies and political forces celebrating market liberalism. Debates about the proper role of the state vis-à-vis the market and the family and about the character of state policies have intensified and broadened out to consider a greater range of policy alternatives; prominently, a range of market or private solutions to social problems for many decades considered properly political concerns. These have led to dramatic changes in social policy, often referred to as 'restructuring', including eliminating or scaling back entitlements and increasing work incentives or requirements. Concerns of gender pervade these social policy debates – about employment opportunities and day care, about how (or even whether) to publicly support care-giving work and single parent families, about the scope of women's choices as to whether and when to be mothers. Should states promote greater social equality? Should government modify or strengthen market forces? Should governments or private entities be the instruments of insurance against social risks? Should states respect 'family privacy' and the decision-making authority of corporations? Should governments recognise any sorts of group rights, or attempt to accommodate systematic differences among social groups? Decisions about gender roles and relations will be inescapable in the current restructuring of social provision.

Contemporary policy shifts are at least partly in response to a perceived need to better harmonise social benefits and labour market policies in the face of economic restructuring and increased

1

international competition. Restructuring of state social provision, trans-formations of labour markets, changing families and households, and political changes all influence each other. The restructuring of work has been associated with shifts to the service sector, the casualisation of labour, increased mobility of capital, and increases in the labour force participation of women, especially married mothers of young children. Changing patterns of paid and unpaid work by women, and to a lesser extent by men, have helped to alter family and household structures, as have partially related trends such as the rising rates of divorce and unmarried parenthood in many countries. Politics has been reshaped by the demands of women and other groups for equality as well as by the demands of employers and bankers for greater flexibility and deregulation. Attempts by political élites to reform social provision to suit the new conditions have meant, on the right, a drive for ever greater marketisation, privatisation and commodification, and on the left, a move towards greater participation in the labour force for all sectors of the population – an 'active society', to use the OECD phrase.

For women, these questions are especially relevant given that states have been so important in translating the demands of feminist move-ments and women citizens (and their allies among men) interested in greater gender equality into material social changes and support for the cultural transformations associated with women's entry into the public spheres of work and politics. One thinks of – to give only a few important examples – guarantees against workplace discrimination, the securing of reproductive rights and other legal rights of personhood, welfare benefits that allow women to support their families when marriages break up or fathers refuse responsibility for their children, and policies to protect job rights when children are born or to promote greater wage equality and access to good jobs. It is policies and programs such as these which have led some analysts to speak of the potential 'woman-friendliness' of the state, to use the term coined by Helga Hernes (1987), and bring political observers to believe that electoral gender gaps reflect women's sensitivity to the appeal of the social policies of the parties of the welfare state. The partisan character of governments has mattered for these policy outcomes, and the capacity of women as citizens to express political power has been critical, increasingly so in the last few decades, in determining the results of political contests. Citizenship appears, then, to have had beneficial effects for women. But of course state programs and social policies have a less friendly side for women as well: systems of social provision which reward citizens engaging in paid labour more than those who engage in unpaid caregiving, workplace policies which ignore workers' caregiving responsibilities, or laws which refuse women the capacity to control their reproductive lives or which fail to protect them from systematic (but 'private') violence.

The contradictory character of welfare states can be seen vividly when we examine policies especially relevant for gender relations in Australia, Britain, Canada and the United States. In these four countries, coalitions involving women's movements have been especially active and social changes in definitions of masculinities and femininities and gender relations quite marked – even as the changes have provoked contentious political debates and struggles over the content of citizenship rights. The United States, Australia, Canada, and Britain are usually characterised as liberal regimes, with a restricted role for the state in the provision of income and services, relative to markets and employers, as compared with the systems of social provision of the other developed countries, such as Sweden, the Netherlands or France. There has been also a tendency to consider many matters relevant for women's and men's relations, such as the division of domestic and caregiving labour within households, as 'private' and beyond the scope of state intervention. (Let us note that we are using the term 'liberalism' as it is understood in most of the world – as a commitment to a minimal state role and a substantial role for private institutions. This is different to the way it is usually used in discussions of US politics, where 'liberalism' connotes what we call 'social liberalism', that is, a willingness to use the state to achieve social purposes, while 'conservatism' connotes what is elsewhere called 'neo-' or 'traditional liberalism', that is, minimising the role of the state.) Today, social changes are both amplifying the sway of markets and opening up family matters for greater public and political scrutiny (the personal has become the political). Over the course of this century, states have led markets in promoting an agenda for gender equality, even as employers' demand for women workers has been a key source of social change. States also have been instruments for reshaping family practices relevant for women's emancipation, while families adapt to changes introduced by women's employment. Surely these are some of the reasons economically and socially conservative forces have been so concerned to gain control of governments and state policy, and have more explicitly opposed feminist demands.

The US welfare state is often excoriated as one inimical to the needs of women and their children. The 'feminisation of poverty' (meaning the high proportion of the poor who are women or children in households maintained by women, and implying their high rates of poverty) and the despised status of 'welfare' in political circles and in popular culture have been invoked to illustrate the ways in which the United States does not care for the poor, and for poor women and their children in particular. And welfare politics are racialised (Quadagno

1994), contributing to a continuing racial divide in living standards and life chances. The US safety net is full of holes: citizens have no guarantee of housing, food or health care, no entitlement to public assistance in times of destitution, no public employment as a last resort. Single parents' entitlement to assistance has been replaced by time-limited, state-run and discretionary welfare programs built around work requirements rather than around supporting full-time caregiving. Analysts point to the distinctive shape of the US welfare state: it has two tiers, one, 'welfare', targeted on the problems of families and serving mainly women, which is stingy and intrusive, and another, 'social security', targeted on the problems resulting from labour markets (for example, retirement) and serving (mainly retired) wage-earning men, their wives and some employed women, which offers more generous benefits and honourable treatment. The working poor (men as well as women) have long been excluded from a welfare state that caters only to narrowly defined categories of needy people – and the retired elderly; and, unlike European welfare states, the middle classes, too, find themselves relying mainly on private sources of welfare.

Do employed women in the United States fare better? Recent expansions of the Earned Income Tax Credit have improved the position of the working poor, including women, with children. But one can point to a relatively large gender wage gap – even women working full-time and all year make only about 75 cents for every dollar earned by similarly employed men. And employed women get few benefits designed to ease the combination of paid work and family work. Parents have only recently gained a limited right to a very short unpaid leave for the birth of a child (or medical emergencies), and public child care provision is scarce. Indeed, caregiving responsibilities are given very little public support or recognition. Comparative researchers often paint the United States as a 'welfare state laggard' – other western countries (including Britain, Canada and Australia) provide paid maternity and parental leaves, health care, along with retirement schemes, and leave substantially fewer members of their populations in poverty.

Yet when one looks at a different set of policies relevant for women and gender relations, one might form a somewhat different picture of US social policy. The United States seems to have made greater inroads in gender integration of occupations than other advanced countries. Women are successful in starting small businesses, and have made substantial progress in entering the professions and management of businesses, even as we see continuing evidence of a glass ceiling at the very top levels. Women are near educational parity with men, notably in tertiary degrees. While affirmative action policies are contested, they seem to have made a positive difference for women of all races, and there is a well-developed legal apparatus directed against gender discrimination in the workplace. And American women's work patterns are converging on those of men, particularly among younger cohorts; women tend to work full-time and for most of their lives. Furthermore, while public provision for child care is limited, employers and for-profit services – encouraged by tax policy – have generated a substantial number of child care slots.

One would also notice that the United States has been an international leader in policies to guarantee women's 'body rights' such as the freedom from domestic violence, sexual assault or sexual harassment at work. Abortion rights are understood as rights of women to control their own bodies – even as this right is contested by those who would elevate the rights of the foetus, and as material support for abortion is not guaranteed. Women's diverse and distinct sexual concerns have been given voice, and have been influential in a number of policy areas as well as in popular culture. A number of different family forms have developed in the United States, and feminists and others have somewhat successfully claimed legitimacy for such households, although this too has been politically contested. The United States has the highest rates of divorce (the majority requested by women) and single parent families among the western states, which, whatever else it reflects about gender relations, bespeaks an unusual level of independence among women.

Observers of the Canadian state might note similar contrasts between social policies on the one hand and, on the other hand, women's workplace opportunities and the cultural legitimacy accorded family diversity and women's body rights – even though, compared to the United States, these have a higher degree of medical entitlement undergirding them. In international perspective, the profile of social spending and social programs in Canada looks quite similar to that of the United States, and private sources of provision are relatively important. Canada in fact preceded the United States in abolishing a citizenship right to social assistance when in 1995 the Canada Assistance Plan was replaced by the Canada Health and Social Transfer, which gives block grants to provinces to run their own welfare programs – with little federal oversight, and no guarantees of coverage. Yet they would also insist that Canada's welfare state has proven more successful in preventing poverty, particularly deep poverty, among all families with children and among the elderly. They would also point to the social right to health care (as Myles and Pierson say, 'Ask a Canadian what distinguishes Canada from the United States and likely as not she will take out her health insurance card'; 1997:13). No Canadian woman will go without pre-natal care, nor will she face harsh trade-offs between welfare with health coverage for her children and paid work with no benefits – as is so common for poor, and many working-class, American women. But she is more likely to be employed, even if a single mother, than are her counterparts in Australia and Britain. And the greater willingness of Canadians than of their American neighbours to use governmental means has had some positive effects for women, including much less poverty among elderly women and greater public support for child care, taking the form of funding to non-profit providers rather than the US strategy of giving tax incentives to employers and for-profit centres. In addition, Canada has paid maternity and parental leaves.

North Americans often look to Britain as providing a better safety net for its citizens, even as private sources are permitted a relatively large role in the overall welfare mix. And it is true that, relative to the United States and Canada, far fewer British citizens, including single mother families and unemployed men, are in poverty. Indeed, despite steady erosion of the safety net under Tory rule between 1979 and 1997, Britain is in the middle ranks of countries in terms of the generosity of aid to all families with children, including single mother families (Bradshaw et al. 1993). And social tolerance for diverse family forms is, in practice, rather well-developed; Britain has relatively high rates of single motherhood and divorce compared to continental Europe. While criticisms of the Income Support system and the supposedly socially disorganising effects of illegitimacy may appear similar to US anti-welfare sentiment, in fact the proportion of all Britons, including single mother families, who claim social assistance is larger than the proportion of all Americans – and they continue to claim it as a social entitlement. In practice, although rhetoric encourages work, work requirements have been rather mild by US standards, and, in particular, women with children younger than school age have not been expected to be at work, certainly not full-time. Yet the New Labour administration of Tony Blair has voiced dissatisfaction about sole mothers' work effort. As part of the administration's 'New Deal' welfare-to-work initiatives, employment incentives, particularly for part-time work, have been enhanced for sole mothers, along with disincentives for receiving assistance.

Women and men in Britain have a social right to health care, provided by the National Health Service. Women's right to abortion services is placed within the context of this medical entitlement, where their requests for abortion must be approved by medical authorities. But there is less opposition to abortion in Britain. British feminists, like their American and Canadian counterparts, have helped to create a well-developed network of women's shelters and rape crisis centres.

Yet British feminist analysts of their welfare state, perhaps taking for granted its anti-poverty effects, complain about the strength of assumptions about the male breadwinner–female caregiver family guiding policy. For example, policies to enhance collection of child support have been passed in a number of countries, but Britain's system is unusual in mandating an amount for the maintenance of the parent with care – almost always the mother – thus reproducing the economic dependency of traditional marriages even after marital breakdown. The British system has institutionalised the expectation that married women will be involved in (unpaid) caregiving across many components of the state system, and some would argue that recently passed community care legislation rests on assumptions about the availability of all adult women for caregiving. Indeed, unpaid caregivers get some public support and recognition, as in the (albeit limited) credits earned for periods of caregiving in the state contributory pension system and the Invalid Care Allowance – although it may be worth noting that the latter was opened to married women only because of a European Union ruling in response to legal action brought by British women. There is very little development of public day care, but private provision of child care is less accessible than in North America, largely because of cost: child care is work to be done in the family. The British system has done better at preventing poverty among stay-at-home mothers with no earnings than have the North American ones, but the incentives this and other programs put in place for women to forgo employment opportunities, particularly full-time ones, have the longer term effect of increasing women's vulnerability to poverty when they no longer qualify for benefits or when they are outside marriage.

British women's situation in employment looks rather bleak as well. Compared to North American and other European women, a very high proportion of British women work in extremely precarious and ill-rewarded part-time work. The labour market in Britain is quite sex-segregated, but in contrast to the United States and Canada, affirmative action policies are less developed while the pay gap is just as large. To be sure, there are celebrated high-fliers, many products of Oxbridge, to be found in The City and elsewhere, but their numbers are relatively lower than in North America, partly because educational opportunity has not been as significant an avenue for women's upward mobility in Britain.

Women in Australia face poverty rates almost as high as the rates in North America – yet their poverty is not so deep. And unlike poor women in the United States, Australian women are not penalised as well by a bifurcated system of social provision in which social assistance is inferior to contributory social insurance, nor is receipt of welfare

generally so stigmatised as in US political culture. But while the beneficiaries of the Australian welfare state are not treated unequally based
on family, marital or labour force status, benefit levels overall are low.
Health coverage is a basic social right. Like British women, Australian
women gain access to reproductive health care, including abortion, as a
medical entitlement; it is mediated by medical authority, but is less
contested politically than is the case in North America. Like North
Americans and Britons, Australians have built up networks of public
agencies for dealing with formerly 'private' matters to do with sexuality
and violence.

In the workplace, Australian women have benefited from the institution of wage arbitration and alliances of women's groups and the
Australian Labor Party (ALP); pay gaps are low in international perspective, comparable to the celebrated Scandinavian cases. The last ALP
administration was responsible for a number of initiatives targeting
women workers' 'special' needs as primary caregivers: special employment training for sole parents and expanding child care provision.
Women workers in the public sector also have access to paid parental
and maternity leave. Notwithstanding these gains, Australian women
tend to work part-time at relatively higher rates than their North
American counterparts, more are housewives, and occupational sex-
segregation levels are higher. Thus, while Australia has produced
'femocrats', feminist women in positions of public authority in national
and state governments, fewer women are to be found in the professions
and business. However, women's gains have been eroded by the spread
of 'economic rationalism' (neo-liberalism) under Labor, but particularly
under the Liberal–National Coalition Government which took power in
1996; this has meant emphases on budgetary restraint, the diminution
of central wage determination in favour of enterprise bargaining, and
compulsory superannuation (mandated private pension coverage,
which has tended to best serve better-paid workers, disproportionately
men). The conservative Coalition Government has already cut back on
spending for child care, and promises to implement changes in industrial relations which will continue dismantling the state apparatus which
was associated with women's pay gains. At the same time, it has attacked
special programs, built up under Labor to deal with the disproportionate poverty and unemployment of Aboriginal women and men and
to compensate for some of the sufferings of the 'stolen children',
indigenous children taken, as a matter of government policy, from their
mothers in the 1940s, 1950s and 1960s.

Are any of these countries 'women-friendly' regimes? We could not
answer the question without asking for which women, and on which
issues? It does seem that there are differences in policy emphasis – on

employment as opposed to protection – among the four, which may reflect differences in what is understood to be important for equality as well as the level of responsiveness to women's concerns. How will economic restructuring affect the ways states can respond to women's demands for greater equality? How are their distinctive profiles related to liberalism? These issues take us to the core of our concerns in this book: the relationships among social policy and gender relations in an era of economic restructuring and associated policy changes. We investigate the policy legacies and the restructurings of social policy across three key policy areas – the labour market, income maintenance, and the regulation of reproduction – in Australia, Canada, Great Britain and the United States of America. Because contemporary debates about the welfare state are shaped by the institutional structures, political alliances and discourses put in place by earlier policy decisions, we seek to make explicit the gendered effects of existing policies, and thus how current policy debates are structured by gendered policy legacies.

States, Welfare and Gender Relations

The character of welfare states has more than just practical political significance. Debates among social scientists and historians have been concerned with the explanations for the origins and development of different specific policies and policy regimes, the effects of such policies and regimes, and what policy outcomes and institutional arrangements tell us about the relationship among states, markets, and families, or democracy, capitalism and gender relations. Indeed, the welfare state has been a favoured site for theorising about state–society relations, and, increasingly, for understanding the connections between gender and politics.

Comparative research has lately been concerned with understanding qualitative differences in the origins and trajectories of social policy, and of institutional arrangements to ask questions about the factors shaping welfare state structures and their effects on economy, society and culture. In consequence, there has also been interest in developing typologies identifying the range of forms taken by welfare states, building on the classic work of Titmuss (1958) and others. The welfare states of Australia, Canada, Britain and the United States are frequently grouped together as representatives of a liberal form of the welfare state, or regime type, in which social provision is limited and shaped so as to preserve maximum scope for individual initiative and market forces. They are seen as similar also because of the relative political strength of neo-liberal economic theory and the relatively strong efforts to cut back spending and social rights. We will explore differences as well as likenesses in social provision in these four countries, evaluating to what extent each resembles the ideal-typical liberal regime as described in the literature on welfare states. Liberalism, affirming the personhood and freedom of the individual, also has important gender dimensions. Feminist analysis of liberalism emphasises the gendered implications of the sharp split between public and private spheres which characterises liberal ideology, and, to some degree, liberal institutional arrangements. 'Feminist' is used here to describe scholarship that uses gender as an analytic category and/or focuses on the situation of women; 'feminist' also describes political orientations in favour of (diverse visions of) gender equality. Thus, it makes sense to ask if policy liberalism is associated with particular gendered effects vis-à-vis the division of labour, power relations and support for specific types of families and households.

Only a few years ago, mainstream comparative research and gender-sensitive work on welfare states were almost mutually exclusive sets, with the result that there was little systematically comparative work on gender and welfare states. This is no longer the case, and we are happy to join with many of our friends and colleagues in developing comparative gendered analyses of welfare states. We have broken with the common practice of having individual scholars analysing only their own countries. (As we are an Irish-Canadian, an American, and an Australian, we were asked many times, 'But who's doing Britain?') Instead, we analysed policies on the labour market, income maintenance, and reproductive rights comparatively, then considered how policies are articulated in the four countries. (When we began, we hoped to help keep the project more manageable by excluding New Zealand, whose social policy history had until that time been similar to Australia's (Castles 1985); the election of James Bolger in 1990 ushered in serious restructuring of social policy. Given the significance of the New Zealand case in some studies of restructuring, we now wish we had included it.) This practice forced us to abandon many preconceptions as we systematically evaluated the dimensions of the policies across all four countries.

Our investigations also contribute to an understanding of the character of contemporary gender relations. Gender relations cannot be understood apart from the state, politics and policy; states influence gender relations, and are in turn influenced by gender relations. While this approach links us to diverse strands of contemporary feminist theory and research, it also sets us somewhat at odds with those who argue that the state is not the most relevant site for investigating gender and other social relations, and prefer instead to investigate local discursive, disciplinary or cultural manifestations of power. Certainly

Michel Foucault (see, for example, 1980) opened up a tremendously important vein of scholarship on the 'capillary', disciplinary mechanisms of power, and its productive character. Many have read Foucault as making the argument that older forms of power – the law and state policy, and the centralised control over the means of coercion upon which it ultimately depends – are of decreasing importance, and of less significance than disciplinary power and normalisation. Other analysts have disagreed with this reading of Foucault, maintaining that while he saw older forms of power as diminishing, he did not argue that they are gone (see, for example, Smart 1989: 6–9; G. Rubin 1994). We accept that states (like all social institutions) have discursive and cultural dimensions (R. Pringle and Watson 1992; Burchell, Gordon, and Miller 1991) – indeed, our investigations of policy regimes are attentive to these dimensions. But we work from the premise that the state is a crucial site for gender and sexual politics, and that investigations of local power should be linked with an understanding of centralised power and the state. Some current manifestations of discursive analysis may be misleading in that they discourage analysis of the state and of links between states and local sites of power (see, for example, Allen 1990). The state has not lost its centrality in institutionally fixing and resourcing particular discursive categories. As R. W. Connell (1987: 130) puts it,

> In managing institutions and relations like marriage and motherhood the state is doing more than regulating them. It is playing a major part in the constitution of the social categories of the gender order ... Through them the state plays a part in the constitution of the interests at play in sexual politics.

Moreover, processes of challenge and contestation are overwhelmingly directed at the state (Connell 1995; Tarrow 1994). Institutionalist scholars, too, see a prominent role for states in gender relations, showing the ways in which varying state and political institutions and organisations have helped to constitute gendered interests, shaped men's and women's political activities and influenced the character of social policies (see, for example, Jenson 1986; Valverde 1991; Deacon 1989; Sklar 1993; Skocpol 1992; Koven and Michel 1993; Orloff 1991; Franzway, Court and Connell 1989). Interest in the state and 'the political' has also come from legal scholars, concerned about the role of law in shaping gender relations, and from analysts of democracy and citizenship, who see in the public sphere a critical ground for contesting gender and other forms of subordination (see, for example, Smart 1989; MacKinnon 1989; Rhode 1994; Fineman 1995; Pateman 1989; Vogel 1991; Lister 1990; Mouffe 1992; Fraser 1997; Yeatman 1990).

We focus on social policy regimes – patterns across a number of areas of policy. Sheila Shaver (1990) has described social policy regimes as institutionalised patterns in welfare state provision establishing systematic relations between the state and social structures of conflict, domination and accommodation. Such patterns refer to the terms and conditions under which claims may be made on the resources of the state, and, reciprocally, the terms and conditions of economic, social, and political obligation to the state. The elements constituting social policy regimes may be economic, legal, political and/or discursive. These regimes are to be found in both individual institutions of the welfare state and in common patterns cutting across domains of social provision, such as health, education, income maintenance or housing. The concept of policy regimes also indicates patterns of public–private divisions of responsibility or oversight for various areas. Earlier formulations of the welfare regime concept have been built largely inductively from empirical analyses of the post-World War II policies of western countries, linked with distinctive class coalitions (see, for example, Esping-Andersen 1990, 1996b; Korpi 1989). Our understanding of regimes has some similarities to these, in that we pay attention to contemporary patterns of policy – albeit in a more gender-sensitive way. But our concept also has affinities to institutionalist concepts of policy legacies or regimes as they developed historically (see, for example, Orloff 1993a; P. Pierson 1994; Leibfried 1992; Weir, Orloff, and Skocpol 1988). 'Regime' thus indicates something broader than the 'welfare state', connoting the full range of domestic policy interventions as well as broader patterns of provisioning and regulation.

The welfare state is typically conceptualised as a state committed to modifying the play of social or market forces in order to achieve greater equality (Ruggie 1984: 11). We prefer to define the 'welfare state' (or 'state social provision') as interventions by the state in civil society to alter social and market forces, but we do not judge a priori that all state social interventions are aimed at, or actually produce, greater equality among citizens. And we use a broad meaning of the term 'welfare state' – we have in mind not just income maintenance programs, but also the state regulatory apparatus (for example, as deployed around reproduction or workplace equality) and public services (for example, day care). We believe that this approach will enable us to move 'from institutional frameworks [alone] towards a larger-scale analysis of the state', situating the institutions of welfare states within larger structures of power and rule (Shaver 1990: 2–3). Here, it will be important to link social policy patterns, as we more comprehensively map these, to the international economic and military activities of states. Indeed, this is beginning to happen as analysts consider the impact for welfare provisioning of globalisation, the fall of socialist states, the development of the European Union, and the end of the Cold War (see, for example, D. Mitchell and Garrett 1996; Rhodes 1996; Esping-Andersen 1996b; Leibfried and Pierson 1995).

While state–society relations are consequential for gender relations, it is important also to investigate not only state–market relations, but also the ways states interact with families, both in terms of provisioning and services and of regulation, as well as how states mediate between families and markets (for example, in income maintenance programs). It is this emphasis that gives us our title.

While many concede that families are sites of gender relations, analysts often treat them as the only sites of gender relations, and therefore treat other social institutions as 'gender-free'. Our perspective is that all social institutions are gendered (Smith 1987; Connell 1987, 1995; Clement and Myles 1994; Scott 1988). Thus, we examine the gendered character of the labour market (for example, patterns of women's as compared to men's participation) and related policies (for example, equal employment policies, day care provision). Similarly, we explore the ways in which state systems of social provision or of legal regulation help to constitute distinctive gendered identities and interests (for example, through processes of making claims on the state as mothers, workers, wives, or of making use of rights associated with legal personhood). We have been influenced by multi-dimensional theories of gender which conceptualise gender as constituted through several different social processes (see, for example, Connell 1995, 1987; Scott 1988). We focus on the gender division of labour and gendered power relations across institutions.

In the following chapters, we do several things in assessing the relations among gender, liberalism and social policy. We explore the liberal commitment to market solutions – which defines the ideal type of the liberal regime in the mainstream literature – and how this affects gender arrangements. We find, for example, that women's disproportionate vulnerability to poverty, present throughout the west, given women's labour market disadvantages and responsibilities for care, is less buffered than in other regimes; poverty rates for women-maintained families and single women are quite high in the United States, Canada and Australia, although this is less the case in Britain (D. Mitchell 1993; see Table 4.1, p. 111). Along the way, we assess the extent to which these states can reasonably be called 'liberal' welfare regimes; we note that the strength and content of liberalism varies across the countries, over time, across different policy areas, and is influenced by partisan shifts. Some might object that we cannot properly assess this claim as we are looking only at so-called liberal regimes and not at other types. We believe it is appropriate and indeed significant to analyse whether or not any particular country conforms to its characterisation as a liberal welfare state regime (for example, in Esping-Andersen 1990); the notion of regime types has been very widely accepted in the literature on welfare states and bears scrutiny. However, we are not setting out to undermine the claim that there is a cluster of liberal policy regimes by presenting an analysis of gender in the four countries. Our focus is on understanding the character of these four gender regimes and the relations between liberalism and gender.

We also take up a significant theme in feminist critiques of liberalism: a gendered division between public and private is a central feature of liberal ideology, and all western states display some elements of this split between family on the one hand and markets and states on the other. Feminists have also noted that the role of families – really, women in families – in providing care has been neglected in mainstream accounts of welfare provision. We agree that what goes on in the 'private' sphere of families – notably the gender division of domestic labour and caregiving, but also sexual and reproductive relations – is actually quite consequential for men's and women's performance in the public spheres of (paid) work and politics. All western countries have a division between what is defined as 'private' and 'public', not just these four 'liberal regimes' (although the depth of the split may well vary). But this feature appears in the Australian, British, Canadian and US welfare states in characteristic ways, and the chapters that follow each deal with the articulation of public and private spheres of social life in particular policy areas. For example, women in the four countries have left housewifery and entered paid work in increasing numbers, despite the dearth of public services as compared to Scandinavia, where a strong public role in providing services formerly performed by women has helped to bring women into the paid labour force. But the lack of almost all but income-tested public services and supports for combining paid and unpaid work means that class differences are quite significant for women workers' material situations and the relative ease or difficulty of organising everyday life.

Further, we argue that liberal ideologies and institutional structures do not completely describe these regimes. Rather, we find that while liberalism does have some distinctive gendered consequences, there are also differences in the character of gender arrangements across states, markets and families among the four countries. With respect to the gender division of labour, we examine the basis upon which claims for social rights are made, the extent to which women as well as men have access to paid work, and the organisation of caregiving work. With respect to gendered power relations, we investigate the character of citizenship rights: the issues of legal personhood as seen in policy around abortion, the individuation or derived character of claims in income security programs, and the extent to which, and how, states secure women's as well as men's personal autonomy or capacity to form autonomous households. Each of the four countries presents a different profile of policies relevant for gender relations. All four have supported women's citizenship rights to a significant degree, but there are differences in how those rights are institutionalised. For example, women's access to abortion occurs in the context of 'medical entitlement' in Australia, Canada and Britain, but is understood as an element of 'body right' in the United States and Canada. Also striking are the differing policy patterns that reflect and shape the gender division of labour. Australia and Britain support elements of gender difference in which mothers are likely to be part-time workers and primary caregivers or full-time caregivers while men are breadwinners. Canada and the United States stress to a greater degree the logic of gender sameness, with women as well as men understood primarily as workers, and caregiving receiving scant public recognition or material support (although women continue to do the bulk of 'private' care work). All four countries uphold a commitment to private provision, but both markets and families fall under the rubric of the 'private' (as do charities or other associations in civil society). And it matters quite a lot which private institution is the locus of provision, or which the state is willing to regulate. For instance, the United States and Britain are both characterised as reflecting a 'maximum private responsibility model' in day care provision (Ergas 1990), but in the United States, market provision is far better developed, while in Britain, 'private' in this case means women caring in the family.

These patterns of similarities and differences in the policy regimes of the four countries speak to the need to develop gendered frameworks for understanding how state social policies, interacting with private forms of provision, affect gender relations. Empirical knowledge of the range and character of variation will be essential to further developments in social theories about gender, politics and the state and in understanding the political constitution of gender relations. Such knowledge is also important to the political project for gender equality, because social politics and the construction of political interests, identities and alliances are decisively shaped by existing policy.

We begin with a review of the literatures on welfare states – plural because the 'mainstream' and gender-sensitive literatures have developed separately, although recently there has been some convergence (Orloff 1996; O'Connor 1996).

Comparative Analyses of Welfare States

Comparative scholarship on the origins and development of modern welfare states has flourished over the past two to three decades. Debate may continue about the importance of potential state autonomy, yet there is broad agreement among scholars about many of the sources of modern social policy (if not about their relative causal importance) – capitalist industrialisation, the political emergence and incorporation of working classes, and the development of greater state capacities for social intervention (see, for example, Steinmetz 1993: ch. 1; Flora and Alber 1981; Orloff 1993a). Likewise, there is greater convergence among scholars about the factors contributing to the expansion of welfare spending and benefit generosity among welfare states in the post-World War II era; strong left-wing governments are especially important, but Christian democratic parties, state capacities, unified political structures and economies that are robust and/or open also emerge as influential factors (Amenta 1993; Hicks and Misra 1993; Huber, Ragin and Stephens 1993). While scholars largely agree about expansionary dynamics, debates are emerging over the most significant factors in restructuring and cutbacks (for example, P. Pierson 1996; Rhodes 1996; Esping-Andersen 1996b). And as gender-sensitive comparative work has developed, there is beginning to be more debate about the role of particular family forms, the organisation of care work, and gendered patterns of political and labour force participation in shaping policy differences across regimes (see, for example, Jenson and Mahon 1993; Lewis and Åstrom 1992; Hobson 1993; Pedersen 1993; Huber and Stephens 1996).

Recently, interest has shifted from the determinants of social spending or of the initiation of modern welfare programs to the qualitative character of state social provision, which in turn is leading to more nuanced explanations of particular policy outcomes. This has been of particular significance for feminist comparative efforts, including our own. First, there has been progress in categorising systems in terms of regime types, including the ways in which different types of welfare states have distinctive political and social effects – a phenomenon many refer to as 'policy feedback'. This is the idea that previous policy choices, as institutionalised in particular programmatic arrangements, affect continuing policy developments. As Paul Pierson (1994: 39) puts it, 'one simply cannot make sense of the contemporary politics of the welfare state without considering how the consequences of preexisting policies structure struggles over social-policy reform' through effects on issue agendas and policy discourses, political coalitions and enmities, and patterns of institutional development (capacities and structures) (Weir,

Orloff and Skocpol 1988). If we are to understand the prospects for gender relations and women's equality in this period of policy change, we need to have a good understanding of how gender relations – including the constitution of distinctive gendered political identities, interests and alliances – have been affected by welfare states and contribute to the politics of restructuring.

Second, rather than simply investigating the determinants of spending levels, which long dominated mainstream quantitative work, recent scholarship builds on T. H. Marshall's (1950) notions of social citizenship, and the ways in which certain types of welfare arrangements may alter power relations. This offers a good bridge to recent feminist efforts to understand how citizenship can affect gendered power.

Influential in promoting these trends has been Gøsta Esping-Andersen's (1990, 1996b) work on the 'three worlds of welfare capitalism': liberal, conservative and social democratic. These regime types are based on how countries cluster along three dimensions of variability: state–market relations, stratification and social rights. Liberal regimes promote market provision of services, encourage dualism between the majority of market-reliant citizens and those who rely on public provision, and offer few alternatives to participating in the market. In social democratic and conservative regimes all citizens are under the umbrella of state provision, but the former states are universalistic, egalitarian, and provide significant public services and decommodification of labour (that is, alternatives to the market), while the latter preserve status and class differentials, offer few public services, and condition benefits on employment. Esping-Andersen classified the Nordic countries and the Netherlands as social democratic regimes and Austria, France, Germany and Italy as conservative regimes. The United States, Canada and Australia are classified as liberal regimes; Britain exhibits some deviating characteristics but tends towards a liberal model. These liberal regimes dedicate lower proportions of GNP to social spending and feature lower levels of net redistribution of income than do European countries (Castles and Mitchell 1993). In all four, private sources of income (work, investment, and private pensions) for the aged – a measure of state–market relations – play a larger role than in other countries (Esping-Andersen 1990: 86–7; Smeeding, Torrey and Rainwater 1993). They exhibit the lowest levels of decommodification among the eighteen OECD countries (Esping-Andersen 1990: 52). The United States, Canada and Australia exhibit the highest degree of liberal stratification principles, Britain a middling degree, reflecting a relatively strong role for means-testing and for markets, private sector welfare and individual efforts. In contrast, they have the lowest scores for conservatism in stratification, as their public pension systems display little occupational or status differentiation. There is variation among the four in the extent to which their liberalism is modified by socialist principles – low benefit inequality and universalism (that is, benefits based on citizenship right rather than labour market participation). Britain, Canada and Australia have middle-range scores on socialist stratification principles, while the United States scores a zero (Esping-Andersen 1990: 76).

Despite their similarities, some analysts also see important variations in social policy outcomes across the four. Francis Castles and Deborah Mitchell (1993) have been prominent in questioning the coherence of the group of low-spending, allegedly 'liberal' regimes, and propose a 'fourth world' of radicalism including Australia, New Zealand and Britain; moreover, Canada has radical tendencies. Radical regimes, they claim, have adopted policy instruments which can promote equalisation without high spending – targeted benefits (which exclude the affluent) and/or progressive taxation. They bolster their case by referring to the historical strength of labourism in Australia, New Zealand and Britain, but in the context of high levels of right-wing party strength and incumbency; right-wing parties block high spending but strong labour movements compel some attention to equalisation. Liberal regimes are those that attempt little or no equalisation; the United States is the only English-speaking country that Castles and Mitchell place clearly in the liberal world. Can this be merely a new way to speak of 'American exceptionalism'? Surely there are reasons to expect differences between the United States and the other three, including a distinctive history of state-building marked by a revolutionary break from Britain, unusual patterns of immigration and settlement, and race relations freighted with the history of slavery. But every country has its exceptionalism. These differing assessments of the extent of similarity and difference among Australia, Canada, Britain and the United States add emphasis to the call to explore in some detail patterns of social policy across the four.

In their own work and in collaboration, Esping-Andersen and Walter Korpi also build on T. H. Marshall's (1950) classic work on the social rights of citizenship, adding an analysis of capitalism and democracy informed by social democratic and Marxist thinking (Esping-Andersen and Korpi 1987; Korpi 1989; Esping-Andersen 1990; Korpi and Palme 1998). The linkage between political rights, power resources and social rights is critical. To the extent possible, workers have mobilised their power resources and utilised political rights to establish social rights. Central to the understanding of how welfare states affect class relations are the concepts of social rights and, for Esping-Andersen, the 'decommodification of labour', understood as the degree to which individuals' typical life situations are freed from dependence on the labour market. These rights affect the class balance of power by insulating workers to some extent from market pressures and by contributing to working-class political capacities. 'Power resources' analysts have questioned whether the state can 'push back the frontiers of capitalism', although more recent work focuses on the maintenance of social rights, and employment, under capitalism (Esping-Andersen 1996b). Feminist analysts raise parallel questions about whether the state can also 'push back the frontiers of institutionalised male dominance', and what the relationship might be between curbing the inequalities and power imbalances of markets and changing the character of gender relations.

Some of the concepts developed in mainstream comparative analysis are compelling, and we work to revise them in light of the findings of feminist scholarship; thus, we make use of the concepts of policy regimes and policy feedback and develop the idea of the potential of social citizenship to alter power relations to consider the effects of social rights on gender relations. But while we find this work suggestive, it is not fully adequate to the systematic, gendered comparative analysis of the welfare states of Britain, the United States, Canada and Australia we hope to accomplish. Thus we propose new frameworks, moving on from where mainstream accounts have left off.

Women and Welfare Regimes

Esping-Andersen's (1990) ideal-typical scheme inspired fruitful research on the variation among regimes as investigators utilised his framework to examine whether or not liberal, conservative and social democratic regime types affect women or the organisation of caring labour in distinctive ways (see, for example, Sainsbury 1994). In subsequent work, Esping-Andersen (1996b) has moved from a focus on male workers' decommodification to incorporating concerns about women's employment – or commodification – and how it can be reconciled with fertility and caregiving. He sees these are central to how countries respond to contemporary political and economic challenges. How services are provided is important to women's capacities to balance paid and unpaid work. Esping-Andersen argues that because conservative regimes promote subsidiarity and do not provide much in the way of services, it is difficult for women to enter paid employment (unless childless), thereby strengthening economic dependence on the principal breadwinner. This adds to insider-outsider tensions in the labour market, as women (and youth) are marginalised by an employment regime revolving around the needs of predominantly male industrial workers. Social democratic regimes promote women's employment by providing services that allow those responsible for care work – mostly married mothers – to enter the paid labour force, and also by employing women in the state service sector. While he sees this as resulting in a desirable mobilisation of women's labour while not undercutting their capacities to bear and rear children, it is costly to the state. Fiscal pressures associated with the globalisation of capital, along with policy decisions taken in the European Union, make high levels of government spending (and running deficits) difficult to sustain. Liberal regimes, he argues, are indifferent to gender relations, leaving service provision to the market. Women are entering paid employment, and are often able to purchase care services in the market, but the quality of these services is far from assured. Low quality child care and policy-related pressures towards commodification rather than education and training may undercut the investment in human capital which is necessary for continuing good economic performance. Moreover, social exclusion is often the price of policy residualism.

Thus, Esping-Andersen links certain gender issues – women's labour force participation, the organisation of care work, and child-bearing – to the political economic outcomes in which he is most interested: competitive economic performance by western democratic countries in a global environment where 'the next South Korea' (that is, low-wage haven) is always on the horizon; the investment in human capital needed to sustain that performance; and the preservation and strengthening of political coalitions for the welfare state, which will preserve democracy, civility and human rights. In analytic terms, there is an implicit claim that the class-related dimensions of regimes determine gender outcomes (although these are rather narrowly defined); an explicitly gendered analysis is not a goal. He focuses on women workers rather than on gender relations, and is interested in relations among states, markets and families because of the implications of caregiving responsibilities for women's capacities to bear children and to enter paid employment, both significant for states' fiscal concerns, but not because of women's aspirations for equality. This makes it problematic to utilise Esping-Andersen's framework – or similarly gender-blind schemes – for understanding policy effects on gender relations.

Analyses of women's poverty and economic dependency using Luxembourg Income Study data have found that women's poverty is partly explained by the policy approaches associated with Esping-Andersen's regime-type categorisation; Germany and Britain show relatively high poverty rates for single mothers and relatively high gender gaps in poverty (that is, the difference between men's and women's rates), but these are most notable in the liberal United States,

Canada and Australia (McLanahan, Casper and Sørenson 1995; also see Table 4.1, p. 111). Policy strategies of countries with low poverty rates for women and low gender gaps differ qualitatively; Sweden reduces women's poverty by promoting their employment, but Italy and the Netherlands – both seen by feminist analysts as conservative regimes – differ, with the former working to reduce poverty by reinforcing marriage and economic dependency, and the latter by providing generous social transfers to all citizens (see also Goldberg and Kremen 1990). But it is notable that gender roles have a significant influence on outcomes apart from differences in regime types: 'marriage and work reduce the risk of poverty for women in all countries, whereas mother-hood increases the chances of being poor. The only mothers who have a better than average chance of staying out of poverty are mothers who combine parenthood and work with marriage' (McLanahan, Casper and Sorenson 1995: 18).

Feminist analysts have been concerned with how care work (broadly defined) is organised and supported (see, for example, Taylor-Gooby 1991; Jenson 1997a). Some analysts found that patterns of service provision reflect regime-type differences; for instance, Siv Gustafsson (1994) determined that public services are best-developed in Sweden, market provision of services is prominent in the United States, and the Netherlands offers little public provision, in effect opting to financially support mothers' caregiving work rather than offering day care. Mary Ruggie's (1984) pioneering study of women and the state in Britain and Sweden had findings broadly compatible with regime-type claims. She revealed that women workers' progress in pay and access to services was affected by the overall relationship between state and society – Swedish women were supported by the state, especially through the provision of day care, while in Britain, the less-developed role of the state left women more likely to remain economically dependent housewives. Similarly, in a comparison of policies supporting care work and caregivers in Britain and Denmark, Birte Siim (1990) argued that the extent to which increased social welfare benefits also increased women's political power depended in part on the organisation of social reproduction. In Denmark, women's dual roles as worker and mother are supported by a social and family policy that gives the state a larger role in organising and financing care for dependants, which facilitates women's integration into the workforce. In Britain, a 'familist' social policy assigns primary responsibility for care work to 'the family', assuming this contains a breadwinner husband and a wife who has time to attend to (unpaid) caregiving work; this seriously undercuts women's capacities to enter the paid labour force on an equal footing with men.

Yet other investigations point to important differences in how care is organised within groups of countries identified as having similar regimes. For example, Arnlaug Leira (1992) and Anette Borchorst (1994) examine variation among the Scandinavian (social democratic) states. Both find that there are significant differences among this group in the level of public child care provision and the characteristics of women's labour force participation – Denmark and Sweden offer greater support for combining motherhood with paid work, particularly for mothers of very young children, than does Norway. This has implications as well for women's economic dependency (Hobson 1990; Hobson 1994: 173). Ilona Ostner and Jane Lewis (1995) point to significant differences between Germany, which supports stay-at-home wives and mothers while constraining women's employment in various ways, and France, which supports mothers working for pay. These analysts suggest that regimes grouped on the basis of state–society relations and other dimensions may well still differ in terms of gender relations. Leira proposes the concept of differing 'models of mother-hood', a notion linked to the gender division of labour and associated ideologies of gender difference or sameness.

Analyses using mainstream regime-type frameworks to understand the relationships between welfare states and gender relations, though promising, cannot fully explain important patterns. They falter partly because they have made 'women' rather than 'gender relations' the targets of their inquiry. We cannot fully tap into states' effects on gender relations simply by looking at how women fare in different regime types using dimensions developed without regard for gender (O'Connor 1993c; Orloff 1993b; Langan and Ostner 1991; Bussemaker and van Kersbergen 1994; Borchorst 1994; Daly 1994; Lewis 1997; Jenson 1997a). Such work reflects key analytic weaknesses: an inadequate theorisation of the political interests of gender and associated political conflicts; and a failure to specify the dimensions of social provision and other state interventions relevant for gender relations. The two weak-nesses are related. If one wants to argue that welfare states help to promote – or to undermine – patriarchy or gender inequality, one needs to grapple with the question of what are the dimensions of the gendered political interests of (different groups of) women and men (that is, what is a benefit and what is a disadvantage?); one also needs to specify the yardsticks for measuring these effects. Indeed, any assessment of the effects of state policies and programs usually implies an evaluation of which groups are empowered or disempowered, whose interests are advantaged or disadvantaged, and whose needs are met or left unfulfilled. But defining needs, interests, subjects, identities and sub-jectivities, or accounting for the constitution of social groups and discerning their shifting and overlapping boundaries are hardly unproblematic, as we see in debates in social theory and political analysis (see, for example, Alcoff 1994; Barrett and Phillips 1992; Butler and Scott 1992; Mouffe 1992; Riley 1988; Yeatman 1994; Fraser 1989, 1997). Such work questions our capacity to specify 'objective' or 'strategic' interests for any groups – 'women', 'workers' or others – and raises as well the political and historical specificity of groups' formation. For example, do women's gender interests lie simply in entering the paid workforce, gaining some relief from unpaid caring labour performed in families through the provision of state services, and obtaining individual rather than derived entitlement to benefits? Do men have gendered interests in welfare state arrangements? Preferring a historically grounded understanding of interests and identities, we eschew any search for women's 'strategic' or 'objective' interests deduced from analyses 'of women's subordination and from the formulation of an alternative, more satisfactory set of arrangements to those which exist' (Molyneux 1985: 232). Moreover, we need to attend to specifically gendered dimensions, based on an analysis of gender relations and gender interests. (Even if one is not interested in gender relations as an object of study, it seems likely that gender-based conflicts will influence other outcomes of interest to welfare state researchers, such as women's capacities to take up employment.) Let us now turn to some of the recent efforts at producing such a gendered analytic framework.

The Gender Regimes of Welfare States

Feminist scholars have shown that gender issues figured prominently in the origins of welfare states, that states have been involved in shaping gender relations in households and workplaces, and that women re-formers, like their male counterparts, were active participants in the development of modern social provision (O'Connor 1996; Orloff 1996; Hobson 1993; Jenson 1986; Pedersen 1993; Roberts 1993; Sapiro 1986; Sarvasy 1992; Shaver 1987; Skocpol 1992). In the last few years, a number of authors have tried their hands at developing frameworks for evaluating the gendered effects of welfare states based on an understanding of gender relations and gender interests. Scholars such as Jane Lewis (1992), Ilona Ostner (Langan and Ostner 1991; Ostner and Lewis 1995) and Diane Sainsbury (1994, 1996) have developed frameworks which focus mainly on gender relations. In our own work, we have built frameworks for analysing welfare states on the assumption that gender is constituted jointly with class, race, nation – in short, within a complex social field which calls for a conceptual framework that recognises heterogeneity among women (as among men), especially with respect to class, race, ethnicity and citizenship status (O'Connor 1993c; Orloff 1993b; Shaver 1989a, 1990; see also Williams 1995). Moreover, as gender relations are multi-dimensional, we must also utilise a framework that examines a variety of effects across several areas.

These efforts have been informed by earlier feminist work on welfare states. A large body of research has developed over the 1980s and 1990s showing that state policies of all kinds are shaped by gender relations and in turn affect gender relations (some of the better collections on this theme include Sassoon 1987; Baldock and Cass 1983; Edwards and Margarey 1995; Brodie 1995; Bakker 1996; Bock and Thane 1991; Koven and Michel 1993; Gordon 1990). This work identifies aspects of gender relations that are not encompassed in mainstream frameworks.

Much early feminist work recognised that welfare states contributed to the reproduction of inegalitarian gender relations, even while providing support to those who suffer from the failures of the welfare state system. Analysts usually focused on a single country, tending to ignore cross-national and historical variation and the possibility that some state social provision – and, by extension, other forms of state intervention – has the potential to advance gender equality. Others, including many analysts of cross-national poverty and state benefit levels, emphasised states' potentially ameliorative impact on social inequality, including gender inequality. Lately, there seems to be among researchers more of a sense that the effects of policy on gender relations can and do vary, sometimes reproducing existing and unequal gender relations, sometimes altering those relations intentionally or unintentionally. The question of whether state policies can have emancipatory, or at least 'woman-friendly', effects has also captured the imaginations of many, even as (or perhaps because) many benefits are being challenged, changed and cut back in different parts of the world (see, for example, Hernes 1987; Piven 1985).

Feminist analysts have focused on several central dimensions of gender relations: first, gendered divisions of labour, with men responsible for economic support of women, children and others, and women responsible for caregiving and domestic labour as well as for bearing children; second, the family wage system, in which men's relatively superior wages (and tax advantages) are justified partly in terms of their responsibility for the support of dependent wives and children and women are excluded from the paid labour force or from favoured positions within it, therefore creating economic dependence on men and a disproportionate vulnerability to poverty for women outside marriage; third, traditional marriage, which implies the gender division of labour and a double standard of sexual morality; and fourth, men's and states' control of women's bodies through legal controls over sexuality and reproduction (including some but not all natalist and eugenic policies).

This view of welfare states as reinforcing women's economic vulnerability and failing to mitigate their economic deprivation is often buttressed by noting the relatively higher levels of poverty among women (that is, single women and women-maintained families) than among men and the increasing proportion of women-maintained households among the poor – the 'feminisation of poverty' identified in the United States in the late 1970s (Pearce 1978). Comparative investigations of the feminisation of poverty showed that poverty levels for women-maintained families, as for other segments of populations, vary considerably (Goldberg and Kremen 1990; Smeeding, Torrey and Rainwater 1988). No matter the measures used, studies consistently find the United States has the highest poverty levels among women-maintained households, followed closely by Canada and Australia; Britain looks better, although rates there are climbing (D. Mitchell 1993; Millar and Whiteford 1993; see Table 4.1, p. 111). Income transfer programs can buffer women's vulnerability to poverty where benefits are more generous than in the United States (Goldberg and Kremen 1990; see Orloff 1996 for discussion of these studies).

While most would agree that the practices described in these central dimensions are involved in the ongoing recreation of sex/gender systems, there have been differences of emphasis among feminist analysts from different countries, reflecting some cross-national differences in emphases of feminist movements. North American, Australian and British commentators have been particularly concerned with women's economic dependency and vulnerability to poverty resulting from their exclusion from paid labour and their responsibility for domestic work (Gordon 1988; Abromovitz 1988; McIntosh 1978; E. Wilson 1977; Cass 1983; Pearce 1978). They have also taken note of a racial dimension, as economic dependency within marriage was reserved for white women, while women of colour were expected to be employed, often in child-rearing and housework for white families (Glenn 1992; Gordon 1994; Quadagno 1994; Roberts 1995). Other analysts, often Scandinavian or British, have emphasised women's responsibility for care work within the gendered division of labour, the continuing dependence of the society on women's unpaid care work, and the ways in which in welfare states care work is less well rewarded than the paid labour that characterises most men's lives, even though women are much less likely to be in poverty there than in North America or Australia (Land 1978; Waerness 1984; Borchorst and Siim 1987; Ungerson 1987, 1990; Balbo 1982; Hernes 1987, 1988; Finch and Groves 1983).

More recently, there has been a greater focus on the ways in which state practices themselves constitute gender relations (Gordon and Fraser 1994; Knijn 1994; Saraceno 1994; Cass 1994; Bryson 1992; Pateman 1989; Lister 1990). This includes: first, women's marginalisation in the polity; second, gendered identities and citizenship with its encodings of male 'independence' based on wage-earning (rather than military service) and female 'dependence', and associated gender-differentiated social provision in which women's and men's basis for making claims differ, and claims based on employment are treated more favourably than claims based on family status; and third, the political and ideological creation of a split between public and private spheres (and women's relegation to the private), which exempts from political consideration and remediation the 'private' processes that affect men's and women's capacities and relative power.

Lewis argues for considering policy regimes in terms of their different levels of commitment to a male breadwinner–female housewife household form, which in ideal-typical form would 'find married women excluded from the labour market, firmly subordinated to their husbands for the purposes of social security entitlements and tax, and expected to undertake the work of caring (for children and other dependants) at home without public support' (Lewis 1992: 162). Women's interests, she thereby implies, are least well served by policies supporting this traditional set of arrangements. Lewis contrasts France, Sweden, Britain and Ireland, finding Britain and Ireland strongly committed to the breadwinner form, France less strongly so, and Sweden only weakly so, with support instead going to dual-earner households; Germany is also categorised as a strong breadwinner regime (Ostner and Lewis 1995). Thus, Lewis's approach underlines the fact that dimensions of variability based on gender relations do not correlate neatly with class-related dimensions (see also Shaver and Bradshaw 1993).

Lewis's exercise highlighted the gendered assumptions of policy-makers about family forms, but was less concerned with outcomes, such as the level of poverty among single mothers (Lewis 1997: 169). Lewis (1997) has since noted that if one looks at more countries, differences in outcomes are clear, even if the logic of supporting male breadwinner–female housewife families is the same. In the male breadwinner regime formulation, women's exclusion from paid work and their subordination within a male-headed family are joined – as they are in male breadwinner ideology. In essence gender difference is assumed to be accompanied by gender inequality and women's lack of autonomy. Given our interest in outcomes, and taking note of first-wave feminists' support of 'equality in difference' through proposals such as motherhood endowments (Lake 1992; Pedersen 1993), we want to think about these issues separately for both men and women, allowing for different articulations of the elements of sameness/difference, equality/inequality and dependency/autonomy.

Diane Sainsbury (1994, 1996) proposes examining states in terms of their similarity to one of two gendered ideal-types: the breadwinner model (similar to Lewis's conception) and an 'individual model', where both men and women are earners and carers, benefits are targeted on individuals, and much caring work is paid and provided publicly. But these ideal-types do not structure her empirical work (1996), which actually focuses on different bases of entitlement drawn from main-stream and gender-sensitive work: need, work and citizenship from the former; and care work or marital status from the latter. She is concerned with how women fare in making claims on these different bases of entitlement across four welfare states, the United States, the United Kingdom, the Netherlands and Sweden, and argues that universal or citizenship claims, which characterise the Swedish regime, produce the most beneficial outcomes for women. In contrast, systems based on work or need and marital status, as seen in the United States and the United Kingdom, are (for somewhat different reasons) much less helpful to women, principally because they treat claims based on work better than other claims, disadvantaging women due to their disadvantaged position in the labour market. We agree that claims bases are significant, yet we argue for systematically assessing social provision and its articulation with other elements of policy regimes such as labour markets and regulation of reproduction, and situating this in the context of a theorisation of gender relations and states. By looking only at social security systems, for example, Sainsbury misses how labour market changes are likely to influence women's capacity to make claims. In countries like the United States, Canada and, to a somewhat lesser extent, Australia, where employment equity programs have opened opportunities for some women, more will be able to make claims as workers. And these changes have also led to greater stratification among women – not all are disadvantaged; indeed, Sainsbury, like Lewis, gives little attention to differences among women or men, paralleling the earlier inattention to (gender) differences among workers. Similarly, it may be Sainsbury's focus on income maintenance apart from labour markets or regulation of reproduction which allows her to avoid confronting some of the unfavourable characteristics of the Swedish policy regime for women, such as a very highly segregated labour market, with a larger 'authority gap' than found in Australia, Canada or the United States (Wright and Baxter 1995), paternalistic rules governing some elements of repro-duction (Jenson and Mahon 1993; Lewis and Åstrom 1992; Ruggie 1988;

Liljestrand 1995), and recently exposed patterns of forced sterilisations on eugenic grounds (*New York Times* 30 August 1997: A22).

Given that gender and other elements of social relations are mutually constitutive, we have been pursuing the strategy of drawing on both mainstream and feminist work, with the aim of developing analytic frameworks that assume the importance of many social relations and identities even as we here focus on how various institutional arrangements and policies affect gender relations among different groups of men and women (O'Connor 1993c; Orloff 1993b; Shaver 1990). Thus, we disagree with Sainsbury's (1994, 1996) argument that building a regime-type framework that can assess gendered effects will proceed best by 'separating gender out' – rather, we want to build dimensions that can assess the specific effects of the state on gender, but consider this in the context of other social relations. Sainsbury (1994) describes our earlier work as though we were interested only in refashioning mainstream concepts to encompass men and women. We think that she has misread our efforts – we do argue for 'refashioning' mainstream concepts by gendering them. But in addition, both Julia O'Connor (1993c) and Ann Orloff (1993b) propose new and specifically gendered dimensions, discussed in greater detail below.

A systematic framework is necessary, one which accounts not only for the basis upon which claims for social rights are made – and the quality of the rights – but also for the overall organisation of services and income (incorporating private as well as public sources), for patterns of class and gender stratification, and for the ways in which labour market policies and the regulation of reproduction affect gender relations, principally through their impact on personal autonomy.

A Framework for Analysing Gender in Policy Regimes

In developing the framework to be used in this book, we draw on our earlier work on policy regimes and the gendered dimensions of state social provision. Shaver (1989a, 1990) argues that social policy regimes have components concerned with personhood and the rights of the individual, with the social organisation of work, and with social bonding in emotional and reproductive relationships. These have close congruence with the terms used by Connell (1987, 1995) to map the structures of gender relations more generally, which are identified as labour, power and cathexis. Shaver shows how the gender dimensions of policy regimes are shaped by state policies and legal frameworks. This approach then calls for an investigation of the gender basis of legal personhood, particularly with reference to 'body rights' such as control over reproduction; how the sexual division of labour is institutionalised in paid employment and affected by related policies such as child care; and how family, reproduction and sexuality are affected by the institutionalisation of dependency or individualisation and the privileging of heterosexuality. We build on these insights by including assessments of a number of policy areas – and their linkages – to allow a fuller than usual evaluation of the usefulness of regime-type frameworks and of the effects of state social provision and intervention on gender relations more generally.

Our choice of policy areas to investigate was informed by earlier feminist and mainstream research on welfare states and by the three dimensions identified by Shaver. We look at three policy areas. The first is the labour market, including the terms upon which women and men have access to paid work and the services that make such work possible for those with caregiving responsibilities, as well as patterns of men's and women's employment. The second is state social provision (cash transfers) as it affects men's and women's material conditions and how social rights are claimed; the ways state provision affects the division of labour, marriage and household formation, and child-rearing, as well as how it affects gendered identities, interests and alliances and reflects particular relationships among states, markets and families. The third area is reproduction, as it is expressed around the regulation of abortion, linked to the concept of legal rights of personhood. The links between labour markets and cash transfer programs have been a staple of welfare state research, and recent work extends this to consider also the impact of services on women's employment. Abortion regulation, however, is often considered apart from the 'welfare state proper'. Yet we would argue that state regulation of biological reproduction narrowly conceived (no pun intended) is influenced by some of the same factors that shape support for the reproduction of populations more broadly, including the cash transfers and services received by families. For example, the value to élites of the children of the poor, of the working classes, or of different racially or ethnically defined populations must be considered when investigating the support given to the mothers (or parents) raising them and women's access to various forms of fertility control.

These areas represent some of the most significant sites of gender politics in western countries over the last three decades. Moreover, by looking at the articulation of these policies within each country, in Chapter 6, we can provide a more comprehensive picture of how states affect gender relations than can be offered by investigations of single policy areas or single countries. We cannot presume to have covered all significant sites of gender politics, although we have attempted to select areas that are strategic and where we could build on our own past research. We see the present analysis as a critical step in developing comprehensive gendered and comparative accounts of welfare state developments, clarifying what are the relevant dimensions of gender policy regimes, and using this analytic framework to reveal the distinctive character of the gendered policy logic in each of the four countries. We also present a preliminary explanation of the patterns we identify by considering the character and strength of political mobilisations by gender equality forces, and the political opportunity structure which they have confronted.

Ann Orloff (1993b) and Julia O'Connor (1993c) build gendered analytic frameworks on the basis of the cumulated cross-national research findings about the relationship between states and societies and about the varying effects of states on social relations and economic inequality. Both have argued for a multi-dimensional approach to understanding the impact of social policy regimes. Clearly, the character of state, market, family relations or social organisation of income and services is significant for the patterning of dependencies and power. Indeed, one of the advances of regime-type analysis is to insist on considering private sources of income and services as well as public ones to get a complete description of welfare state types. Women's labour force participation is affected by how care is organised and whether there is a public component. But the mere absence of public provision of care does not tell us which private source – markets, voluntary organisations or families – will provide care. We hope to extend our understanding of states' impact on gender by this examination of countries where differences in the role of the state are not as pronounced as has been the case in earlier comparative studies. We expect that this will both allow us to develop a fuller understanding of the gendered effects of liberal institutional arrangements and to explore differences within this group related to other dimensions of gender regimes.

The stratification dimension is concerned with both gender differentiation, that is, the reinforcement of the gender division of labour, and inequality, that is, differences in access to valued resources. We attend as well to differences among women and among men based on gender roles (for example, paid worker, unpaid caregiver) or other social positions (for example, based on race or class). Regimes contribute variably to gender differentiation and politically salient gender identities on the systemic level (for example, through creating different programs for labour market and family 'failures') and individually (for example, through processes of making claims on the state, where men have typically made claims as individuals and workers, and women have often made claims as dependants and family members). Of course, gender differentiation, at least theoretically, may be compatible with gender equality (see, for example, Fraser 1997). Regimes also contribute to inequalities in the resources available to different groups (based on gendered identities or position in the division of labour, but also on other social differences such as class and race).

Finally, there are the gender effects of social provision on power relations of all kinds. Social rights are significant in that they provide a basis for citizens' personal and household autonomy and may insulate them from exploitable dependencies in families and markets (O'Connor 1993c; Orloff 1993b; Fraser 1997; Goodin 1985). Welfare states are usually understood to be organised on the basis of social citizenship rights; that is, effective claims on the state for particular benefits or services under specified conditions. But most systems retain varying levels of discretionary social assistance, which bears greater or lesser resemblance to poor relief (Eardley at al. 1996). Such aid, while preventing utter destitution, is less effective as a counterweight to dominant social forces in markets and families than are programs that take the form of social rights. Political and civil rights form part of the context for the claiming of social rights, and, for women's movements, the legal rights of personhood (for example, reproductive rights) have been an especially important goal.

In theory, social rights could be effective against all dependencies; arguments for a citizen's wage have sometimes been justified by considering its 'independence effects' vis-à-vis both markets and families. (Rights to be cared for, however, seem not to have been considered in this context; Kittay 1997.) Social provision based on need, if need were construed broadly and if programs were designed to protect recipients' dignity, might also work in ways that partially secured this end. But it is also often the case that social rights are effective in one sphere, but do not carry over to others, or are assigned to one group but withheld from others, or depend for their effectiveness on 'private' arrangements (for example, caregiving in the family). It is important to look at the whole ensemble of state interventions, along with market–family relationships, to understand their impact on gender relations. For example, women's caregiving allows men to participate in paid work without the encumbrances of caregiving responsibilities. Or women's paid work – making them less 'insulated' from the market – usually allows them greater independence in choices about family formation.

Social rights vis-à-vis the labour market are critical for workers in capitalist societies. Esping-Andersen (1990) focused on decommodification, which 'protects individuals, irrespective of gender, from total dependence on the labour market for survival ... [a] protection from forced participation, irrespective of age, health conditions, family status,

availability of suitable employment, [that] is obviously of major importance to both men and women' (O'Connor 1993c: 513), although
benefits allowing people to be outside the labour market affect men and
women differently given the present gender division of labour (Orloff
1993b: 317). Others emphasise rights to employment under specified
conditions of pay, safety, job satisfaction and the like. Given that not all
social groups have equal access to jobs that allow personal independence and access to benefits, critical gender dimensions of welfare
regime variability include access to paid work and to the services that
facilitate employment for caregivers. These are especially notable when
one considers women's historic exclusion from employment and the
linkage of citizenship rights to employment. We examine not only the
public supports for mothers' employment (as do Gornick, Meyers and
Ross 1997), but also how such supports may be provided through
markets. State efforts to open good employment opportunities to
women through anti-discrimination and employment equity policies
also affect women's access to work and their possibilities for personal
autonomy.

Rights may also be effective in subverting familial dependencies – not
those that are the result of a need to be cared for because of age or
disability, which Kittay (1997) and Fineman (1995) termed 'inevitable
dependency', but those resulting from the economic dependence, or
'derived dependence', that so often accompanies caregiving.

Welfare benefits, provision of services, and employment regulations
affect the capacity to form and maintain an autonomous household,
a dimension which indicates an individual's ability to survive and support their children without being forced to marry or enter into other
family relationships (Orloff 1993b). We prefer 'capacity to form an
autonomous household', or the shorter 'autonomy', to 'defamilisation',
suggested as an analogue for decommodification (McLaughlin and
Glendinning 1996; Lister 1994a). Some have argued that 'capacity
to form and maintain an autonomous household' does not attend to
women's situation within marriage. On the contrary, by referring
to 'capacities' for autonomy, we indicate whether people have the
resources to choose household forms freely, whatever their current
situation (in or out of partnerships of various sorts). We fear that
'defamilisation' will suggest a preference for substantive autonomy –
no families – and conjure up exactly the sort of illusions about individuals' capacities to operate without interdependencies for which
traditional advocates of liberalism have been criticised by feminist
political theorists. We believe that a key issue for contemporary gender
relations is whether women – like most men – are in a position of
being able to choose freely whether or not to enter marital or other

relationships, and to some extent to have a voice in their character. Such a capacity enhances women's power vis-à-vis men, especially within marriages and families. Thus, we are concerned with procedural autonomy – women's as well as men's rights to make decisions free of coercion – rather than expressing a preference for substantive autonomy (see Marilyn Friedman 1997).

There are at least two possible sources for a capacity to form an autonomous household. Paid work is a principal avenue by which women have sought to enhance their independence from husbands and fathers in families – thereby undermining the breadwinner–housewife family form – and claim full status as 'independent' citizens in the liberal democratic polity. Others are cash benefits from the state for staying at home to care for children or others, a citizen's wage, or a combination of employment and state benefits. But this dimension could be generalised to ask how different sorts of supports for diverse households affect the balance of power between men and women within marriages and families as well as outside them, and is therefore relevant for men's as well as women's situations.

Different groups gain access to capacities for household formation and maintenance in distinctive ways. In all western states, the vast majority of men gain this capacity through their market work; most income maintenance programs, since their inception, have served as 'back-ups' to the family wage system, allowing men to continue to support their families when they lose their wage-earning capacities temporarily or permanently. Until recently, however, women did not have equal access to such programs, principally because they were not in full-time employment, although in some cases because of discriminatory rules. Even now, most men retain a significant amount of freedom of choice relative to family and household formation given advantaged labour market positions and welfare state back-ups, even as some of the family-supporting components of income maintenance programs have been cut back. Women's sources of support typically have been more mixed and more varied across groups of women and cross-nationally. Many women continue to rely on wage-earning men to support them in part or entirely, while others have turned to states or to labour market participation. Benefits for sole parents are not usually generous enough to merit being called a 'citizen's' wage, but they do offer a bottom-line capacity for household independence (critical in cases of domestic violence). State policies have differed in how – and if at all – the capacity to form and maintain households is supported for men and for women, or for some groups of men and women. (For example, some regimes have promoted stay-at-home motherhood and supported breadwinning for men for a favoured 'race'/ethnicity or class whose reproductive capacities are valued, while denying such supports to others.) Moreover, the dimension of capacity to form an autonomous household implies more than individual independence; it also gets at whether women and men are allowed to have, as well as to support, families, thus reflecting the character of regulations of sexuality, custody, reproduction, marriage, divorce and household composition. (We might call this 'access to family', to parallel access to work.) Thus, the concept has relevance for other groups which have been denied the rights and resources to form and maintain families: people with disabilities, immigrants and refugees, minority ethnic or racial groups, or gays and lesbians.

For many analysts of the welfare state, the state's emancipatory potential resides in rights that counteract the power of the market (for example, Korpi and Palme 1998; Offe 1984; Esping-Andersen 1985, 1990), as they are concerned mainly with the situation of (implicitly male) workers, not about men and women in terms of their position in gender relations, and because they link social rights to the political mobilisation of workers. Demands for social rights supporting other forms of autonomy are related to a particular understanding of women's interests and are linked to specific currents within contemporary political mobilisations. Recent work cautions against deducing politically salient identities and interests from social structures; rather, these must be understood in specific historical, political and discursive contexts (see, for example, R. Pringle and Watson 1992; Weir, Orloff and Skocpol 1988).

With what grouping, and with what understanding of women's gender interests could one link social rights for personal autonomy? Feminist analysts are wary of assumptions that there is a unitary and natural category 'women' with a set of already constituted common interests and homogeneity of experience, noting conflicts of interests among women based on class, race, ethnicity, nationality, sexual orientation, and so on as well as historical differences in how the category 'woman' was constituted (see, for example, Collins 1990; Molyneux 1985; Riley 1988). We might instead consider gender interests, that is, the interests of men and women that have their basis in gender relations across a series of contexts and including positions within the gender division of labour, sexual relations, gendered political power and so on (for example, Mouffe 1992; Young 1994). This allows one to treat gender relations as a (not 'the') primary means of structuring social relations without assuming that all women or all men are positioned in the same way. Indeed, we should expect differences among women, and among men, in gender interests.

We take a contextual approach to the construction of interests and identities. We expect differences across the nationally specific institutional and political settings represented by the concept of 'social policy regime', as well as across socially significant groupings based on race, class and the like, in at least some aspects of men's and women's gender interests. Once particular sets of arrangements are institution-alised, political actors build up expectations and understandings, and make decisions and investments of time and resources that are not easy to revise or undo. This is important for understanding women's 'choices' about part-time versus full-time work, for instance. Moreover, the preferences or interests developed within one national context may not translate into another.

Bodily and economic autonomy have been central themes in women's movements' demands on the states of Australia, Britain, Canada and the United States. Autonomy is usually taken to imply the freedom to make choices about reproduction, family and work and the resources to act on one's choices. Some formulations of such demands incorporate a pervasive individualist liberalism characteristic of modern societies, reflected in both the welfare state itself and in 'radical', 'liberal' and other feminisms. Feminists have criticised liberalism for failing to take account of interdependencies and the need for care faced by all of us at some points in our lives (see, for example, Kittay 1997). Others have argued for the value of caring and mutuality which seems missing in much liberal thought and political practice and, indeed, in some versions of feminism (see, for example, Tronto 1993; Gilligan 1982). Yet, while recognising these values, and the dangers of a false independence, others – and we would include ourselves here – want to insist on the necessity of sharing care work in a just manner. It is critical to avoid the imposition of the obligations, burdens and costs of care on only some groups, which has sometimes taken the form of better-off women 'off-loading' care work onto other women of less-advantaged social status (for example, immigrants, poor women) which in the framework of dominant market liberalism may be construed as 'voluntary' (Folbre 1994; this phenomenon is discussed in Glenn 1992 and Windebank 1996). We affirm the importance of social arrangements which while supporting interdependency also give scope for individual choice in commitments to the self and others. By no means have all women accepted the goal of autonomy; indeed, the phenomenon of 'right-wing' women, or women mobilised around defending 'traditional' gen-der relations, has been investigated extensively (see, for example, among many, Luker 1984; Kandiyoti 1991; Klatch 1990); such women would reject notions of interests based on increasing 'choice' (see, for example, Jónasdóttir 1988). However, we think 'autonomy' corresponds with some of the political demands of contemporary movements for gender equality and reflects the strategic logic of modern feminist political projects vis-à-vis the welfare state – projects with which we sympathise, and the influence of which we may assess as reflected in states' support to autonomy.

After describing analytically the gendered logics we find in the four countries – that is, the gendered patterns of stratification, social and civil rights, and the social organisation of income and services – we turn to an examination of the relationship between the political forces of gender equality and these patterns. We examine both how gender equality issues have been understood and represented in the four countries since the 1960s, and some of the key factors (in addition to liberalism) that have affected the orientations and success (or lack of it) of women's movements. For example, the US political context has been quite encouraging to liberal feminist civil rights claims, in terms of available allies and established political discourse, but less open to claims for social rights. Canadians have found increasing space for civil rights claims, and, like Americans, have found encouragement for an orientation based around access to employment. British feminists, in contrast, have been able to rely on stronger traditions of social rights, including allies within the labour movement and labour parties, but find less space for distinctively gendered civil rights claims; moreover, during the 1980s and early 1990s, they confronted a dismal political opportunity structure for influencing state policy. Australians enjoyed a more encouraging political climate than did Britons, but also built upon a distinctive tradition of social rights and labour activism unlike the American one. We also assess how trends such as increasing globalisation and economic restructuring affect the prospects for women's equality projects.

Ultimately, feminists may want to link analyses of the character of gender policy regimes and historical accounts of policy developments with theorisations of women's power or of the ways in which the distribution of power flows along gendered lines, but we attempt a more modest account which will, we hope, offer a mapping of the explanatory terrain awaiting future researchers of gender and welfare states. We would stress that a full explanation of these gender regimes or other gendered policy outcomes will require not only an examination of women's political mobilisation, but also an examination of the forces which already have been shown to be influential in earlier accounts of policy developments: the character of economic production, demographic characteristics and family and household forms, ideologies and discourses of welfare, the structure of gender interests and the mobilisation of forces around those interests, political institutions and opportunity structures, state capacities, and the like. Future research might well rely on the exemplars of Jane Jenson (1986) and Susan Pedersen (1993), who trace the development of British and French family policies comparatively, and situate the forces mobilised around different gender identities, interests and ideologies – feminists, Catholics, trade unionists and others – in the context of geopolitics, élite fears about declining fertility, different economic profiles, employers' variable demand for women workers, trade unionists' variable strength to enforce a family wage, state capacities and discourses of the family, state and economy.

What of the effects of social policy regimes on relations of race, ethnicity, nationality, immigration status, language and other identities? This has been an issue of much concern for feminist and other scholars who are attempting to avoid overgeneralising about women (and men). For example, notions about imagined communities of class, race, ethnicity, and nationality have also shaped policies for the support of mothers, parents and children. In the United States, Australia and Canada, maternalist programs – mothers' pensions, maternal health programs, and the like – were not consistently accessible to African-Americans, other women of colour and indigenous women (Bellingham and Mathis 1994; Lieberman 1995; Goodwin 1992; Gordon 1994; Roberts 1993; Boris 1995; Lake 1992; Little 1995). Our focus is on understanding states and gender relations, and we do not attempt to fully map states' impacts on class relations, race relations, or other aspects of social difference and inequality (but see Omi and Winant 1994). But it is possible – and important – to highlight gender relations analytically, while attending to variations in how states affect the gender relations of different social groups. This kind of work will complement case studies of particular countries, regions or localities which can examine the interworkings of class, race, gender, nationality and sexuality (see, for example, Boris 1995; Mink 1994; Roberts 1995; Williams 1989), as well as analyses which foreground the construction of other social relations, while attending to gender differences across groups (but see Shaver 1989a; Williams 1995).

Comparative Strategy

States clearly do differ to some extent in their effects on gender relations. We know that the United States, Britain, Canada and Australia differ from Sweden, and, for that matter, from any other European country, but we don't know well enough just how much – and along which dimensions – they may or may not differ from each other. By comparing four countries with significant similarities, of course, we will not be in a position to evaluate precisely how different they are from other developed countries. Most work to date on gender and policy regimes has compared countries with very different institutional features. From this research, we have learned about the importance of certain regime characteristics, particularly the broad patterns of state–society relations, for explaining variation in gendered outcomes. But conclusions based on analyses which contrast countries purporting to represent different regime types are very likely influenced by which country is chosen to 'stand in' for any given regime cluster, when we have not carefully assessed their differences and similarities across dimensions relevant for gender. Moreover, while there have been analyses of the Scandinavian countries and some attention to whether some specific cases (such as the Netherlands) fit into the social democratic or conservative corporatist groups, less attention has been given to the liberal countries as a group although each has been studied extensively as an individual case. Liberalism is too often treated simply as a residual category – the 'not-social democratic' or 'not-conservative'. We attempt to give more substance to liberalism as a set of ideologies and institutional arrangements, built up over time, which shape current patterns of policies, and thereby contribute to understanding substantively the impact of policy liberalism on gender relations, a concern we have as scholars and as participants in liberal polities.

The impact of liberal ideologies and institutional arrangements on gender relations has not yet been assessed empirically in a systematic way. Clearly, commodification is a feature of all varieties of capitalism, but nowhere in the developed west has commodification yet been applied to women on the same terms as men, running into competing imperatives of social reproduction and the interests of most men and some women in encouraging women to marry and maintain responsibility for domestic work. Yet liberal social policy is said to do more than other types to promote the commodification of labour and the reliance of citizens on markets. We investigate whether the stronger reliance in liberal countries on private forms of provision and the concomitant lesser development of the state has distinctive gendered consequences. Women's increasing participation in wage labour is not limited to the so-called liberal countries, but it may exhibit distinctive patterns related to the institutional and policy features of this type of welfare regime. Similarly, the tradition in the United States, Britain, Canada and Australia of individualism and attachment to 'negative' liberty – that is, freedom from state interference in personal (as well as economic) affairs – may well be associated with distinctive patterns of family and reproductive policies and practices. And, of course, different variants of liberalism may be associated with distinctive views about proper gender relations, or gender ideologies may vary independently.

These four countries have been shown to have a number of commonalities in terms of the social, economic and political factors thought to influence the historical development of social policy. Most obviously, they share a British cultural and political heritage – albeit one which is enriched by varying degrees of ethnic and racial heterogeneity, including the continuing presence of indigenous peoples in the three settler societies; the 'French fact' of Quebec; the descendants of African slaves in the United States and to a much smaller degree in Canada and, as immigrants from former British colonies, in Britain; substantial numbers of immigrants from Europe (Irish immigrants being notable in all four), Latin America and Asia. Indeed, relative to other developed countries, the four, and particularly the United States, have historically had heterogeneous populations (Omi and Winant 1994; Stasiulis and Yuval-Davis 1995). In all four, landed classes were relatively weaker and bourgeoisies relatively stronger than in continental Europe (Moore 1967). Their (historically) more protected geopolitical position relative to the nations of continental Europe resulted in less-developed state capacities for domestic interventions and thereby reinforced preferences for private as opposed to state provision (Orloff 1993a). Liberalism and liberal parties have played strong political and ideological roles (Hartz 1964), while church-related parties analogous to the Christian democratic parties of Europe are absent (Lipset 1979). Indeed, because we are interested in liberalism, gender and policy, we chose not to focus on certain parts of these countries: Quebec and Northern Ireland, where Catholicism and separatist nationalisms, and a history of colonial subjugation in the latter, complicate the picture considerably. Feminism has been historically a relatively strong social movement in all four countries (Koven and Michel 1993), and suffrage for women came relatively earlier than in continental Europe, particularly in Australia and the western states of the United States (Sivard 1985: 28). In combination with strong individualist currents in the cultures of the four, this is reflected in distinctive family arrangements and strong affirmation of women's independence. The liberal countries, especially the United States, feature relatively high rates of divorce and proportions of single parent families (see Table 4.2, p. 156). As across the west, women's labour force participation has increased. In these four, levels are higher than anywhere but the Scandinavian countries (see Table 3.1, p. 68).

Canada, Britain, the United States and Australia share some impressive similarities in terms of the political factors found to be significant for contemporary policy outcomes that distinguish them from other western countries with democratic institutions, capitalist economies and high standards of living; we discuss this more thoroughly in Chapter 6. Political configurations in the four include relatively high levels of right party incumbency (Castles and Mitchell 1993: 117), linked to their two or two and a half party systems based on first past the post or modified plurality electoral arrangements (Castles 1993). In place of social democratic and communist parties, one finds labour parties in Australia (ALP) and Britain; and, in Canada, the social democratic New Democratic Party (NDP), one of Canada's minor parties, promotes some policies similar to the ALP and Labour. In the United States, we see the 'exceptional' (and much remarked upon) absence of socialist or social democratic parties of any sort, although the Democratic Party contains (but is far from dominated by) social democratic currents. Corporatist arrangements have not, for the most part, found fertile ground in the four. A key exception was the Accord between the unions and the Australian Labor Party that has been a significant feature of recent Australian political arrangements, and one which is implicated in some of Australia's unusual policy features relative to women's paid work, although the 1996 election of a Liberal-led Coalition Government is likely to undercut the influence of the unions (Castles 1994, 1996a). Finally, these four countries are notable for the extensive mobilisation among women of maternalist and feminist movements which championed state support and political recognition for women's mothering activities in the early years of the welfare state (Koven and Michel 1993; Skocpol 1992; Lake 1992; Pedersen 1993). Feminism remains today a strong social movement and popular cultural presence (despite backlash) in all four countries (Katzenstein 1987; Klein 1987; Curthoys 1994; Randall 1987; Adamson, Briskin and McPhail 1988; Nelson and Chowdhury 1994). In contrast, women's political representation is relatively low, reflecting largely (but not exclusively) the structural barriers imposed by the electoral and party systems in these countries; women have a somewhat better representation in public administration, particularly in Australia, Canada and the United States (Norris 1987: ch. 6; United Nations 1995: 171–5).

   While we can note the significant political similarities among the four countries, it is also critical to take notice of the changing partisan character of governments. The fortunes of different political parties remain central to understanding policy developments. A commitment to restructuring and economic rationalism have come to characterise parties of both right and left, the result of intense ideological and organisational battles over the 1980s and 1990s (P. Pierson 1994; Pusey 1991; Cooper, Kornberg and Mishler 1988). Yet partisan differences remain with regard to how much of a role the state should have in steering restructuring efforts and buffering its effects on citizens and regions, and parties differ as well in their programs relevant for gender relations (for example, the Australian Labor Party favours the expansion of public child care, the Coalition Government has offered assistance for housewifery; see Mitchell 1997; the US Democrats by and large support abortion rights, while the Republicans' platform does not; Ontario's Progressive Conservatives have attacked the wage equity scheme of the previous NDP Government). In addition, political groups both right and left are to some extent divided by differences about gender; even though organised feminist groups are for the most part allied with left or centre-left parties, concerns about gender relations have affected the right as well (for example, internal splits over abortion in the US Republican Party). Restructuring of social policies will occur whatever the outcomes of the next few elections, but the shape these policies ultimately take will surely be influenced by which parties and which factions are in power when critical decisions have to be made.

In the following chapters, we take on the task of empirically describing and analysing the cross-national variations among these four welfare states across the three policy areas – labour markets, income support, and regulation of reproduction. Our examination of labour market policy in Chapter 3 begins with gendered patterns of labour market participation (a key feature of the gender division of labour), then focuses on women's employment rights, an essential area of citizenship rights. We cover service provision and parental leave policies, and employment equality strategies, including anti-discrimination, affirmative action and comparable worth initiatives. Our analysis is distinctive not only in accounting for public–private division in service provision, but also in considering the institutional roles of states, markets and families, revealing important distinctions among the four even within the overall emphasis on 'private' provision. We also explore patterns of gender stratification (sameness/difference) linked with employment patterns and policies, and document the emergence of stratification based on distinctions between good jobs and bad jobs which partially replaces, and partially overlaps with, gender differences. Chapter 4 examines the major income maintenance programs: old-age (retirement) and survivors' coverage, unemployment benefits, sole parents' benefits, support for families and support to caregiving. We describe the roles of states, markets, and families in the provision of income, the creation or reinforcement of gender (and class) differentiation and inequality (stratification) within cash transfer programs in terms of the benefits and treatment accorded to different beneficiaries, and the institutionalisation of social rights for household support and personal autonomy – or lack thereof. Chapter 5 presents material on how abortion rights are secured, provided and understood, situating this legal right of personhood in the context of social rights to health care.

Our focus is on carefully delineating the features of policy in each area, utilising elements of the analytic frameworks we have described above in order to accurately capture the states' gendered effects.

Although we have been guided by a common framework in analysing the policy areas, we allow the specificities of each policy area to shape each discussion. We draw on a range of primary sources – mainly government documents and reports – and secondary analyses of gender relations and social provision. Before proceeding to the comparative analysis, we explore more fully the gendered dimensions of liberal ideology in Chapter 2. We want to draw out the implications of different variants of liberalism for gender relations, as well as to discuss how historically liberal social policy has affected gender relations. In Chapter 6, we discuss the distinctive character and articulation of these policies – the overall gendered policy logic – in each country, and assess the similarities and differences of the four policy regimes. Here we also link these gendered policy logics with the differing patterns of political mobilisation by women's equality forces in social movements and political parties in the context of distinctive political opportunity structures across the four countries. We close with our reflections on the significance of these patterns for social theory and political strategy.

CHAPTER 2

Liberalism, Gender and Social Policy

The ideology of liberalism is a defining element of the liberal welfare state type (Esping-Andersen 1990: 41–4), yet what this ideology implies for social policy institutions has been largely taken for granted. Comparative analysis has focused on the economic dimensions of liberalism, primarily the liberal valuation of the individual and the central roles of the market and voluntary effort in social provision. Typically, liberalism's broader social policy content has been evoked with general references to Titmuss's (1974: 30–2) model of residual social policy, in which public policy has a role only when market and family fail. Discussion of the liberal type has given little attention to those aspects of liberal ideology which refer to gender and the relation between state and family, and to the way these aspects are expressed in social policy institutions. This chapter addresses that gap.

Interestingly, the comparative literature has had rather more to say about the relations between state and family which characterise other regime types. It has noted the importance of religious principles in shaping these relations in the corporatist policy regimes of continental Europe (Flora 1986: xviii). The Catholic concept of subsidiarity sees the relation between state and family as a hierarchy of governance, with authority supposed to remain at the lowest level possible. Its Protestant counterpart in the doctrine of sphere sovereignty views family, state and church as separate and distinct spheres of authority. Both principles entail state support for traditional family structure, and these states have been less responsive to women's demands than their liberal counterparts (Ostner 1993). In sharp contrast, Scandinavian social democratic policy regimes have drawn on a communitarian tradition in which state and society are seen as mutually interlocking. This tradition legitimates state intervention to foster gender equality, primarily through the

43

provision of services to harmonise work and family life in dual-earner households (Sainsbury 1996: 26; Esping-Andersen 1996a: 10–13).

There is a sense in which liberal ideology pervades all capitalist welfare states, whatever their type. Represented in it are key terms of cultural meaning which describe human identity in the modern west (Taylor 1989). Fundamental to these terms is the notion of the person as an individual self capable of introspection, freedom and moral action. There is, further, an affirmation of ordinary life, including commercial activity but also an idealisation of marriage and family life independent of control by the wider society. As well, there is a valuation of sentiment and a notion of nature as an inner moral source. This notion, in its Victorian forms, extended to ideals of equality, universal benevolence and a moral imperative to reduce suffering.

These terms of cultural meaning suffuse the defining conception of person and society at the heart of the liberal political tradition. Gray (1995: xii) describes this conception as having four unifying tenets. Liberalism is individualist, giving primacy to the person over the social group; it is egalitarian, regarding all persons as having the same moral status; it is universalistic, valuing the moral unity of the human species above particularities of association and culture; and it is meliorist in regarding all social institutions and political arrangements as capable of human improvement. Affinities between liberal ideology and the welfare state are further evinced in the centrality to both of the notions of right and the just claims of the individual on the state given by such rights. Liberalism posits individuals as having natural rights to freedom and property, and assigns to the state the role of elaborating and enforcing those rules necessary to reconcile conflicts among the rights of individuals. Liberals disagree, however, about the extent to which such rules can express a common vision of social justice (Plant 1991: 79).

The origins of modern welfare states lie in the 'liberal break' of the late eighteenth century, when core liberal ideas such as the free individual, equality and self-help lent impetus to the replacement of paternalistic poor relief with the beginnings of modern national welfare arrangements (Rimlinger 1971: 35–86; Flora and Alber 1981: 48). With the liberal break, British poor law reform gave liberal ideology a new legislative authority, affirming the principles of less eligibility and the workhouse test. These adapted the modern forms of social protection that began to be established at the end of the nineteenth century to the needs and ethos of industrial capitalism. This was the case not only in England, France and the United States, where liberalism was strong, but also in Bismarck's Germany, where it was much weaker (Rimlinger 1971: 122; see also Polanyi 1957). Liberalism also had a strong influence on the early formation of Scandinavian welfare institutions (P. Baldwin 1990: 55–65; Castles and Mitchell 1993: 120).

In the discussion of welfare states, liberalism is more often understood in the specific sense of an ideology of market capitalism which has constrained the role of the state in countries of British political heritage. This is the economic liberalism which Karl Polanyi (1957) identifies with laissez-faire and English poor law reform, and whose key ideas C. B. Macpherson (1962) identifies as the ideology of possessive individualism. Liberalism in this sense has a far narrower meaning. As compared with liberalism in general, individualism and universalism are exaggerated in its conception of person and society, while the meliorist orientation to human institutions is weakened by extreme distrust of public politics and the role of the state.

This is the meaning Esping-Andersen (1990: 41–4) evokes to distinguish between liberal welfare states and their corporatist and social democratic counterparts. The hallmarks of the liberal welfare state are benefits shaped by the principles of less eligibility and voluntarism. According to the first, a framework of means-tested social assistance drawn from the old poor laws ensures that social protection does not interfere with the workings of the labour market. The commitment to voluntarism stresses charity and self-help, the latter institutionalised in contributory social insurance or collectively bargained social benefits for wage earners. Esping-Andersen maintains that liberalism has proved highly flexible, devising ways of accommodating social protection which are not only compatible with the commodity status of labour but may also strengthen it.

Feminism has given important insights into the gender content of liberalism. Its critique centres on the dichotomy between the public and the private at the foundation of liberal thought. Because it divides the public world of state and society from the private domestic life of home and family, this separation is inherently gendered. Liberalism portrays the public and private spheres as independent of one another when in reality they are inextricably connected, and so obscures a fundamental source of power and inequality in relations between the sexes (Okin 1981; Burton 1985: 41–56; Pateman 1989). This separation provides the starting point for understanding the distinctive ideological grounding for gender relations in welfare states of the liberal type.

Liberalism itself has had several distinctive historical inflections. This chapter examines three successive variants of liberalism which have influenced welfare state development in these and other countries. These are classical liberalism, new or social liberalism, and neo-liberalism. The discussion considers how the division between public and private has been understood in each of these variants and the way such understandings have been translated in the policy regimes in the United States, Great Britain, Canada and Australia. The meaning of this division for women's place in the public world of economic and political life has changed as liberalism itself has changed. The shift from classical to new liberalism opened the parameters of liberal individualism to allow real, though limited, recognition of social interdependency. These parameters were institutionalised in liberal social policy regimes in all four countries. The social interdependency these parameters recognised has come under challenge again with the neo-liberal reassertion of the primacy of market individualism. However, the apparent circularity of these shifts conceals more linear development within liberalism in the way it has understood relations between state and family and the individual personhood of women. Classical liberalism assumed a division between the public world of state and civil society and the private family household of male head and dependent family members. This division was carried over into new liberalism and the nascent welfare state, where it shaped social policy regimes in terms of family wage principles. Those principles have become increasingly problematic in the current period, not least because of challenges from feminism and its assertion of women's claim to equality as liberal individuals. Family wage principles have comparatively little place in the social policy prescriptions of contemporary neo-liberalism.

Classical Liberalism

For the welfare states of Great Britain and her former colonies the legacy to which Rimlinger refers was that of liberalism itself, and in particular the tensions between its classical and new liberal variants (Orloff 1993a: 163–7). The classical liberalism of the 'liberal break' drew directly on the heritage of Enlightenment thought and political philosophy in the tradition of Hobbes, Locke and Smith. Sheldon Wolin (1961: 294) characterises liberalism as at once an attack on traditionalism and a defence against radical democracy. Finding the source of social authority in human beings themselves, it was secular and rationalist in temper. In this sense liberalism and conservatism were born together, for, as liberalism broke with tradition, conservatism was defined by its defence. Robert Nisbet (1966: 9) refers to radicalism, liberalism and conservatism as the three great ideologies of the nineteenth and early twentieth centuries. Liberalism viewed all men (as Nisbet saw it) as equal in nature, and perhaps equal in political authority; it did not see them as necessarily or appropriately equal in status and wealth.

The key terms of classical liberalism were freedom and the rights of the individual. The state existed to protect the natural rights of its citizens, and its power was properly limited to this function. Macpherson (1962: 263–77) sets out seven assumptions comprising the ideology of possessive individualism. These begin with the premise that human freedom requires independence of the wills of others, more specifically freedom to enter into relations with others voluntarily and with a view to one's own interests. The individual is thus the proprietor of his or her own person and capacities, owing nothing to society, and in practical expression of such freedom has the right to alienate his or her capacity to labour. In the ideology of possessive individualism human society consists of a series of market or market-like relations. The role of the state is to protect the individual's property in his or her person and goods, and to maintain the orderly relations of exchange between individual societies on which society-as-market depends. It may abridge the freedom of the individual only to the degree necessary to ensure that all individuals have the same freedom.

Liberalism was first of all about the emancipation of the individual from the restraints of tradition and the rule of the crown, aristocracy and church. Its rationalism and the equation of social with market relations came out of its infusion with ideas from classical economics. This infusion replaced the older notion of a common good posited by reason with that of a society rooted in desire, and the interior self of conscience with the exterior one of interest. The ends of action were a product of the passions, and rational conduct lay less in moral restraint than in the calculation of self-interest and the sacrifice of present pleasures for future ones. Liberal ideas about the state reflected anxieties about property and its preservation in social conditions of scarcity and inequality. The primary object of social policy was thus security – the security of property rather than of the life circumstances of the poor (Wolin 1961: 331–3).

Liberal social policy found an uncompromising expression in the English poor laws of 1834. In the eyes of the liberal Nassau Senior, a member of the Poor Law Commission, they represented emancipation from the servitude of laws designed to restrict the freedom of the working class for the benefit of their masters, laws which imprisoned them in their parishes and dictated their employment and wages (Rimlinger 1971: 42–3). However, while assistance might be allowed to the aged and incapable, aid to the able-bodied poor was to be subordinated to the market. The principle of less eligibility and the workhouse test ensured that aid to the poor not only did not intrude on the incentives of the labour market but reinforced them. Orloff notes a remarkable similarity in liberal ideologies of social policy in Britain, Canada and the United States by the 1870s, a result in part of constant communication between their leading figures. Two basic approaches were at play in all three countries. Classic or laissez-faire liberalism favoured deterrent poor relief to enforce the work ethic and discourage dependency. Scientific charity saw a positive role for the emerging field of social work in distinguishing the deserving from the undeserving poor and developing expert methods for rehabilitating the former. There were institutional differences in the three countries. While Great Britain developed state administration, charitable bodies played a larger role in the United States. Canada's later development meant that the shift in policy was less marked in that country (Orloff 1993a: 161–7).

When it came to women, the affirmations of the natural equality and freedom of individuals at the heart of classical liberalism were problematic. Susan Okin (1981) shows how stubborn were the contradictions these assumptions raised for the development of liberal philosophy. The new value which modern culture placed on sentiment, marriage and family life has already been noted. Okin argues that the idealisation of the sentimental domestic (and patriarchal) family gave a new rationale for the subordination of women in a society premised on equality. Women were now to be idealised as the mistresses of the domestic haven, creatures of sentiment rather than rationality, and united with their husbands in upholding the interests of household and family. Women's lack of political rights was an obvious expression of their exclusion from the society of individuals. Explicating the hidden clauses in the social contract, Carole Pateman (1989; see also Vogel 1991) reveals fraternal assumptions in the metaphor of legitimate political authority: the parties to the social contract are patriarchal heads of households, and they consent to political order on behalf of other family members. She argues that the incompleteness of women's individual personhood, including their subordinate status in many of the provisions of the welfare state, is a testament to the power of the fraternal social contract.

Mistresses of the domestic haven were the economic dependants of husbands and fathers. Most adherents of classical liberalism assumed women's proper dependence within a family headed by a male bread-winner. Yet some early liberals – John Stuart Mill as well as Mary Wollstonecraft and Harriet Taylor – believed women as well as men were entitled to individual civil and political rights and to the means of independence (Eisenstein 1981). The meaning of dependency, central to liberal ideology, has itself undergone transformations (Fraser and Gordon 1994: 314–19). Classical liberalism recognised gender difference in terms of the sentimental family and the pedestal: men and women were different, and women's difference distanced them from the liberal individual of the market and competitive society. As individuals and the heads of families, men were physical participants in labour markets and actors in political life. As wives, at least, women's natural dependency placed them in the private domain of home and family, removed from both politics and the market. In actuality, women also laboured, in or outside the market, but were not widely forced to work under poor relief until the 1870s (Orloff 1993a: 121–51). (In the United States gender differences were not given the same meaning for all racial groups. Women of colour were not exempted from work requirements, and often could not achieve economic independence.) For both men and women, the claim to poor relief disqualified the individual from the respect and entitlements of citizenship. Since women (and certain groups of men) did not share in the key to such entitlement, the franchise, these effects had gender contours also.

New Liberalism

The ideological foundations of the liberal welfare states lie less in classical liberalism than in the new liberalism and kindred movements of the late nineteenth and early twentieth centuries. Among the impulses to reform, Rimlinger (1971: 57–60) identifies the Fabianism of Sidney and Beatrice Webb, the Victorian conscience, the settlement house movement, and Booth and Rowntree's research documenting the failures of poor law and charitable provision. Orloff (1993a: 167) also notes changes in the character of the state itself, giving it new capacities to intervene in and regulate economic activity. Originating in England, the currents of new liberal ideology were also influential in shaping social policy in North America and Australasia.

New liberalism was one of a number of overlapping bodies of social thought which arose in the period, including idealism, positivism and especially socialism. It was particularly significant in social policy (Freeden 1978: 195). The impetus to its emergence is debated. Gaston Rimlinger (1971: 57) attributes it to the growing strength of organised labour and Britain's Labour Party, while Freeden (1978: 21) sees it as a modernisation of the liberal tradition generated from within liberalism itself. They agree about the importance of changing attitudes among sections of the middle and upper classes. Jose Harris (1993: 228–9), who considers idealism the more significant variant of progressive thought in the period, attributes the upsurge of new liberalism to the social dislocations of the times and loss of confidence in the doctrines of classical economics.

New liberalism, sometimes also called social or social democratic liberalism, was a synthesis of individualist and collectivist values. It shared classical liberalism's concern with the freedom of the individual, but took much greater notice of the social circumstances which conditioned individual choices. New liberalism understood freedom as more than the negative freedom of classical liberalism: it also included the positive freedoms of opportunity and personal development. It brought to liberalism a new concern with the ethical character of society, which it viewed as an organic whole. Drawing on scientific discourses of evolution, it saw this whole as motivated by the co-operative spirit that replaced the competitive instincts of natural selection in higher order species. The new liberals saw industrial society as creating new circumstances of social interdependency, in which government was an indispensable support for individual endeavour. They recognised poverty, especially among the aged, as less evidently a failure of the individual and more probably a consequence of social and economic processes. As a political philosophy of reform, new liberalism sanctioned actions benefiting the majority, centrally the working classes, as the expression of common rather than class interest (Freeden 1978; Dickey 1980; Harris 1993: 11–13; Orloff 1993a: 167–81).

In consequence, new liberals rejected the deterrent poor law in favour of social provision with at least the flavour of right. Unlike the poor law assistance of classical liberalism, social protection was constructed as a feature of citizenship, an enhancement rather than a negation of civil and political status. State-sponsored old-age protection recognised dependency among aged people in honourable terms analogous to those applied to soldiers (Orloff 1993a: 173–9). New liberal reformers were attracted to contributory social insurance because it could reflect liberal principles such as foresight and thrift in universal provision. Often, however, means-tested benefits were a more practical basis for initial developments (Freeden 1978: 200–6; Shaver 1991). New liberal values also underpinned industrial regulation, workmen's compensation and, in Britain, also unemployment insurance. Poor relief remained for those whose needs were still not considered deserving.

New liberalism came in the wake of multiple feminist reform movements, among them abolitionism, temperance and women's suffrage. New liberalism's reform responded to women's needs in terms that were in some respects equal to those of men. Orloff (1993a: 176–7) notes, for example, that most American, Canadian and British proposals for old-age pensions called for women to receive the same coverage as men, as they also did in Australia (Shaver 1991: 109). The organisation of women's trade unions occurred in the same period (Jenson 1990; Ryan and Conlon 1975), and in Britain reforms attempted to regulate the wages of female outworkers (Pedersen 1993: 50).

The dominant pattern, however, was for the familial assumptions of classical liberalism to be systematically carried over into new liberal reform measures. These upheld the male breadwinner household and the support of children through the male family wage, and their effect was often to benefit male workers disproportionately while marginalising women's employment (Pedersen 1993: 49–52). Such effects were particularly pronounced in the family wage established under the Australian system of judicial wage determination early in the twentieth century. The male wage was set to provide for the 'matrimonial condition' of the worker, and the wage of the female worker, who was partly provided for in the wage of her husband or father, was to be only half the male wage (Macintyre 1985: 54–8).

New liberalism was not alone in this; such familial assumptions pervaded most thought of the period. Importantly, such carryovers also expressed the views of many women of the time. Many women supported trade union demands for a male wage sufficient to enable wives to leave the paid labour force, and for legislation limiting the hours and conditions of female and child labour. Maternalist movements were influential in maternal and child welfare policies in a number of countries. These movements extolled the private virtues of domesticity while also seeking to legitimate women's participation in public policy arenas (Michel and Koven 1990; Skocpol and Ritter 1991; Skocpol 1992).

Alone or in combination with other influences, the ideology of new liberalism shaped the development of post-war welfare states and the social rights of welfare citizenship (Marshall 1950). It was fundamental in shaping the Keynesian commitment to state action moderating inequality and maintaining full employment. Keynes (1963: 372–80) himself argued that an extension of the traditional functions of government was essential for both avoiding destructive social conflict and enabling the successful functioning of individual initiative. He argued that this could be achieved without undue loss of the scope for individualism, private initiative and personal liberty.

Keynesian welfare states typically assumed the desirability of the family of male breadwinner and dependent spouse, and this family form was encoded in many of their frameworks of provision. Developments in feminist critiques of the treatment of gender in new liberal ideology have paralleled those of the welfare state itself. The first generation of feminist critique focused on the failure of the welfare state to accord full liberal personhood to women (Land 1976; E. Wilson 1977; Brown 1981; Baldock and Cass 1983). These writings pointed to welfare state support and the reinforcement of a sexual division of labour in which women were defined as primarily wives and mothers and only secondarily as participants in paid employment. More recent feminist arguments have been concerned to defend women's entitlement to support and assistance in their own right, and have drawn on new liberal ideology to make the case. Such arguments have been various. Some have stressed women's claims to full and equal personhood as the bearers of social rights, including the right to be full-time mothers. Others have relied on new liberal understanding of social interdependencies to argue women's special needs for support and assistance. The professional histories of social work, nursing and midwifery centre on demands for the recognition of women's work (E. Wilson 1977). The case for anti-discrimination legislation has been more closely confined by classical liberal individualism (Thornton 1990; Bacchi 1990). Women's physical vulnerability has proved a viable ground for feminists to develop gender-specific services for women facing domestic and sexual violence, but it has been harder for feminists to argue that these services must be provided in a distinctively feminist way (Johnson 1981; Withorn 1981; Melville 1993).

Contemporary Neo-liberalism

Contemporary neo-liberalism is a restatement of classical liberalism, reasserting the liberal principles of freedom, market individualism and small government. Like classical liberalism it is an ideology of possessive individualism (Macpherson 1962). Neo-liberalism has gained strength in the last two decades, taking up political ground between conservatism and the 'socialist' collectivisms of the welfare state and monopoly capitalism. As a movement neo-liberalism has been strongest in the English-speaking countries, and particularly in the governments of Reagan in the United States, Thatcher in Great Britain and of Bolger in New Zealand. It has drawn added strength from the collapse of socialism in the former Soviet Union and Eastern Europe.

Friedrich Hayek (1944) elaborated the perspective most convincingly in objection to the growth of state powers and particularly to the movement of the 1930s and 1940s toward economic planning; Milton Friedman's (1962) arguments have also had wide currency (Barry 1990: 50–68). Like classical liberalism, neo-liberalism gives primacy to freedom, which it understands in the narrow and negative sense of minimal restriction of the individual by the powers of the state. It sees such freedom as enacted through the actions of individuals in voluntary relations with one another. Barry Hindess (1987: 120–67) points out the weaknesses of these conceptions in a society of highly developed interdependencies, including those of transnational capitalism: they fail to recognise the inhibitions on freedom that follow from lack of resources and opportunities in an unequal society, and the inequalities of power among individuals when these include not only economic actors of differing economic position but also corporations. Hindess argues that neo-liberalism understands the market in highly abstract, idealised terms devoid of the institutional details which configure it in actual social life. It is only in this way that market exchange can be pictured as the index and essence of freedom in society.

Though it favours the voluntarism of private charity, neo-liberal thought does allow a limited welfare role for the state. So long as it does not involve coercive powers for government, Hayek, for example, does not see this as infringing liberty. To the extent that state welfare extended beyond a minimum level of adequacy, however, it would undermine the rule of law, which requires the establishment of impersonal, known rules of legitimate action. A 'limited security which can be achieved for all and which is, therefore, no privilege' is permissible. This must be distinguished from 'the assurance of a given standard of life'. Hayek objects in principle to the kind of welfare state that aims at 'social justice' and becomes 'primarily a redistributor of income' (1944: 159–260; cited in Hindess 1987: 136–7).

Neo-liberalism attained its widest currency only after the end of the post-war boom and sustained expansion of the welfare state, and has had its greatest resurgence after 1980. Its thrust has been directed at restraining the continued growth of the state and in particular of its welfare apparatuses. A key goal has been to restore market forces to areas of social life in which they have been displaced or altered by the state. It has been one spur towards privatisation and the contracting of public services to the private sector, trends which have been by far the most pronounced in the English-speaking liberal welfare states.

In principle, neo-liberalism is subject to the same contradictions as classical liberalism with respect to women's problematic status as liberal individuals and the privileged place of the family in society. The high value neo-liberalism places on freedom tends if anything to reinforce the separation of public and private life. In practice, neo-liberal opinion is usually allied with conservative political forces, diluting its market individualism with resurgent conservative doctrines about the need to safeguard traditional family life (Gilder 1981). These arguments some-times have feminist variants affirming the positive status of women's traditional roles. But neo-liberalism itself claims to be blind to ascribed characteristics of individuals such as age, sex and race. It has grown up while married women were entering the labour market in steadily increasing proportions, and while liberal feminism has forcefully asserted women's full personhood in law and the market. Where its conservative political allies have allowed, neo-liberalism has been more

willing than classical liberalism to recognise women as individuals in
their own right.

Even in its neo-liberal guise, some aspects of the ideology of possessive
individualism resonate with some of the central themes of contemporary feminism. Key among these is its affirmation of individual
freedom and personal autonomy. Such resonances sound very clearly
in feminist demands for equal opportunity in employment, and for
freedom and choice in areas of personal life, including sexuality,
marriage and household formation; in independence and authority
with respect to the control of one's body, sexuality and reproductive
capacities; and in the assurance of physical security on the streets and
in personal relationships. Where the mainstream of contemporary
feminism differs from the ideology of possessive individualism is in
asserting that such autonomy owes nothing to society. Feminist demands
can be understood as claims to autonomy in its procedural sense, as
assuring women choice or decision in circumstances that are free of
coercion and manipulation, rather than to autonomy in the sense
of aspiring to self-sufficiency or to independence of or indifference to
the needs of others (Marilyn Friedman 1997: 51–7; see also Yeatman
1994). Neo-liberal individualism gives no ground for reconciling the
claim to autonomy with the constraints of human interdependency
and the connectedness to others that is most fully developed in the
lives of women.

Under neo-liberal conditions, the price of women's liberal individualism is that their needs and satisfactions are defined by the market paradigm. Neo-liberalism has been vocal in its opposition to welfare state
support for women on grounds of gender and gender disadvantage. It is
frequently argued, for example, that intervention to address race and
gender discrimination is undesirable because it contravenes individual
freedom, and is moreover unnecessary because in time such problems
will be overcome by the rationality of the market. Neo-liberals see
supports for the dual-earner family, such as child care, as best provided
through the market, though they often accept a degree of regulation to
ensure minimum quality of care. More unambiguously than its contemporary new liberal counterpart, neo-liberalism pictures women in
the same terms as men, equally possessive individuals. Neo-liberalism in
Australia, Canada and Britain is more ambivalent than in the United
States about the wholesale commitment of women to the public world of
the market, particularly in the case of single mothers.

The classical, social and neo-liberal versions of liberal ideology have
succeeded each other in the formation and development of modern
welfare states. In what ways have they informed the welfare states of
Australia, Britain, Canada, and the United States?

Social Policy Liberalisms

The origins of the 'liberal break' lie in Europe, principally Britain and France, as do the nineteenth-century liberal social policy innovations of poor laws, the workhouse and charity organisations. British liberalism and its ideas about social policy institutions spread to the United States, Anglophone Canada and Australia during the nineteenth century. In all three the English Poor Law Amendment Act of 1834, and in particular its commitment to the principles of deterrent poor relief and less eligibility, gave influential social policy models in the classical liberal mould. These included the acceptance of poor relief as a public responsibility, its organisation on a local basis, and the principles of kin responsibility and the assignment of pauper children to apprentice labour (Katz 1986: 13–14).

The ideological legacies of classical liberalism are strongest in the United States. Its nationhood came at the moment of the 'liberal break', and its leaders wrote its founding documents in liberal language. Seymour Lipset (1990: 8) suggests that liberal values of individualism and achievement were crystallised in the Declaration of Independence, reinforcing their centrality in the nation's political culture thereafter. Louis Hartz (1955: 6) describes the United States as having 'a natural liberal mind'. The failure of effective social democratic and socialist parties to develop in the United States is one manifestation of a liberal hegemony unparalleled in the other three countries. This has been associated with strong individualism and pervasive distrust of the state and state solutions to social problems. The tradition of the poor house, described by Michael Katz (1986: 4) as the cutting edge of poor relief policy, dominated its early welfare history. This was drawn directly from English models of outdoor relief and the workhouse.

Canada took shape as a nation rather later, and did not embrace liberalism to the same degree. Continuing differences of culture and national values have been widely noted. Lipset (1990: 13–16) maintains that if the founding political culture of the United States was Whig (liberal), that of Anglophone Canada was Tory (conservative). Francophone Canada was less strongly marked by libertarian ideology than France itself (Hockin 1975: 10; cited in Kudrle and Marmor 1981: 89). Canadian political culture has owed more to conservatism than liberalism, but at the same time has also supported a viable, if minority, social democratic tradition. In consequence Canada has been more open than the United States to an active role for the state in social policy as in other areas. Its early welfare development followed British and French models of poor relief. Liberal variants of these were more important in some provinces than others, with the institutions of the workhouse and the almshouse strongest in New Brunswick and Nova Scotia (Guest 1980: 9–17; see also Orloff 1993a: 240–68).

Australian liberalism, like its Canadian counterpart, had to contend with the centrality of the state to all of colonial life from its earliest importation. This was truest of those colonies which began as penal settlements, but applied to considerable degree also in those established as colonies of free settlement. In the early years convicts and free settlers alike depended on the state for services such as health and education, and for land and labour with which to make their fortune. Classical liberal ideology came rather later than elsewhere, and was more closely embraced by colonial administrations and the bourgeois society formed around them than by the populace drawn from working-class England and Ireland. While Hartz (1955: 20–1) characterises the societies of the United States and English Canada as 'bourgeois fragments', sharing the liberal individualism of their English founders, he describes Australia as a 'radical fragment', imbued with the working-class ideologies of the time. Like those of Canada, Australian social policy models were pale imitations of English philanthropy and poor relief. Philanthropy relied less on voluntary donation than on state subsidy to fund good works, while the relief model largely did without the workhouse and the need for settlers to pay a poor rate (Dickey 1980: 1–66; Macintyre 1985: 25).

The modern machinery of the twentieth-century liberal welfare states is new liberal, and those of Australia, Britain, Canada and the United States are much more alike in this respect. The social policy visions of the 1930s and 1940s, each identified with a national social policy figure, elaborated social policy frameworks compatible with Keynesian economic policy ideas, though largely before these were known as such. The social policy prescriptions identified with Roosevelt (United States), Beveridge (Britain), Marsh (Canada) and Chifley (Australia) were similarly new liberal in framing collective social protection which was nevertheless tailored to preserve the exigencies of possessive individualism and the market. They differed in the comprehensiveness of social protection, its structure, and the way it was to be associated with the wage-earning individual.

The social liberalism of Roosevelt's vision for old-age security was clearly expressed in his advocacy of contributory old-age insurance in 1929, before he became national President. He saw poverty in old age as neither a disgrace nor a fault of the individual, but as a consequence of modern industrial life. He favoured social insurance because it could support various standards of living in old age which reflected the effort of different classes to save through contributions (Rimlinger 1971: 212–13; Orloff 1993a: 172–4). Beveridge (Great Britain, Interdepartmental Committee on Social Insurance and Allied Services 1942:

6–7) made much the same case for contributory social insurance in Britain. His 1942 Report posited co-operation of the state and the individual as a central principle of social security. He saw this as giving security in exchange for the citizen's service and contribution. The state should ensure a national minimum, but leave scope for the individual through voluntary effort to provide for himself and his family above that minimum. Much the same sentiments were expressed in Canada and Australia. In Canada Leonard Marsh, commissioned to write 'Canada's Beveridge Report' (Canada, House of Commons 1943: 12), cited Beveridge to the effect that social insurance meant the sharing of risks across all classes and opined that its particular merit was to enlist the direct support of those classes most likely to benefit while avoiding the evils of pauperisation and excessive state philanthropy. The main body of the 'Australian Beveridge Report' appeared just before Beveridge published his Report. Actually a series of documents written by a Parliamentary committee, it lacked the unity of vision of its counterparts. Here and elsewhere, Australian new liberalism has been tinged with labourism (Castles 1985; Castles and Mitchell 1993: 120; Beilharz 1994). The Australian Report shared most of the ideas of its counterparts elsewhere but declined to endorse the principle of contributory social insurance, favouring instead a standard minimum pension funded from a progressive income tax (Kewley 1973: 234–45; R. Watts 1987; Shaver 1987).

These visions of the 1930s and 1940s also gave social policy prescriptions for the sexual division of labour in paid work and the family home. The norm these envisioned was of married women leaving paid work to be full-time wives and mothers, and they recommended remarkably similar social policy support for this arrangement. They also foresaw support for women solely responsible for children. The vision was elaborated most fully in the British Beveridge Report (Great Britain, Inter-departmental Committee on Social Insurance and Allied Services 1942). Among the eight 'primary causes of need' which Beveridge identified were the 'marriage needs of a woman', defined by her dependence on her husband and her consequent vulnerability to the loss of his support or his incapacity to provide it. This involved exchanging the rights she had acquired in employment before marriage for new rights flowing from her status as wife and mother. The expectation of married women's dependence was revealed most clearly in the 'married women's option', which provided that a married woman in employment could elect not to contribute to social insurance, in which case she would not be entitled to unemployment or retirement benefits except through her husband, 'as one of the married team'. The married woman who kept up her contributions was to have a pension of her own (Great Britain, Inter-departmental Committee on Social Insurance and Allied Services 1942: 124, 131–5). In that women's benefits were to be the same as men's, it was also fairer than the arrangements prevailing at the time (see Land 1976). The insurance principle could be applied to widows, but separated or deserted mothers would be supported through social assistance.

Very similar prescriptions were offered in the Beveridge Report's Canadian and Australian counterparts. Canada's Marsh Report (Canada, House of Commons 1943: 28–9, 92–9) followed the same line of argument but was much less explicit about the particulars. A man's contributions were to be regarded as providing for himself and his wife, actual or potential, and a married man would receive a benefit for her support. Women who were wage earners, whether married or single, would have the same entitlements as men to unemployment and sickness benefits. The Report foresaw the possibility that provincial mothers' pensions might be replaced by children's allowances, social insurance benefits to survivors and modernised public assistance. It opined, however, that widows without children might be required to undertake training for gainful employment. Australian proposals centred on the desirability of establishing widows' pensions, for which separated wives were also to be eligible, and of providing age and disability pensioners with allowances for the support of their dependent wives and children. Recommendations for unemployment benefit contemplated a woman qualifying for benefit, but provided also for an allowance for the dependent wife of an unemployed person (Shaver 1987: 420–1).

Though their sources were more divided, very similar social policy prescriptions for gender relations and the sexual division of labour had been offered in the United States in the 1930s. A maternalist vision stressed women's particular capacity for nurturance. They favoured the family wage principle and the support of women and children through male wages, and support to widows so they could care full-time for their children. Maternalists argued that social policy assistance should be directed to women rather than their husbands. Advocates of social insurance were also committed to the family wage, and saw social insurance programs for husbands and fathers as providing for their dependants, in much the same way as did Beveridge (Gordon 1995; Kessler-Harris 1995).

There was considerably more diversity in the measures implemented in the four countries than the rhetoric of their formative periods might suggest. The 'two track' United States social security system established something of both visions. It based support for mothers with children and some other groups on the public assistance tradition established with mothers' pensions. Initially this applied to all women with sole responsibility for children, including single mothers, widows and separated wives. In 1939, spouses and survivors were incorporated into the old-age insurance system. For workers and their dependants, social insurance provided income-related benefits for the aged and unemployed, yet also retained substantial 'welfare capitalism' in which significant parts of social protection are provided by employers. This coverage only became comprehensive, and racial exclusions eliminated, in the 1960s and 1970s (Rimlinger 1971; 193–244; Quadagno 1988: 99–124; Orloff 1993a: 269–98). The social protection afforded by social insurance in Britain was more comprehensive, and its early development and substantial universality in some respects likens it to the social democratic social provision of Scandinavia (Flora and Alber 1981). However, its limited flat-rate benefit structure left ample scope for supplementary protection through the market. Australia embarked on its distinctive path towards comprehensive social security funded from general taxation and allocated on the basis of generous means-testing (Kewley 1973; R. Watts 1987; Shaver 1991). Except for family allowances and limited unemployment insurance, Marsh's hopes for Canada went without issue during the 1940s, and the development that took place afterwards owed little to Marsh's particular vision. It has combined social democratic elements, such as a two-tier age pension combining a universal and a wage-related component, with continuing social policy residualism in other areas (Guest 1980; Kudrle and Marmor 1981).

The liberalism of these formulations has since come under challenge in all four countries, first in the welfare state expansions of the 1960s and 1970s and again in the contractions of the 1980s and 1990s. The ideologies of expansion intertwined new liberal and social democratic thought, while those of contraction have been compounds of conservative and neo-liberal argument. Common to both have been ideological accommodation to changing gender relations and the liberal separation of public and private life.

Neo-liberal social policy prescriptions have had some currency in all four countries, but have been most prominent in Britain and the United States (Murray 1984; Williams 1989: 166–77; C. Pierson 1991; P. Pierson 1994). Such prescriptions have centred on reversing the growth of the welfare state and restoring the play of market forces in these and other sectors of the economy. While most directly concerned with employment and the labour market, the neo-liberal agenda has been far broader. Typically it has also included benefit reductions and targeting, reduced levels of taxation, deregulation, privatisation, the contracting out of public services, and the reassertion of the responsibilities of family and community in the long-term care of the aged, and people with disabilities and mental illness. Governments of many kinds are following strategies of this kind to restructure welfare states in the 1980s and 1990s. Their neo-liberal variants have been distinguished by an ideological commitment to market individualism and particular emphasis on tax reductions and benefit cutbacks. In the case of single mothers especially, but also of unemployed men, charges that welfare spending is excessive have at times carried hidden references to race. This is most clearly vocalised in the United States, where the stereotypical 'dependent' welfare client is depicted as a black teenage mother (Fraser and Gordon 1994: 327; see also Roberts 1997); British discourse has been more oblique (Phoenix 1996).

In isolation from conservative influences, neo-liberal policy formulations usually treat women in the same terms of possessive individualism as they treat men, and construct issues about their participation in paid employment as matters of rational market choice. American neo-liberal opinion asks: 'Why should the [welfare] mother be exempted by the system that must affect everyone else's decision to work?' (Murray 1984: 231). There has been concern about low rates of employment among wives of unemployed men in both Great Britain and Australia (Cooke 1987; King, Bradbury and McHugh 1995). However, neo-liberal policy proposals to move the care of elderly and disabled people out of institutions and back to the 'community' continue to reflect liberal divisions between public and private life. These proposals assume that the women are able to accept these caring responsibilities because they have the primary economic support of a husband (Ungerson 1997: 216–25; Groves and Finch 1983).

Anna Yeatman (1996) observes the emergence of a new mode of individualised, contractual governance across the Anglophone liberal democracies. By the new contractualism, she refers to a mode of individualised regulation which treats the parties to relations of governance as individuals and constitutes them as consenting equals. She sees governments instituting contractualism of this kind in employment relations, where individual contracts replace collective agreements; in the contracting out of publicly funded services to non-government organisations or other external suppliers, including by competitive tender; and in new, individualised modes of 'case management' for clients of services such as employment assistance and supported home care. The ethos of this new contractualism is to be found in the UK Citizen's Charter, the 1991 New Zealand Employment Contracts Act, and the 1994 Australian Employment White Paper. According to Yeatman, some versions of this new contractualism – as in the neo-liberal social policies of Thatcher, Reagan and Bolger – do little more than restate nineteenth-century utilitarianism. Others, however, are not necessarily bound by liberal assumptions about the asocial nature of the individual. Yeatman believes these others may represent the beginning of a transformation in modes of governance beyond liberalism and towards a more substantive individualism.

Liberalism and Gender

Feminists see liberalism as having failed to accord full liberal person-hood to women. This is because the freedom of the liberal individual is a product of the separation of civil society from the authority of the state. Feminist critiques of the division of society into public and private spheres have not applied to liberalism alone. They have taken a number of forms, representing this division as a dichotomy between nature and culture, between morality and power, and between the personal and the political (Burton 1985: 33–56). They have been sharpest with respect to liberalism. The individualism and universalism of liberal thought are both flawed on this account. Liberal individualism acknowledges only the bounded self of the public sphere, and so denies recognition to the interdependencies and social connectedness of human society that are relatively more important in the lives of women than of men (Graham 1983; Hartsock 1983: 252–9). Liberalism's claim to be universalistic is false on the same account, for the liberal individual tacitly refers only to the male actor of the public sphere. Kathleen Jones (1990) suggests that the liberal citizen is modelled on the behaviour of white male élites, measuring all citizens against a standard defined by particular race, gender and class characteristics. She specifies three dimensions in which the particulars of male identity are falsely universalised: the body in both its symbolic and corporeal senses; the division of social life into public and private domains in which the sphere of private life is perceived as 'outside' both state and civil society; and the recognition of political behaviour only in the competitive, individual terms of electoral activity, obscuring women's relations to the state as claimants and low-level service workers. These problems also weaken liberalism's claims to be egalitarian and meliorist. How can it treat individuals as having equal worth without recognising the particularities of individual and group identity (Vogel 1988: 136; Yeatman 1994)? How can social and political institutions be improved without such recognition?

Feminist critiques of liberalism have been sharpest when discussing the welfare state. In her essay, 'The patriarchal welfare state', Pateman maintained that, 'since the early twentieth century, welfare policies have reached across from public to private and helped uphold a patriarchal structure of familial life' (1989: 183; see also E. Wilson 1977). She argued that welfare states have formed around ideals of citizenship based on 'independence', in which independence is defined by masculine attributes and abilities. Women's citizenship is framed as womanly dependence and is accordingly defective. Pateman identifies three elements of independence through which patriarchal structures are encoded in welfare state citizenship: the capacity to bear arms, the capacity to own property, including property in one's own labour, and the capacity for self-government, including as protector of the family unit.

Nancy Fraser's (1989) analysis of social provision in the United States shows the centrality of the gendered division between public and private to its liberal character. She finds this in the distinction between social insurance typical of most welfare states and the social assistance programs which are particularly prominent in the liberal version. Fraser argues that social insurance programs construct beneficiaries as rights-bearing possessive individuals and hence paradigmatically male, while social assistance arrangements frame theirs as clients and hence paradigmatically female. She sees this as a double distinction, in that the rights of social insurance recipients have the contractual status accorded to free liberal individuals while the entitlements of social assistance claimants subject them to the guiding authority of welfare caseworkers. Fraser's argument leans heavily on the American example, and the nature of both social insurance and social assistance varies a good deal from one country to another, even among those of the liberal type (Eardley et al. 1996).

The peculiarly liberal character of welfare arrangements in Britain, North America and Australia stands out especially clearly when they are viewed from the perspective of the more highly developed welfare states of Scandinavia. Scandinavian feminists have seen their sisters in liberal countries as unduly pessimistic about the role of social policy institutions in the lives of women. Helga Hernes (1988: 202–9) in particular argues that Scandinavian social policy arrangements do more than other types to bridge the liberal division between public and private life. In these countries the mobilisation and political incorporation of women in the second phase of welfare state development has led to a 'public/private mix'. While these writers are not uncritical of social policy in the countries of the region (Waerness 1984; Leira 1992), the comparative accounts suggest that Scandinavian welfare states differ from others in this respect. Birte Siim (1988: 176–9) distinguishes between women's dependency as clients and as consumers, and suggests that their dependency as clients predominates in Britain and the United States while dependency as consumers is more the norm in Denmark and Sweden. She regards the Danish welfare state as having fostered a partnership between state and family, and to some extent between women and the state, while the British welfare state still largely leaves the support of reproductive life to the family.

Feminist responses to liberalism are complicated by the fact that the movement's own origins lie in the liberal tradition. While mainstream feminism arose as a recognisably liberal movement, its socialist, radical, and cultural variants have also shared many liberal tenets (Eisenstein 1981: 4). The claim that woman is an independent being, common to most variants, is premised on the eighteenth-century liberal conception of the independent and autonomous self. As critiques have moved beyond analysis of the classic liberal texts, feminists have begun to acknowledge greater complexity in the liberal tradition. These discussions continue to interrogate the liberal separation of public and private spheres of social life, but do so with greater awareness that its implications are double-edged. This separation constructs citizens as if they were equal when they are not, and reserves all difference and particularity to a realm conceived as private and hence non-political; at the same time, however, it also gives the foundation for citizenship and democratic self-government. This discussion includes a degree of self-scrutiny: it recognises, for example, that the early movement's focus on 'the personal is political' in small-group participatory decision-making had an oppressive and undemocratic side (Phillips 1993: 110). Most have agreed in seeing the liberal separation between public and private as a source of women's disempowerment, but some have, nonetheless, valued the secluded space it has afforded for women-centred values and culture (Parvikko 1991).

Many feminists nevertheless regard liberalism and liberal democracy as a viable foundation for women's claims to gender equality, and some writers have begun to reappraise the liberal tradition in the light of the resources it may offer, in whole or in part, in the struggle for more robust forms of democracy. The common theme underlying such reappraisal is a recognition that political identities and interests, including those shared by and among women, are not pre-given but socially constructed in the play of political participation and democratic decision-making. Whatever aspirations one may hold for the longer term, liberal democracy stands as the actually existing form for such politics at the present time. Both Phillips (1993) and Fraser (1997), for example, see even limited liberal democracy as affording women some scope to construct diverse political identities and interests through its participatory processes. Fraser (1997: 70) argues that an enhanced version of Habermas's concept of 'the public sphere', referring to a discursive space in modern societies in which political participation is enacted through the medium of talk, gives a way of formulating these possibilities and considering how they might be enlarged. Iris Young

(1990) argues that group representation for minority interests would enhance the scope of the democratic process to recognise and accommodate difference in the formation of such identities and interests; although Chantal Mouffe (1995) rejects Young's formulation of group rights, she similarly calls for conceptions of democracy which acknowledge and value conflict and plurality as inherent in democratic processes.

Whatever the form it takes, liberalism sits uneasily with contemporary understandings of gender relations and the sexual division of labour. There is an enduring contradiction between the liberal individualism of economy and society, in which men and women are separate and equal persons with individual rights, and the collective bonds of private life joining men and women in marriage, kin relations and the upbringing of children. Operating at the conjunction of state and civil society, social policy mediates this contradiction.

Pateman sees liberalism's implications for women as fraught with 'Wollstonecraft's dilemma', in which demands for gender-neutral inclusion on equal terms with men seem to conflict with wishes for recognition of gender-specific talents, needs and concerns. She sees the welfare state as oppressing women, but at the same time as responsible for important improvements in their circumstances and democratic opportunities. In particular, she sees welfare state support as opening choices for women about their economic dependence on men, and opening the matter of their rights to public politics. Scandinavian feminists such as Hernes (1988: 199) and Siim (1988: 182) have similarly seen women's active political participation as a potential counter to the rendering of women as clients of welfare state authority. Fraser (1987; see also Yeatman 1990: 139–48), pointing to the mediating role of administrative authority, is less optimistic about the democratic potential of the welfare state.

The balance between the four key tenets to which John Gray (1995) ascribes the unity of the liberal tradition – individualism, egalitarianism, universalism and meliorism – has shifted through the succession of classical, new and neo-classical approaches to social policy. While shifts associated with the role of the state in the market economy have remained within the liberal bounds of limited government, those concerning gender and the family have shown a more profound recasting of the liberal tradition. As one variant has succeeded another, the family group has come into sharper focus, and the persons comprising it have acquired greater recognition as distinct individuals.

According to Gray, the liberal tradition gives priority to the person over the social group. Feminist critics such as Okin (1981) and Pateman (1989) have shown this priority to be muted in the case of dependent

family members, in particular married women. It has, however, become less so in successive variants of social policy liberalism. Classical
liberalism sentimentalised the family and, as denizens of the domestic
order, its female members had little claim to the liberal personhood
of the public world. Nor was the private society of the family an
appropriate object of the public concern of the state. In contrast, new
liberalism recognised family members as the dependants of wage
earners and the state as legitimately concerned with their support and
protection through the family wage principle. Its key terms also enabled
women to claim personhood as individuals in their own right, and to use
social policy discourse to pursue those claims. In its turn, neo-liberalism
has begun to define both men and women as possessive individuals, but
to see the sexual division of labour in paid and unpaid work as matters
of private choice by marital partners rather than a concern of the state.

All three variants have affirmed both liberal egalitarianism, in considering all individuals as having the same moral status, and liberal
universalism, in valuing the common human attributes above particularities of association and culture. The inclusion of women in the
ambit of liberal personhood has driven these principles further apart
than in the past. The individuation of married women is a strengthening
of the egalitarian tenet of the liberal tradition. To do this in the universalistic terms of possessive individualism is to exacerbate the contradiction between the public world of the market and the private world
of the family, and hence to provoke conflict between different groups of
women. Social policy development fostering the full liberal personhood
of married women is consistent with the meliorist tenet of liberal theory,
identified with the idea of social improvement, in so far as it remains
within the bounds set by the liberal commitment to limited government
(Gray 1995: 88).

Liberalism has never been the only ideology influencing social policy,
even in those countries where its influence has been greatest. It has
been compounded with others, including social democratic, labourist
and even corporatist elements in periods of expansion, and conservative
and corporatist elements in times of contraction. Of the four welfare
states considered here, the influence of liberalism, especially in its
classical and neo-liberal forms, has been most dominant in the United
States. It has arguably been weakest in Canada, where it has been
tempered by both conservative and social democratic influences. Historically, new liberal values have had greatest influence in the British
and Australian welfare states. These have taken somewhat different
directions in the recent period, with neo-liberal ideology driving a
reduction in spending on welfare in Britain and labourist values
moderating the reshaping of institutions in Australia.

CHAPTER 3

The Labour Market and Social Policy

The primacy of the market is the hallmark of the liberal policy regimes but reliance on the labour market for survival does not take place independently of relations of caring and dependence within households. Consequently, analysis of policies and services related to the organisation of daily life, which may facilitate or militate against labour force participation for those with caring responsibilities, is essential to a rounded analysis of particular social policy regimes. In addition to such policies as maternity and parental leave, and the availability of child care and facilities for caring for other dependants, policies relating to pay and employment equity, which may enhance the quality of participation, are also important to the character of social policy regimes and should be part of a comprehensive analysis. The analytical framework outlined in Chapter 1 allows us to examine labour market patterns and associated policies in terms of three dimensions. Through the lens of the state, market, family dimension we identify the relative importance of state, market and family individually and in interaction, in service provision, organisation and regulation. Utilising the stratification lens we analyse gender differences in labour force participation and associated characteristics, including the extent and nature of part-time work and the impact of service provision and regulation on gender stratification. Through the social citizenship rights lens we analyse the extent and quality of social rights as they facilitate labour force participation and enhance its quality.

In this chapter we consider gender differences in labour force participation and associated characteristics. This provides the context within which we can analyse the action taken by countries to sustain or mitigate the identified patterns of gender-based labour force stratification. We concentrate on policy responses and services within the USA,

Great Britain, Canada and Australia, in particular within services that address gender differences in labour force participation and services that facilitate labour force participation, namely child care and maternity and parental leave. We outline briefly the employment equality strategies pursued in these four welfare states. This entails identification of the extent and quality of social citizenship rights as they facilitate labour force participation and/or enhance its quality, and identification of the role of the state, market and family in service provision and regulation. The stratification dimension, while not the primary focus in this part of the analysis, is important in sensitising us to the extent to which benefits and services, in particular the level and nature of their provision or absence, reinforce the gender division of labour and/or gender inequality. Stratification again takes primacy in our analysis of the outcomes of equality strategies.

Gender and Labour Force Participation

In outlining patterns of labour force participation and associated characteristics our focus is on identifying key dimensions of gender-based labour force stratification. We situate Australia, Canada, the United Kingdom and the United States within the context of the eighteen OECD countries widely analysed in comparative welfare state research and which include the suggested exemplars of other social policy regimes (discussed in Chapter 1). Because of data availability issues we use the United Kingdom rather than Great Britain in these and other quantitative OECD comparisons but our qualitative analysis throughout the chapter concentrates on Great Britain in the context of the three other liberal social policy regimes.

The general pattern of increased female labour force participation and decreased male participation associated with earlier retirement over the 1960 to the mid-1990s period has resulted in an increase in the female share of the labour force in all OECD countries, with the exception of Japan which already had a 40 per cent female share of the labour force in 1960 when the median for the eighteen OECD countries listed in Table 3.1 was only 32 per cent. By the mid-1990s most OECD countries had reached the 40 per cent female share and the median for the eighteen countries was 43. Despite these trends, there is still some clustering of countries around levels of female participation and share of the labour force in the mid-1990s. The general pattern is that the social democratic welfare states – the Nordic countries – have the highest levels of participation and female share of the labour force, the liberal cluster comes next and the conservative corporatist cluster exemplified by France, Germany, Austria, the Netherlands and Italy

Table 3.1: Selected Labour Force Statistics for Eighteen OECD Countries, Ranked by Female Share of Labour Force, 1994 (Percentages)

| | Labour Force Participation as a Percentage of Population Aged 15–64 | | | | | | Female Share of Labour Force | | | Labour Force in Services | | | Labour Force in Government | | |
| | 1960 | | 1990 | | 1994 | | 1960 | 1990 | 1994 | 1968 | 1990 | 1994 | 1968 | 1990 | 1994 |
	Male	Female	Male	Female	Male	Female									
Sweden	98.5	50.1	85.3	81.1	78.1	74.4	33.6	48.0	48.0	49.8	67.5	71.6	18.4	31.6	32.0
Finland	91.4	65.6	80.6	72.9	77.1	69.9	43.7	47.1	47.0	41.1	60.6	64.9	11.0	29.1	25.1
Denmark	99.5	43.5	89.6	78.4	84.2	73.8	30.9	46.1	46.0	49.9	66.9	68.1	15.2	30.4	31.0
USA	90.5	42.6	85.2	68.1	85.3	70.5	32.5	44.9	45.6	59.4	70.9	73.1	17.0	14.6	14.5
Norway	92.2	36.3	84.5	71.2	82.7	71.6	28.2	44.9	45.5	48.0	68.8	71.2	15.4	27.6	30.6
Canada	91.1	33.7	84.9	68.2	82.6	67.8	26.6	44.5	44.7	59.7	71.2	73.3	18.6	19.4	20.4
New Zealand	93.8	31.3	80.8	62.1	83.9	65.0	24.5	43.3	43.8	49.0	64.8	64.6	18.4	18.1[2]	18.1[2]
France	94.6	46.6	75.2	56.6	75.9	59.1	33.3	42.9	43.8	45.8	64.0	68.4	17.4[1]	22.8	24.8
United Kingdom	99.1	46.1	86.4	65.1	83.3	65.6	32.7	42.8	43.7	51.3	68.9	72.4	17.5	19.4	15.0
Austria	92.0	52.1	80.1	55.4	81.0	62.1	39.4	41.0	42.9	43.1	55.3	59.6	12.8	20.6	22.4
Germany	94.4	49.2	80.7	56.6	80.8	61.8	37.3	40.7	42.4	43.0	56.8	59.1	10.9	15.1	15.1
Australia	97.2	34.1	86.1	62.3	85.5	63.8	25.1	41.3	42.2	54.1	69.0	71.3	23.8	23.0	20.9
Belgium	85.5	36.4	72.7	52.4	72.5	51.6	30.2	41.6	41.2	51.2	69.0	68.2	14.0	19.3	19.4[3]
Netherlands	97.8	26.2	79.6	53.0	79.1	57.4	21.5	39.2	41.1	54.1	69.1	73.0	11.9	13.5	12.7
Switzerland	100.0	51.0	93.6	59.3	97.5	67.5	34.1	38.1	40.7	43.8	59.5	67.2	7.4	11.0	14.1
Japan	92.2	60.1	87.8	60.4	90.6	62.1	40.7	40.6	40.5	45.7	58.7	60.2	6.3[1]	6.1	6.0
Italy	95.3	39.6	78.1	44.5	76.9	43.4	30.7	36.8	36.4	39.3	58.6	59.7	13.4	15.6	16.2
Ireland	99.0	34.8	82.2	38.9	81.8	43.9	25.6	31.6	34.7	41.7	56.2	60.4	12.6	14.1	14.0[3]

Notes: We use 1968 as a base year for both services and government because government employment as a percentage of total employment is not available for most of the countries until then.

[1] Figure is for 1974.
[2] Figure is for 1985.
[3] Figure is for 1993.

Source: OECD 1996.

includes countries with the lowest female share. But there is considerable overlap between clusters. For example, the female share of the labour force is as high in the United States as in Norway and is higher in France than in Australia. While female labour force participation is still consistently lower than male participation in all OECD countries, we find a process of convergence in male and female levels of participation, although varying in intensity, in all countries. These changes tell us nothing of the character of participation, however. This is where we find considerable differences between men and women and also among women, although the patterns differ cross-nationally.

A review of the characteristics of labour force participation and its quality indicates some broad similarities across our four countries in terms of the patterns of gender differences: a high percentage of the labour force, and high concentration of women, in service sector employment, the predominance of women among part-time workers and gender-based occupational segregation and pay differentials are noteworthy. Yet, these patterns are not distinctly different from those in several other OECD countries and there are some significant differences across the four countries. These differences and the persistence of gender stratification in participation can be illustrated by the patterns of participation by family type and continuity of employment and also by patterns of part-time employment.

The most recent data on labour force participation of men and women by family type are from the Luxembourg Income Study and relate to the mid-1980s. While the exact figures have undoubtedly changed since then, it is unlikely that the patterns, illustrated in Table 3.2, have fundamentally altered. For comparative purposes we include figures for Sweden, whose female participation rates approximate those of males in Australia, Canada, the United Kingdom and the United States, irrespective of family type. These data indicate not only consistent gender differences in participation in the four countries irrespective of family type but also significant cross-national differences in participation, especially participation by women. The most marked gender differences, irrespective of country, are for sole parents, followed by those married with children, whereas the least gender differences are for those married without children. Despite the similarity in gender patterns across countries there are some marked cross-national differences. With the single exception of the married with no children category, where the United Kingdom has relatively high female participation, the United States and Canada have the highest levels of female labour force participation and the least gender differences in participation. In contrast, Australia is characterised by the most marked gender differences irrespective of family type.

Table 3.2: Labour Force Participation of Women and Men by Family Type in the Mid-1980s

	Women				Men			
	Single	Sole Parent	Married (with children)	Married (no children)	Single	Sole Parent	Married (with children)	Married (no children)
Australia (1985)	66.9	35.3	53.1	52.5	76.6	76.9	90.9	77.4
Canada (1987)	74.7	57.7	61.3	62.9	78.8	71.1	90.1	79.5
United Kingdom (1986)	54.5	43.7	54.3	63.7	76.0	70.7	89.9	81.7
USA (1986)	74.8	56.9	59.3	63.3	82.4	78.8	90.6	80.4
Sweden (1987)	75.7	88.2	88.1	81.8	80.8	89.4	97.7	89.9

Source: Mitchell 1993: 56, Table 2; analyses of the Luxembourg Income Study.

A noteworthy characteristic that emerges from these data is the high level of dual-earner units: irrespective of country, over 50 per cent of women in family units with children are in the labour force. This has significant implications for services to support labour market participation. Even more important in this regard are the relatively high percentages of female sole parents in the labour force in both the United States and Canada. It is noteworthy that these figures are markedly higher than those for Australia and the United Kingdom but still considerably lower than those for Sweden.

The ranking of countries on participation by family type is consistent with the patterns evident in relation to continuity of employment across the employment life cycle. OECD analysis indicates that by the end of the 1980s a female labour force participation curve in the form of an inverted 'U' or 'plateau' characterised the United States and Canada whereas in the United Kingdom and Australia female labour force participation was still characterised by two peaks: the first, in the age range of 20 to 24, reflects high participation before child-bearing; the second peak, in the age range of 35 to 44, reflects married women returning to employment as their children get older (OECD 1994: 54–62). These are separated by a valley at around age 30, which is 'the predominant age band for mothers of young children' (OECD 1988: 134). Data for the United Kingdom indicate that participation is linked to both education and family size. Despite the persistence of the two-peak pattern in the United Kingdom and Australia it is noteworthy that this pattern is less pronounced in the early 1990s in both countries and this is true of several other OECD countries, which traditionally have had low levels of female participation (OECD 1994). The inverted 'U' or plateau pattern represents a situation where labour force participation is generally combined with child-rearing. The patterns evident for Canada and the United States are now coming close to those of Sweden, where withdrawal from the labour force is infrequent and ongoing participation is facilitated by long maternity and parental leave, extensive child care provision and the option of reduced working hours. France, which also has extensive child care provision, demonstrates a similar pattern of participation. Significantly, the United States and to a lesser extent the Canadian patterns of participation are being achieved with low levels of public support in terms of child care and parental leave. Before analysing these services, we consider part-time work, which is of major significance in the labour force participation of women: they are still disproportionately in part-time employment and this employment tends to compare unfavourably with full-time employment in terms of quality.

Table 3.3: Part-time Employment in Eighteen OECD Countries, Ranked by Part-time Employment as a Proportion of Female Employment, 1995 (Percentages)[1]

| | Part-time employment as a proportion of total employed | | | | | | | | | Women's share of part-time employment | | |
| | Men and Women | | | Men | | | Women | | | | | |
	1979	1990	1995	1979	1990	1995	1979	1990	1995	1979	1990	1995
Netherlands	16.6	33.2	37.4	5.5	15.8	16.8	44.0	61.7	67.2	76.4	70.4	73.6
Switzerland	–	23.2	28.3	–	7.3	8.6	–	40.5	54.7	–	83.7	82.7
Norway	25.3	26.6	26.5	7.3	8.8	9.4	50.9	48.2	46.6	83.0	81.8	80.8
United Kingdom	**16.4**	**21.8**	**24.1**	**1.9**	**5.0**	**7.7**	**39.0**	**43.8**	**44.3**	**92.8**	**87.0**	**82.3**
Australia	**15.9**	**21.3**	**24.8**	**5.2**	**8.0**	**11.1**	**35.2**	**40.1**	**42.7**	**78.7**	**78.1**	**74.4**
Sweden	23.6	23.2	24.3	5.4	7.3	9.4	46.0	40.5	40.3	87.5	83.7	80.1
New Zealand	13.9	20.1	21.2	4.9	8.5	9.3	29.1	35.2	36.1	77.7	76.1	75.7
Denmark	22.7	23.7	21.6	5.2	9.0	10.4	46.3	41.5	35.5	86.9	79.4	73.3
Japan	15.4	17.6	20.1	7.5	8.0	10.1	27.8	31.9	34.9	70.1	73.0	70.1
Germany	11.4	13.2	16.3	1.5	2.1	3.6	27.6	30.6	33.8	91.6	90.5	87.4
Belgium	6.0	10.2	13.6	1.0	1.7	2.8	16.5	25.0	29.8	88.9	88.6	87.5
France	8.2	12.0	15.6	2.4	3.5	5.0	16.9	23.8	28.9	82.2	83.1	82.0
Canada	**12.5**	**15.4**	**18.6**	**5.7**	**8.1**	**10.6**	**23.3**	**24.4**	**28.2**	**72.1**	**71.0**	**68.8**
USA	**16.4**	**16.9**	**18.6**	**9.0**	**10.0**	**11.0**	**26.7**	**25.2**	**27.4**	**68.0**	**67.6**	**68.0**
Austria	7.6	8.8	13.9	1.5	1.6	4.0	18.0	20.0	26.9	87.8	88.8	83.8
Ireland	5.1	8.1	11.3²	2.1	3.8	5.1²	13.1	17.1	21.7²	71.2	68.2	71.5²
Finland	6.7	7.2	8.4	3.2	4.4	5.7	10.6	10.2	11.3	74.7	67.8	64.7
Italy	5.3	5.7	6.4	3.0	3.1	2.9	10.6	10.9	12.7	61.4	64.7	70.6

Notes: [1] Based on country definitions of part-time work. Data for the United Kingdom, Belgium, Denmark, Germany, Ireland and Italy are from the annual European Labour Force Survey. Data for all other countries are from national Labour Force Surveys.

[2] Figures are for 1994.

Source: OECD 1996: Table E.

The interpretation of the figures in Table 3.3 must be handled with caution since OECD statistics on part-time work are not directly comparable due to cross-national differences in the cut-off points used. In some countries the part-time work cut-off is thirty-five hours per week, as in Australia and the United States, in others, such as Canada, it is thirty hours, and in several European countries, including the United Kingdom, it is self-defined. More problematic is the fact that these cut-off points do not indicate the average hours worked by part-time workers. There is a considerable difference in the character of part-time work of eight or ten hours duration, on the one hand, and thirty to thirty-five hours duration on the other, not only in terms of relationship to the labour market but also in terms of the levels of state, market and/or family support needed to facilitate participation. Despite these caveats, the quantitative data are useful in pointing to labour market stratification in all countries and gross cross-national differences and trends.

The total percentage of the labour force in part-time work in OECD countries in the mid-1990s ranged from 37 per cent in the Netherlands to 6 per cent in Italy. The liberal welfare regime cluster came mid-way, with 19 per cent of the US and Canadian labour forces in part-time work, compared with 24 per cent in the United Kingdom and 25 per cent in Australia. But women are the vast majority of part-time workers in all OECD countries, ranging from a low of 65 per cent in Finland to 88 per cent in Belgium. Women's share of part-time employment has decreased in three of the four liberal regimes, the United States being the exception since 1979 and especially since 1990, due to the increase in part-time work among males. But in 1995 female predominance still ranged from 68 per cent in the United States, through 69 per cent in Canada, 74 per cent in Australia to 82 in the United Kingdom – only Germany, Austria, Belgium and Switzerland are higher in terms of female predominance within the OECD. Only six OECD countries had above 40 per cent of their female labour force in part-time work in 1995 – the Netherlands (67 per cent), Switzerland (55 per cent), Norway (47 per cent), Sweden (40 per cent), the United Kingdom (44 per cent) and Australia (43 per cent). The corresponding figures for the United States and Canada are 27 and 28 per cent respectively. Despite the differences in cut-off points for part-time work, the marked difference in the extent of part-time labour force participation, especially by women in the United States and Canada on the one hand, and Australia and the United Kingdom on the other, cannot be denied: the United States and Canada have relatively low rates of part-time work among women in OECD terms while Australia and the United Kingdom have relatively high rates.

There is now an enormous literature on part-time work. Three broad sets of issues are pervasive in this literature: the characteristics and quality of part-time work and the influence of institutional structures on these; the influence of flexibility on the decisions of employers and employees; and the orientation of part-time workers in terms of labour market commitment.

First, the characteristics and quality of part-time jobs vary within and across countries but there is strong evidence that in Canada, the United States and especially the United Kingdom the majority of part-time jobs are 'bad jobs', that is low wage, low skill, of relatively few hours duration, with high turnover and poor working conditions (Economic Council of Canada 1990; Tilly 1991; Schoer 1987; Dex and Walters 1989; Ellingsaeter 1992; Dex 1992). The characterisation of part-time work in the Australian Women's Employment Strategy Report indicates clear similarities. That Report states that part-time jobs tend to be restricted to the lower grades within occupations which are unskilled or for which the skills involved are basic and non-transferable. Part-time workers face more limited promotion prospects and receive less training than their full-time counterparts (DEET, Women's Bureau 1988: 36). In addition, part-time workers are less likely to belong to a trade union, to be permanent or to receive the non-wage employment benefits accorded to permanent employees; they are also less likely than full-time workers to be covered by an industrial award or to be aware of their award entitlements (DEET, Women's Bureau 1988 ABS 1991: 178). But there are exceptions to this scenario, for example permanent part-time workers in the public service (Commonwealth of Australia 1992a: 120) and part-time workers covered under the award system which character-ised the Australian labour market up to the early 1990s (Hawke 1992). Wages for part-time workers were usually based on the hourly rate for full-time employees and some awards provided for premium rates for part-time workers, typically 10–15 per cent of the full-time hourly rate but sometimes considerably more (ABS 1994). Vacation and benefits were usually pro-rated to full-time hours (ILO 1989: 59–60).

The phenomenon of lesser pay and conditions for the majority of those working fewer hours is common to all four countries, as is the association between hours and quality – the fewer the hours the lesser the pay and conditions. In an analysis of wage differentials between part-time and full-time workers using Luxembourg Income Study data for the mid-1980s, Gornick and Jacobs (1996) demonstrate that women part-time workers earn significantly less than their full-time counter-parts in all four countries, but the part-time pay gaps, both gross and net, are greatest in the United States and the United Kingdom fol-lowed by Australia and Canada. They associate these differences with institutional factors, such as government wage-setting policies, including minimum wage regulations, and the extent of unionisation and union practices in relation to part-time workers (Gornick and Jacobs 1996: 19–22). Other analysts have also identified the importance of institutional factors in explaining other cross-national differences. For example, the extent of part-time work in the United Kingdom approximates Scandinavian levels but differs considerably both in the average hours worked and the conditions and level of integration into the labour force – part-time work in the Scandinavian countries is typically of thirty hours duration and subject to standard employment protection, part-time work in the United Kingdom tends to be of ten to sixteen hours duration and is often not well protected (Ellingsaeter 1992; Employment Gazette 1992; A. Dale and Glover 1990: 60–2). While several countries may have one or more specific factors that are conducive to influencing supply of and/or demand for part-time workers, the United Kingdom appears to have a whole configuration of factors that are conducive to part-time work. These include both supply and especially demand side factors with a long history such that short-hours part-time work is a structural characteristic of the contemporary labour market (R. Crompton, Hantrais and Walters 1990; Dex 1992). In summary, institutional structures influence the level of part-time work, its quality and the variation in pay and conditions among part-time workers not only across countries but within countries.

Second, flexibility is regularly cited as a contributor to part-time work but the reasoning varies since flexibility is both a demand and supply side influence. Restructuring of the economy and growth of the service sector in all developed economies are associated with an emphasis on flexibility by employers and this is conducive to an increase in part-time work. Evidence from the United States indicates that much part-time work is demand driven, especially that element in the service sector, and is associated with a desire for flexibility on the part of employers (Tilly 1991), yet the extent of part-time work is relatively low in the United States by international standards. However, while the overall percentage of the labour force in part-time work was the same in 1990 as in 1960 it increased over the first half of the 1990s (see Table 3.3). Dex (1992) argues that flexibility is less likely to be reflected in part-time work in the United States than in the United Kingdom because employers can achieve flexibility through the greater prevalence of contract agencies – these offer employers part-time services but offer workers full-time jobs; it is important to bear in mind that these are often contract or home-work jobs, that is, merely a different type of non-standard employment. It is noteworthy that the negative reaction to the 1994 striking down of the United Kingdom Employment

Protection Act (1987) centred on the limitation of flexibility for employers. The 1987 Act gave weaker rights relating to redundancy and unfair dismissal to employees working fewer than sixteen hours a week and none to those who worked fewer than eight hours. Those working between eight and sixteen hours a week had to work five years to qualify for rights, compared with two years for full-time workers. In March 1994 the House of Lords, in response to a case brought by the Equal Opportunities Commission, ruled that the legislation breached European Community law on equal pay and equal treatment at work for men and women. However, part-time workers still do not enjoy the same rights as full-time workers in relation to pension and maternity rights. Conservative Party spokespersons and industry representatives claimed that the mandated change would lead to a lessening of flexibility for employers and to job losses (*Guardian*, 4 March 1994).

Flexibility on the part of employees is often cited as an influence on the supply of workers; it is argued that employees, in particular women employees, choose part-time work. This has been an issue of some contention in recent debates (Hakim 1996; Probert 1997). In discussing the British situation Hakim argues that 'the majority of part-timers actively prefer their shorter working hours and that many full-timers would prefer shorter hours, even at the price of a drop in earnings' (Hakim 1993a: 104). However, it is important to ask to what extent part-time work is the optimum choice and to what extent it is a best possible option because of caring responsibilities in the context of absent or unsatisfactory supports, such as child care, and/or care for other dependent people. It is noteworthy that in the United Kingdom, where female economic activity rates and employment type (that is, whether full- or part-time and number of hours worked) vary strongly with the age of the youngest child and are particularly low for mothers of 0 to 4-year-old children, there is a marked under-supply of adequate child care for pre-school children (Ellingsaeter 1992: 27). This contrasts with Denmark, which has the best public child care in the European Union, 'where a disconnection between motherhood and part-time work has become manifest' (Ellingsaeter 1992: 25). Similarly, in France where public child care services are well-developed, there is far less variation in female labour force participation and type over the life cycle (Hantrais 1993: 134–5).

Third, associated with the choice issue, Hakim (1996) argues that part-time work in Britain is qualitatively different from full-time work; that the primary identity of part-time workers is not worker but other identities, such as homemaker or student, that part-time workers are highly satisfied with their jobs and that they tend to be secondary family earners. She argues that these characteristics and the concentration of part-time workers in a few occupations, primarily clerical, retail sales and personal services, contribute to the low profile of part-time work and the qualitatively different work orientation of part-time workers (Hakim 1996: 67). In contrast to the British data cited by Hakim in support of her argument that part-time workers choose the present patterns, evidence from Australia, which has equally high rates of part-time work although generally better remunerated, indicates an increase in involuntary part-time work: Australian labour force survey data indicate that 28 per cent of part-time workers were under-employed in 1991, that is, they did not work as many hours as they would have liked. This represented a 61 per cent increase in under-employment over 1988. Thirty-seven per cent of under-employed part-time workers 'would have preferred to work 10–19 hours more per week whereas 14 per cent would have preferred to work an extra 30 or more hours per week' (ABS 1991: 2). These contrasting positions indicate that we have a situation of heterogeneity not only within countries, in the characteristics of workers – well-integrated full-time workers and part-time workers many of whom are in bad jobs – which is recognised by Hakim (1996: 215), but also across countries, in the characteristics and conditions of part-time workers, a minority of whom are in high-skill, well-remunerated jobs and the majority of whom are in insecure, poorly remunerated jobs. As with full-time workers, institutional structures and individual resources, both in terms of scarce skills and ability to engage supports, contribute to the ability to make choices in relation to the quantity and quality of labour market participation and the stratification of part-time workers. This issue of heterogeneity is also important to a consideration of other labour market characteristics.

The literature on part-time work strongly indicates that the predominance of poor quality part-time jobs is a characteristic of all four countries. This relatively bleak scenario has significant implications for gender-based labour force stratification: part-time workers are predominantly female and the quality of part-time jobs in these four countries tends to be relatively poor. This must be recognised as a significant contribution to perpetuating gender-based labour force inequality whatever the extent of choice of part-time work by individuals. It must also be recognised that, as with full-time work, part-time work comprises a range of jobs in terms of quality and conditions in all countries. The distribution along this range is not available for the four countries but the indications are that institutional structures, in particular government policy in relation to labour market issues and trade union density and policy orientation towards part-time workers, may influence the distribution. In view of the predominance of women among part-time workers these institutional structures have a major impact in the stratification of the labour market by gender.

This review of key aspects of labour force participation in Australia, Canada, the United States and the United Kingdom indicates both similarities and differences across countries. While the labour force participation figures indicate convergence in male and female levels of participation in the 1960 to mid-1990 period in all four countries, there has been a persistence of marked gender-based stratification. This is evident in part-time work, which is predominantly female, and labour market participation by family type and continuity of employment, both of which demonstrate gender differentiation. But all of these are characterised by cross-national variation: women are more likely to work full-time in the United States and Canada where participation over the life cycle approximates the inverted 'U'-shaped pattern of Sweden, reflecting the typical combination of labour force participation and child-rearing irrespective of family type. In contrast, the United Kingdom and Australia still demonstrate a two-peak pattern with a significant percentage of women leaving the labour force during the early years of child-rearing, and this is especially true of sole parents, although the two-peak pattern is becoming less marked.

Measures Facilitating Labour Force Participation

In analysing the actions taken to facilitate labour force participation and the equality strategies pursued to enhance the quality of employment, we are primarily concerned with two dimensions of our analytical framework: namely, the social citizenship rights dimension in terms of the extent and quality of rights, and the state, market, family dimension in terms of service provision and regulation. We have identified child care and maternity and parental leave as the key measures to facilitate labour force participation.

Child Care and Employment

Child care is only one aspect of the broad range of caring work in all societies. Caring work is organised on a formal basis within welfare state institutions, but is largely informal and performed within households and communities. Given the gender inequality in its distribution, how it is valued and facilitated is an important aspect of all welfare states in terms of the gender distribution of work and welfare (see Ungerson 1990) and in terms of gender-based labour market stratification.

In its review of child care published in 1990, the OECD identifies two extremes in terms of child care policy. At one extreme are those countries which adopt maximum public responsibility for child care and have generous and well-funded leave provisions – the Nordic countries, although there is variation among them, and France. At the other end of the continuum, where the United States and Britain are the best exemplars, maximum private responsibility for child care is imposed, leave provision is meagre and/or subject to widespread exclusions, and wage replacement is non-existent or relatively low (OECD 1990). The aims of child care services in those countries which impose maximum private responsibility are '(i) to provide a "safety net" of child-care services for the poorest families, as well as for children at risk of physical abuse or neglect; (ii) to encourage the use of private or voluntary services; and (iii) to guarantee a minimum level of quality child care' (OECD 1990: 139). This approach is consistent with the philosophy of the liberal social policy regimes where 'the proper sphere of state behaviour is circumscribed by the functioning of market forces' (Ruggie 1984: 13). Australia and Canada conform to a lesser extent than do the United States and Britain with the maximum private responsibility categorisation. While child care is not considered within a framework of social citizenship rights in any of these countries, in Australia there is more of a recognition of child care as an element of the social wage (Brennan 1994: 10). There has been mobilisation around child care by equality advocates to varying degrees in all four countries over the past few decades (see Chapter 6) and since the late 1980s it has become an issue of political concern in all four.

In the United States much of the political concern has centred on the working poor, high public assistance dependency and the needs of children in low-income families (*Congressional Digest* 1990: 33–7, 64). This increased interest was reflected in federal legislative action in 1990 in the form of the US Act For Better Child Care which authorised matching grants to states over three years to help improve the availability, affordability and quality of child care, primarily for low-income families. Tax credits to individuals and tax breaks for employers are intended to encourage market provision and facilitate parental choice for those further up the income scale. Michel (forthcoming: 551) argues that such policies have, to a large extent, achieved their objectives: market-based provision, whose quality varies by ability to pay, has increased significantly. This supplements family care for working-class and lower middle-class families and voluntary-run centres for middle-class families. At the upper end of the market there is considerable choice of high quality care, including nanny care and nursery schools. The result is a multi-tiered system along class lines (Michel forthcoming: 559).

Increased political interest in child care in Britain is due in part to 'a developing labour shortage, arising from falling numbers of school leavers, and the perceived need to employ more women with children' (European Commission Childcare Network 1990: 36). This increased interest is reflected in exhortation by government for provision by employers, the school system and the private non-profit sector, with the government's role being exclusively as regulator (European Commission Childcare Network 1990: 36–7). The Labour Government, elected in May 1997, has put considerable emphasis on the role of child care in facilitating labour force participation for low earners and especially sole parents. It introduced a tax credit for child care costs targeted at low earners in its 1998 Budget. This is part of its welfare-to-work package and is expected to increase the labour force participation of sole parents. As in the United States, the system is multi-tiered, but it differs in the relative importance of family and market solutions. Public pro-

Table 3.4: Level of Responsibility and Type of Public Child Care Measure

	Overall responsibility	Responsibility for services	Subsidies	
			Direct	Indirect
Australia	Central government	Local authorities	To parents and service providers	To employers
Canada	Provinces	Public and private profit and non-profit institutions	To parents and service providers	To parents and employers
United Kingdom	Central government	Municipalities	To service providers	To employers
USA	States	Public, private and community institutions	To service providers	To parents and employers

Notes: Direct subsidies refer to payments made directly to service providers and to parents according to income. Indirect subsidies refer to payments made in the form of tax credits or tax exemptions which cover part of the cost of child care. The imputed value of employer child care benefit is not taxable in the hands of employees in any of the countries – this is a recent change in Australia and the United Kingdom. In Canada there is a tax exemption of $C5000 per child up to 6 years and children with special needs; there is an exemption of $C3000 per child 7 to 14 years; a credit is granted to parents with non-taxable income. In the United States there are tax credits of $US2400 per child for the first two children; 30 per cent of deductible expenses are allowed if income is less than $10 000, and 20 per cent of deductible expenses if income is greater than $28 000.

Source: OECD 1990: 123–51, Annex 5.C.1, and 151–2, Annex 5.C.2, adapted and updated.

vision is strongly targeted to sole parents and other low-income families (Ruggie 1984). Despite the recent interest in encouraging collective solutions, the mainstay has been, and still is, family provision. As in the other three countries, high quality market-based solutions are available to those with the necessary financial resources.

Canada is close to the maximum private responsibility end of the continuum but there are some significant differences between its approach and those of the United States and Britain (see Table 3.4). In Canada child care is the responsibility of the provincial and territorial governments and the extent of provision varies considerably among them as does the commitment to publicly funded and non-profit child care (Goelman 1992; O'Connor 1998a). Most children of employed parents are in informal care arrangements, which includes care by friends, neighbours, relatives and for a minority nanny care – the latter is tax deductible and is used primarily by high-income couples. It is estimated that in 1990 only 12 per cent of children were in licensed child care arrangements, mostly licensed day care or licensed home care. Twenty-one per cent of those children in day care were subsidised to some extent with subsidisation restricted to low-income families (S. Crompton 1991). Most public funding of child care is given in the form of subsidies to low-income families and, consequently, publicly funded child care tends to be seen as a welfare service rather than a right (National Council of Welfare 1988: 7–8). Yet, most families who qualify for subsidised care do not get it because of the absence of licensed spaces. As in the United States the system is multi-tiered with choice and financial resources being closely linked. Another similarity is the growing corporate involvement in child care provision although this is still outweighed by the involvement of the non-profit sector.

For a brief period Canada had a National Child Care Strategy. This was announced in December 1987 by the Conservative Government, following two decades of intensive lobbying by women's groups, supported by the labour movement, and a long series of reports and task forces on child care (Status of Women, Canada 1986; M. Mitchell 1987; Canada, Special Committee on Child Care 1987; Pepin 1987). This strategy, which did not involve the creation of a national child care system, included improved tax relief for child care and a seven-year program to create 200 000 new child care spaces through cost-share arrangements with the provinces. The tax relief aspects were implemented; these disproportionately advantage high-income earners, not only because of marginal tax rates, but also because they are more likely to use child care options, including nannies, for which receipts can be obtained. The strategy to create new child care places was abandoned in April 1992 using the argument that 'there are other priorities that must come first. These include addressing the problems faced by children at risk – child physical and sexual abuse, poor nutrition and health, low income' (Canada 1992). This statement clearly confirms Canada's location within the maximum private responsibility category.

In terms of commitment, Australia has embraced a mixed public/private/community approach to child care and, in contrast to the other countries, since 1988 has had a National Child Care Strategy. This was a response to considerable political pressure from gender equality advocates and the trade union movement and reflects the political commitment of the Labor Government, which was in power from 1983 to 1996. The key achievements are that almost two-thirds of the demand for work-related child care for 0 to 4 year olds was met by the early 1990s as was about 40 per cent of the demand for work-related child care for school-age children and there was a commitment to meet all the need by the year 2000 (Department of Community Services and Health 1992, cited by Brennan 1994: 207). Since 1984 child care fee relief has been available to low- and middle-income families and since 1991 this has been available to families using private and employer-sponsored child care services. A Childcare Cash Rebate Scheme, which came into effect in July 1994, was designed to assist with the cost of work-, study- or training-related child care expenses for children under the age of thirteen in informal as well as formal child care arrangements. This was introduced as a non-income-tested scheme on the grounds that the cost of child care is 'a legitimate expense for parents earning an income' (Minister for Family Services, quoted in Canberra Times 3 May 1994: 13). This was consistent with the shift in emphasis on child care in Australia from a women's issue and/or a welfare rationale to an economic rationale under the Labor Government (Summers 1994: 24). Under the succeeding Liberal–National Coalition Government the scheme has been changed to an income-tested one. This has paralleled other changes directed to benefiting full-time carers.

An additional contrast between Australia and the other three countries is that, unlike those national governments, the Australian Commonwealth Government plays a major role in funding child care services and Australia has more government provision of child care than any of the other countries (Commonwealth of Australia 1994: 6, Table 1.4). Yet, there has been a consistent shift towards private sector provision and in the early 1990s almost 80 per cent of the planned new places for pre-school children were commercial and/or employer-sponsored (Brennan 1994: 209).

Over the past decade there has been an emphasis on the provision of work-related care arrangements, especially child care, in several countries including all of the liberal welfare states. This interest is reflected in statements encouraging such provision and more concretely in tax relief to employers for costs of provision and in the non-taxation of employees for the imputed cost of company-provided child care. The latter is a recent change in both Australia and the United Kingdom. There is now a major emphasis in Australia, by both government and the Australian Council of Trade Unions, on the provision of employer-supported child care (ACTU 1990; Office of the Status of Women 1993). Unions in all of these countries have to varying degrees focused on child care as an element of the social wage over the past decade but this emphasis has been more consistent in Australia. There is an increasing recognition by business and governments of the economic costs and benefits associated with child care and this is reflected in the arguments of advocacy groups in all countries (Brennan 1994: 206–7; *Financial Times* 3 November 1997; National Council for One Parent Families 1997).

This interest in work-related child care is also reflected in the activities of business representative groups, such as The Conference Board. While this organisation is strongest in the United States and Canada, it 'strives to be the leading global membership organisation that enables senior executives from all industries to explore and exchange ideas that impact on business policy and practices' (D. Friedman 1991: 2). As such it is influential in the development of best practice in relation to employment conditions. It is clear in its research report, *Linking Work-Family Issues to the Bottom Line*, which includes discussions of child care, parental leave and elder care, that the focus is on large, well-established and economically strong companies. The same is evident from a Labour Canada (1990) report, on *Work-related Child Care in Canada*, which demonstrates that work-related child care is a phenomenon confined to the public sector and large, well-established private sector employers. The growth of this kind of provision in situations where care is extremely limited is both a reflection of the division of jobs into 'good' and 'bad' and a reinforcement of differences in the material conditions of workers in different parts of the labour market (Economic Council of Canada 1990). Good jobs are characterised by standard work forms, high levels of unionisation and/or internal labour markets – internal labour market practices include formal job description, performance evaluation, salary classification systems, job ladders, employment and promotion testing. Bad jobs are characterised by unstable, non-standard work forms and very low levels of unionisation. Women, visible minorities and young people are over-represented in bad jobs. It can no longer be assumed that bad jobs are confined to the economically weaker sector of the labour market although they are more prevalent there. There is still a continuum of jobs in terms of quality but there is also considerable evidence of a 'declining middle' stratum of employment in several countries including the liberal welfare states (Myles 1991a).

The provision of work-related child care and associated occupational welfare measures for those in good jobs lessens pressure for public provision from that socio-economic sector most likely to be effective in exercising political pressure for such provision. This is also the sector most likely to employ nannies for in-home child care, for whom a large part of the cost can be deducted as a child care expense in some countries, for example, Canada and the United States. Child care illustrates very clearly the working out of class differences among labour force participants and the way in which failure in public policy to recognise the linkages between status in the household and status in the market is associated with a reinforcement of class and gender inequalities. This failure also contributes to a reinforcement of the good jobs–bad jobs division.

Maternity and Parental Leave

Since the Clinton administration passed the Family and Medical Leave Act in 1993 all four countries have had maternity leave and some part of this leave has been paid for some workers in all but the United States (see Table 3.5). Australia has the longest leave – fifty-two weeks – but it is unpaid except for federal and some state public sector workers and a minority of private sector workers who get full pay for twelve weeks; the total covered is estimated to be 17 per cent of the labour force. Under the 1994 Wage Accord between the Australian Council of Trade Unions and the federal government it was agreed that all employed women would receive twelve weeks' paid maternity leave (*Sydney Morning Herald* 3 June 1994). However, this decision was subsequently modified and the result is a maternity allowance. This is a one-off tax-free payment of $A870 (1996) conditional on the individual qualifying for Family Payment which is both income and asset tested.

With effect from October 1994 the European Union Directive on the Protection of Pregnant Women at Work has been reflected in United Kingdom law. This resulted in an improvement in the minimum statutory entitlements. The existing provision of forty weeks' leave with six weeks paid at 90 per cent replacement rate was maintained. A further twelve weeks is paid at a statutory maternity benefit rate which is set at the same level as sickness benefit. Eligibility was, and continues to be, conditional on two years of continuous employment of sixteen hours or over with the same employer. As a consequence, a large proportion of women are excluded or eligible only for lesser benefits. There is no paternity, parental or care of sick children leave in the United Kingdom (Moss 1991; European Commission Childcare Network 1990: 34–5) but the Labour Government has reversed the policy of the previous

Table 3.5: Maternity and Parental Leave (Universal Government Measures)

	Maximum duration (weeks)	Replacement rate	Eligibility criteria
Maternity leave			
Australia[1]	52	Nil, except for federal and some state public sector workers who get full pay for 12 weeks	Coverage by conciliation and arbitration award, that is, 83% of women and all workers in 2 states
Canada[2]	17–18	Up to 60% of a maximum determined annually; first 2 weeks unpaid	Employment Standards legislation for leave; benefit eligibility same as unemployment insurance
United Kingdom	40	90% for 6 weeks; statutory maternity benefit for 12 weeks	2 years' employment with same employer
USA[3]	12	Nil	Employment in company with 50 employees or more
Parental leave			
Australia	51 (in lieu of maternity leave)	Nil	Coverage by federal conciliation and arbitration award; legislation promised to cover all workers
Canada	10	Up to 60% of a maximum determined annually; first 2 weeks unpaid	Employment Standards legislation for leave; benefit eligibility same as for unemployment insurance
United Kingdom	None		
USA	None[4]		

Notes: Data are for general provisions in each country's national labour legislation. Workers may have additional benefits under collective agreements.

[1] Maternity leave is an industrial relations matter and various awards stipulate various provisions; length, qualifying period and paid or unpaid. A maternity allowance, introduced in February 1996, is paid to meet some of the costs of the birth of a child. It is income- and assets-tested and paid in a lump sum ($A870.60 in 1996), equal to six weeks of the Parenting Allowance paid to families where a partner cares for children at home.

[2] Duration varies by province.

[3] Care leave was introduced in 1993 and applies to birth, adoption and sick child leave. Some states already had unpaid maternity leave.

[4] The United Kingdom Government is committed to implement the EU Directive on Parental Leave not later than December 1999. This will guarantee men and women workers an individual non-transferable right to at least three months' parental leave for child care purposes (as distinct from maternity leave) after the birth or adoption of a child until a given age of up to eight years, as defined by the Government and/or management and labour (*Employment Equality Review* February 1998: 1–2).

Source: OECD 1990: Table 5.8, 144, adapted and updated.

Conservative Government and agreed to implement the European Union Directive on Parental Leave and Leave for Family Reasons. The deadline for implementation is December 1999. This directive was first put forward by the European Commission in 1983, when it was vetoed by the Conservative Government. The proposals were reactivated in 1993 and again opposed by the Conservative Government on the grounds that they would impose 'added burdens on employers without regard to their impact on jobs' (Michael Forsyth, Employment Minister, quoted in *Labour Research* March 1994: 9). The Maastricht social policy agreement, from which the British opted out, allowed its adoption by the other member countries in 1996 with an implementation deadline of June 1998, or June 1999 in exceptional circumstances. The main provision of the agreement is that men and women workers must have an individual, non-transferable right to at least three months' parental leave for child care purposes (as distinct from maternity leave) after the birth or adoption of a child until a given age of up to eight years, to be defined by member states and/or management and labour (*Employment Equality Review* February 1998: 1–2). It is noteworthy that despite the Conservative Government's consistent opposition this directive was supported throughout the 1980s and early 1990s by the Equal Opportunities Commission, several trade unions and voluntary organisations. In addition, improvements in maternity and parental leave in collective bargains over this period were widespread and company-initiated programs were also reported – often directed at the retention of people at the high end of the occupational spectrum (*Labour Research* September 1992; *Labour Research* August 1993: 17–18; Heitlinger 1993: 196–8).

Maternity leave in Canada varies by province but is generally seventeen to eighteen weeks, fifteen weeks of which are paid at 60 per cent replacement rate and subject to a fairly modest weekly limit. The level and duration of payment are often increased through collective bargaining. Leave provision is governed by employment standards legislation, federal or provincial, and benefits are governed by the Unemployment Insurance Act; this has the effect that one may be entitled to benefits and not to leave. Despite this, in 1987, 92 per cent of all maternity leaves were compensated; in 1980 it was 77 per cent. Unemployment insurance benefits were the only compensation in 72 per cent of cases in 1987, and 20 per cent of women received other benefits such as full or partial pay from employers or group insurance; only 14 per cent of women received these kinds of payments in 1980 (Moloney 1989).

The United States was the last country in the OECD to grant care leave that would cover maternity needs – some states had introduced unpaid maternity leave earlier. The 1993 provision of twelve weeks of unpaid leave is progressive in applying to men and women and covering a wide range of care needs – it may relate to childbirth, adoption or sick child leave. On the debit side, it reinforces labour market stratification in that it only covers employees in companies with fifty or more employees. Since it is unpaid it is firmly market reinforcing.

Australia and Canada have parental leave. Canada has a ten-week parental leave and benefit, with the same eligibility as for maternity benefit – this was introduced following a legal challenge by a natural father to the maternity leave provisions. One week unpaid paternity leave and fifty-one weeks unpaid parental leave, the latter in lieu of maternity leave, were granted in 1990 by the Australian Industrial Relations Commission. At the same time, a one-time only option of part-time employment at pro-rata full-time pay for either parent up to the child's second birthday was granted. In addition a female employee may work part-time during pregnancy. These decisions apply only to workers covered by federal level awards, but these influence state level awards. Legislation has been promised which will cover all workers. This legislation is linked to Australia's commitment to ILO Convention 156, the Convention on Equal Treatment of Workers with Family Responsibilities, which Australia ratified in 1990 and which none of the other three countries has ratified.

In all four countries some collective agreements include both leave and benefit provisions which improve on national standards. In addition, payments may be made and/or increased and the length of leave may be extended by employers. This generally happens in the public sector and in jobs at the higher end of the occupational spectrum (Ries and Stone 1992: 385–6; Heitlinger 1993: 196–8; Glezer 1988). In other words, supplementary leave and benefit provisions reinforce the good jobs–bad jobs segmentation of the labour force.

The policy options adopted in relation to facilitating labour force participation have significant similarities but also vary in significant respects across the four countries. Child care does not have the status of a social citizenship right in any of these countries, nor is it discussed in these terms, despite considerable pressure from gender equality advocates over the past twenty years and the emergence of child care as a political issue, to varying degrees, in all four countries since the late 1980s (see Chapter 6). There is some discussion of child care as an element of the social wage in all four but this is minimal except in Australia, which has a strong commitment to meeting child care needs; this commitment is increasingly being exercised through the market rather than through public and/or community/voluntary sector provision which was emphasised in government statements in the 1980s and early 1990s. While all four countries support private responsibility over public responsibility for service provision the extent of the support for public provision varies not only cross-nationally but also over time in individual countries and across sub-national units. The form of private responsibility supported – market or family – also varies cross-nationally. The United States has the strongest market orientation, the United Kingdom has the strongest family orientation. The former reinforces occupational stratification, while the latter reinforces gender stratification. Maternity leave in Australia, Canada and the United Kingdom and care leave in the United States have a stronger social rights orientation than does child care but eligibility criteria and/or coverage are associated with limited scope and short duration. The status of benefits is even more tenuous – there are no care benefits in the United States, eligibility for maternity benefits is relatively stringent in Britain, and is confined to certain categories of workers in Australia. Canada is best in terms of eligibility and benefit access criteria, although the leave duration possible is better in Australia and Britain.

Measures facilitating labour market participation are one element of labour market equality strategies. Of equal importance are strategies relating to the equalisation of the quality of participation.

Employment Equality Strategies

Pay inequity and gender-based occupational segregation, with their associated inequity in quality of employment and compensation, are two of the most obvious manifestations of gender-based labour market stratification (OECD 1985; 1988; 1994). These are also two of the areas in which mobilisation by gender equality advocates has been most in evidence since the 1960s (see Chapter 6).

While the public policy employment equality strategies pursued in the four liberal welfare states under discussion have some significant cross-national similarities, they differ in some significant respects. For example, all except Australia have equal pay legislation but only some states in the United States and some provinces in Canada have strong legislation on equal pay for work of equal value or comparable worth (Weiner and Gunderson 1990: 110–14, 138–9) and in most of these jurisdictions it is confined to public sector workers. Equal pay measures are directed to the underpayment of women doing the same or broadly similar work as men in the same employment. Equal pay for work of equal value is directed to the effects of horizontal segregation and the undervaluation of work done primarily by women; equal value or comparable worth is generally based on a composite measure of skill, effort, responsibility and working conditions and may be arrived at through a process of job evaluation (Kahn 1992: 3). Depending on the interpretation it may allow for comparison of occupations in the same workplace or across workplaces.

All four countries have legislation relating to equal employment opportunities and the prohibition of discrimination but the approaches adopted vary from anti-discrimination through affirmative action to expanding opportunities through training and child care provision (OECD 1988; Steinberg and Cook 1988; O'Donnell and Hall 1988). Legislation in these areas is directed to the effects of vertical segregation and seeks to remove barriers to the integration of women into all areas of the labour force; barriers which may be in hiring, training and/or promotion procedures.

Equal Pay and Pay Equity

The action taken to remedy gender inequality in pay is conditioned by the vastly different industrial relations structures in Australia on the one hand and Canada, the United States and the United Kingdom on the other. Up to the early 1990s the system in Australia was highly central-ised through federal and state Conciliation and Arbitration/Industrial Relations Commissions, which ruled on pay issues. Since 1969 the Commissions have accepted the principle of equal pay for equal work and since 1972 the principle of equal pay for work of equal value, that is, that 'award rates for all workers should be considered without regard to the sex of the employee' (Equal Pay Decision Print B8506 1972: 7; quoted in Burton 1991: 130). Equal pay for work of equal value, which was implemented in three phases up to 1975, has been associated with a significant reduction in the wage gap (R. Gregory and Duncan 1981; Burton 1991: 146–8). The principle of comparable worth was rejected in 1986, in a ruling relating to nurses' pay, on the grounds that it would result in too broad a range of work value comparisons and hence would 'strike at the heart of accepted methods of wage fixation ... and would be particularly destructive of the present Wage Fixing Principles' (Conciliation and Arbitration Commissioner's ruling; quoted in O'Donnell and Hall 1988: 58). The Commissioners pointed out that Canada, the United States and the United Kingdom, where the prin-ciple is applied, although with different approaches in each country, have very different industrial relations systems to the Australian one. Their systems are highly decentralised and considerably lower per-centages of their labour forces are covered by collective agreements. In May 1990, 80 per cent of Australian wage and salary earners (83.5 per cent of women and 77.3 per cent of men), including all public sector employees, were covered by awards made by the Commonwealth and state industrial tribunals or by collective agreements registered with them. In Canada it is estimated that only 50 per cent of the labour force are covered by collective agreements, and in the United States less than 20 per cent of the labour force are covered (Ries and Stone 1992: 369). In the mid-1990s it is estimated that only 45 per cent of the British labour force are covered by collective agreements compared to about 70 per cent in the 1980s.

The United States, Canada and the United Kingdom have adopted a legislative approach to pay equity. The US legislation on equal pay dates from 1963 but the emphasis on comparable worth did not arise until the late 1970s. In Canada, equal pay for equal work legislation has been in existence federally and provincially since the 1950s and was embodied in the Canada Labour Code in 1971. Pay equity was adopted as part of the Canadian Human Rights Act in 1977 and has been adopted, or legislated for, by half of the provinces and two territories in the intervening period. The 1970 Equal Pay Act in the United Kingdom came into effect in 1975; it was amended in 1983 following a European Court of Justice ruling that the original act did not meet the requirements of European law as embodied in Article 119 of the Treaty of Rome, which mandates equal pay for equal work, and subsequent equality directives, which have broadened this to equal pay for work of equal value. The effectiveness of a legislative approach is dependent on several factors, the most important of which is whether the legislation is proactive or complaint-based. Proactive approaches are more effective than complaint-based approaches. Under a complaint-based approach an individual, group or their representative is obliged to initiate a complaint and go through the process of demonstrating unfair pay. The national legislation in all three countries is complaint-based. The effectiveness of legislation is also dependent on political support and willingness to review and strengthen the legislation if necessary. Political support has varied over time in all countries as has trade union support (J. Gregory 1992; England 1992; Kahn 1992; Rubery 1988; Fudge and McDermott 1991a).

The equality strategies pursued in the four countries are based on similar principles. Equal pay for equal work was accepted first in all countries; later the principle of equal pay for work of equal value was accepted. Despite the formal acceptance of the comparable worth principle in the United States, Canada and Britain, their progress in reducing pay differentials has been less than Australia's, although substantial gains have been made by some workers in all countries. This difference is consistent with the findings of quantitative cross-national analyses which demonstrate that collective approaches to wage determination are more effective in equalising the wages of women and men than are the legislative approaches pursued to date (Whitehouse 1992; Rosenfeld and Kalleberg 1991). It is important to recognise that there are serious limitations to the legislation in all three countries. The complaint-based characteristic of the national legislation in the United States, Canada and Britain means that it is the responsibility of the individual employee to prove unequal pay. Comparable worth is still subject to legal challenge in the United States, where claimants are often obliged to prove intentional discrimination (England 1992: 225–52). In all countries the process of determining comparable worth through job evaluation is fraught with difficulties, especially for workers without collective representation (England 1992; Acker 1989; Fudge and McDermott 1991b). In the United States class actions are possible and most cases are brought in this way, but the courts can, and frequently do, disallow these (Blum 1991: 23). In the United Kingdom, unless the employer agrees to treat a particular claim as a test case, each claim must be pursued separately and the findings of Industrial Tribunals do not set legal precedents. The widespread application of comparable worth has been limited to public sector workers in some states in the United States and some provinces in Canada. A collective approach to implementation is similarly limited and, with the exception of the Canadian province of Ontario, this applies only to public sector workers.

Employment Equity

Australia, the United States, Canada and the United Kingdom initially adopted an anti-discrimination approach in which 'labour market inequality is perceived to result from specific unfair treatment or discrimination toward employees by employers and others, including unions, employment officers, counsellors, and so on. Policy is formulated in terms of what employers or others are prohibited from doing' (Steinberg and Cook 1988: 319). This is extremely limited in its impact on barriers to employment equity. In contrast, the affirmative action model 'shifts the locus of discrimination from individual behavior inside and outside the labor market to the structure and functioning of the labor market – in particular, to the systemic behavior of all parties acting in it. This new model has implications for changing the power relationships in the market' (Steinberg and Cook 1988: 320). The United States has the longest experience with such an approach but each of the countries has eventually incorporated some elements of affirmative action, or an employment equity approach, as it is called in Canada. All four also have some form of contract compliance programs, whereby government contractors have to subscribe to some form of employment equity, although the level of commitment and enforcement varies over time and across countries.

The United States combines the anti-discrimination and affirmative action approaches. Title VII of the 1964 Civil Rights Act, which came into effect in 1965, prohibited discrimination in employment practices and established the Equal Employment Opportunity Commission (EEOC) 'to investigate and conciliate complaints and grant complainants the right to seek remedies in court' (Blum 1991: 22). The institutional and legal frameworks developed in the United States are important resources and have proved effective when political commitment has encouraged their use. The strength of this political commitment has varied – it was weak during the Nixon and Ford administrations, strong during the Carter administration, and weak during the Reagan and Bush eras (Blum 1991: 23). It is noteworthy that the gains made in the public sector have been considerably better than those in the private sector and have been consistent throughout this period. The importance of the political complexion of the Supreme Court for achievements under the 1960s measures are reflected in the push for the Civil Rights Act 1991. This legislation was directed to countering 'the effects of nine Supreme Court decisions from 1986 to 1991 that made it harder for workers to bring and win job discrimination lawsuits' (*CQ Almanac* 1991: 251). In addition, it established a four-year Glass Ceiling Commission 'to study how business filled management and decision-making positions, the developmental and skill-enhancing practices used to foster qualifications for advancement, and the pay and reward structures used in the workplace' (*CQ Almanac* 1991: 259). In its first report the Commission concluded that despite three decades of affirmative action women and minority groups are to a significant extent blocked from top management with women constituting less than 5 per cent of senior managers. They point to the difference between the rhetoric and practice of inclusion (Glass Ceiling Commission 1995).

Canada, like the United States, combines an anti-discrimination and affirmative action approach, the former being covered by the Canadian Human Rights Act (1977). The Canadian Charter of Rights and Freedoms, which forms part of the Constitution Act, 1982, constitutionally affirmed the right to equality in employment and explicitly permitted legislation such as employment equity. The 1986 Employment Equity Act, which covers four groups – women, visible minorities, disabled people and aboriginal peoples – states that employment equity 'means more than treating persons in the same way but also requires special measures and the accommodation of differences' (Section 2). In addition to the Employment Equity Act, which covers only 5.5 per cent of the workforce, Canada's federal government has a contract compliance policy requiring employers of 100 or more workers bidding for federal contracts of $200 000 or more to commit themselves to employment equity. The program applies to about 880 companies employing about 7.5 per cent of the labour force, primarily in manufacturing and such businesses as engineering services, printing, cleaning services and university research. A special parliamentary committee, which reported on the operation of the Act in May 1992, made several recommendations for broadening its scope and increasing its effectiveness through such measures as training and child care; this indicates that there is a recognition that some of the sources of women's labour market inequality lie outside the labour market (Special Committee on the Review of the Employment Equity Act 1992). A revised Employment Equity Act, incorporating some of the recommended changes, was passed in 1995. In particular, it extended coverage to all employees in the federal public sector, that is, the federal public service, agencies and commissions; it empowered the Canadian Human Rights Commission to conduct audits of all public and private employers under the legislation to verify compliance and to empower the Canadian Human Rights Tribunal, acting as the Employment Equity Review Tribunal, to ensure final enforcement when needed in both the public and private sectors (Canada Human Resources Development 1994). This answers one of the major criticisms of the original Act, that is, non-enforceability of employers' obligations. The inclusion of the federal public sector brought an additional 10 per cent of the labour force under coverage of the Act and answered the criticism that the public service affirmative action policy was not being strongly enforced.

The Australian federal Sex Discrimination Act was passed in 1984, although the earliest state legislation dates from 1975. The federal legislation is complaints-based but does contain provisions against apparently neutral employment requirements that disadvantage women. It was amended in 1992 to cover federal industrial awards and variation in industrial awards made after the date of the legislation. This was introduced to guard against discrimination in the changed climate of decentralised bargaining arrangements. The Affirmative Action (Equal Employment Opportunity for Women) Act was passed in 1986 and was fully operational by February 1989. It focuses on the removal of systemic discrimination. It covers all private sector employers with 100 or more employees, as well as higher education institutions; it requires employers to set goals and timetables for achieving a representative workforce (OECD 1988; O'Donnell and Hall 1988: 78). In 1992 it was extended to cover voluntary bodies with 100 or more paid employees, elected union officials and trainees employed through group training schemes. With effect from January 1993 companies in breach of affirmative action legislation for women workers are ineligible for

Commonwealth government contracts, which are worth $A10 billion annually. The Australian Commonwealth legislation differs from the Canadian federal legislation in being focused exclusively on women while the Canadian legislation covers four designated groups. It is broader in scope than the Canadian federal legislation in covering all firms with 100 or more employees. It covers 45 per cent of the labour force compared to the 23 per cent covered in Canada. Until 1993, when the contract compliance provision was introduced in Australia, the only sanction for non-compliance was naming in Parliament.

The legal basis of employment equity in the United Kingdom is the 1975 Sex Discrimination Act as amended in 1986, which was introduced to meet European Community equality requirements as reflected in Article 119 of the Treaty of Rome. Industrial tribunals, which are quasi-judicial bodies explicitly established to deal with labour relations disputes, are central to the United Kingdom system. The Equal Opportunities Commission is involved only when a dispute raises a question of principle or when a complainant cannot pursue a claim unaided. The EOC is also charged with monitoring the Equal Pay and Sex Discrimination Acts and recommending amendments to the laws. While the legislation in the United Kingdom reflects an anti-discrimination approach, there is encouragement of voluntary affirmative action. This action is for the most part confined to a relatively small number of companies and is often targeted at the upper levels of the occupational spectrum, for example, the Opportunity 2000 campaign which was strongly supported by Prime Minister Major. An investigation by the Equal Opportunities Commission indicates that due to under-funding, training is extremely limited in the United Kingdom and some programs are being cut back (*Labour Research* May 1993: 30).

In summary, all four countries have adopted an anti-discrimination approach; the United States, Canada and Australia have affirmative action/employment equity legislation. Australia has adopted the most extensive approach to expanding employment opportunities through training and child care provision, but there is some emphasis on these in all these countries.

Gender-based Pay Differentials and Occupational Segregation

Recent directly comparable earning figures for the four countries are not available. However, the available gender wage differential measures from the mid-1980s to the early 1990s give a consistent ranking with Australia at the high end, followed by the United Kingdom, the United States and Canada (OECD 1988; OECD 1991: Table 2.16; Gornick 1992; J. Gregory 1992). The figures presented in Table 3.6(a) are not directly comparable because those for Australia and the United Kingdom are based on hourly earnings, those for the United States are based on weekly earnings and those for Canada on annual earnings. Since the latter two include overtime earnings, which men are more likely to have, the exact male–female differential may be less than indicated. Despite these caveats these figures reflect the ranking of countries for the mid-1980s to mid-1990s in the sources cited above. In that context the current figures also reflect decreases in male–female differentials over time. Across all OECD countries women have generally achieved larger increases in real earnings than have men over the past decade, narrowing somewhat the earnings gap. These increases are not confined to the earnings of highly qualified women. Wages for the lowest decile of female workers have improved relative not only to the lowest decile of male workers but also to the median earnings of male workers (OECD 1996: 63). However, as with every other aspect of labour market participation it is important to recognise that these aggregate measures of gender differences conceal considerable variation in the experience of workers in the public and private sectors, in different occupations, in unionised and non-unionised employment and in full and part-time work.

Data for all four countries for the early 1990s illustrate marked differences in gender pay differentials between public sector and private sector full-time employees (see Table 3.6(b)). The female–male pay relativity is higher for government sector workers in all four countries – it is highest in Australia, at almost 90 per cent, and lowest in the United States, at 74 per cent – but the biggest percentage advantage enjoyed by public relative to private sector workers in terms of gender equity in pay is in Canada, followed by the United Kingdom, Australia and the United States. The greater gender equality in pay in the public sector can be explained by a number of institutional factors. For example, there is generally greater visibility of procedures in relation to pay scales and settlement in the public sector than in the private sector, unionisation is higher and the application of pay equity measures is facilitated by both of these characteristics. The public sector advantage is also to a significant extent built into the employment equality measures in all of these countries.

Notwithstanding data and measurement limitations, there are some clear indications of over- and under-representation of women and men in different occupations in all countries. Women are generally over-represented in clerical and service occupations and in the service sector, and men are over-represented in the transport and communications and manufacturing sectors, and these patterns have changed little over the 1980s; however, the representation of women in managerial and

Table 3.6: Ratio of Female to Male Earnings for Full-time Workers

(a) Mid-1990s

Australia (1996)	84.4 (Hourly earnings)
Canada (1995)	73.1 (Annual earnings)
United Kingdom (1996)	80.0 (Hourly earnings)
USA (1996)	75.0 (Weekly earnings)

Sources: Australia: ABS, *Labour Force Surveys*, Cat. No. 6203.0, Canberra, ABS; Canada: Statistics Canada 1995; United Kingdom: 1996 *Labour Force Survey*; United States: US Bureau of the Census 1997, *Employment & Earnings* (January).

(b) Public and Private Sectors, Early 1990s

	Sector		Total Full-time
	Private	Public	Workforce
Australia (1992)	79.1	89.6	84.5
Canada (1992)	67.9	79.8	71.8
United Kingdom (1991)	65.8	76.7	71.9
USA (1991)	67.2	74.1	71.0

Sources: Canada: Statistics Canada, Household Surveys Division, 'Survey of Consumer Finances', unpublished data; Australia: ABS, *Labour Force Surveys* Cat. No. 6203, Canberra, ABS; United Kingdom and United States: calculated from Table 4, Gornick and Jacobs 1997, which is based on Luxembourg Income Study micro-data.

administrative occupations and to a lesser extent in professional occupations varies markedly across the liberal welfare states. Despite these facts, women have made gains in all these countries – what is at issue is the location and extent of these gains.

Table 3.7 outlines the percentage of women in the major occupational groups and the percentage of female employment accounted for by each group. Differences in classification across countries makes exact comparisons impossible; however, a review of the country distributions in the early 1990s indicates some marked similarities and differences in the female share of occupational groups across countries and a comparison with the early 1980s indicates some marked differences in the rates of change. The most marked similarity across countries is the predominance of women in clerical employment, which ranges from 75 per cent in the United Kingdom to 81 per cent in Canada. Apart from this, there tends to be a difference between the United States and Canada, on the one hand, and Australia and the United Kingdom, on the other, in terms of the percentage of women at

Table 3.7: Percentage of Women and Percentage Share of Female Employment in Major Occupational Groups, the United States, Canada, United Kingdom and Australia, 1990

Occupational groups	USA	Canada	United Kingdom	Australia
	Women in group (%)			
Managers and administrators[1]	42	41	32	24
Professional	53 ⎫		40 ⎫	41 ⎫
	⎬ 52	50	⎬ 45	⎬ 45
Para/semi-professional[2]	49 ⎭		50 ⎭	47 ⎭
Clerical	79	81	75	77
Unskilled service	60	57	67 ⎫	
			⎬	64
Sales	48	47	66 ⎭	
	Share of female employment (%)			
Managers and administrators[1]	11	11	11	6
Professional	16	21	9	13
Para/semi-professional[2]	4		10	6
Clerical	28	30	26	32
Unskilled service	18	17	15 ⎫	
			⎬	23
Sales	12	10	12 ⎭	
Other occupations[3]	11	11	17	20

Notes: [1] Managers is categorisation for United States, Canada and United Kingdom; managers and administrators is categorisation for Australia.

[2] United States: technical and related support; United Kingdom: associated professional and technical occupations; Australia: para-professionals.

[3] This includes the following occupational groups: United States: precision, production, craft and repair (9%), operators, fabricators and labourers (8%), primary (1%); Canada: processing/machining (2%), product fabricating/assembling/repairing (4%), construction and transportation (1%), materials handling/crafts (2%), primary (2%); United Kingdom: craft and related occupations (3%), plant and machine operators (4%), other (10%); Australia: labourers and related workers (13%), plant and machine operators (3%) and trades persons (4%).

Sources: Statistics Canada 1993; United States, Bureau of the Census 1993: adapted from Table No. 644, p. 405; 'Women in the Labour Market', *Employment Gazette*, November 1993; ABS 1992, *August Labour Force Australia*, Canberra, ABS.

the higher end of the spectrum. While in Canada and the United States in the early 1990s over 40 per cent of managerial/administrative jobs were held by women, in the same period women in Australia and the United Kingdom held only 24 per cent and 32 per cent respectively. In professional and semi-professional occupations the differences are considerably less: the percentage of jobs held by women in the United States and Canada was 52 and 50 per cent respectively, compared to 45 per cent in Australia and the United Kingdom. Considering the percentage share of female employment in various occupational groups and despite the differences in classification across countries, the very low percentage share of female employment in managerial and administrative positions in Australia – 6 per cent compared to 11 per cent in the other three countries – is noteworthy. We identify contributory factors below.

A comparison of country-specific major occupational distributions for the early 1990s and the early to mid-1980s indicates that segregation has declined in all the liberal welfare states, but at a slow rate, and then only at the upper end of the occupational distribution. With the exception of the United States, where it remained static, women's representation in clerical, sales and service occupations increased slightly over the decade. The only occupational groups that showed substantial increases in the representation of women are the managerial/administrative and professional occupational groups. For the United States and Canada, the most marked increase in female representation was in the managerial/administrative occupational group; the representation of women increased in both countries by 28 per cent over the decade from 1982 to 1992. Representation in the professional occupational group also increased over the decade, but by far lower percentages – 9 per cent in the United States and 11 per cent in Canada. While this means that women in the United States and Canada make up 50 and 52 per cent respectively of each country's professional and para/semi-professional occupational groups, it is important to recognise that women are concentrated in nursing, teaching and social science professions in these countries as in the United Kingdom and Australia.

In the United Kingdom there was a 45 per cent increase in the percentage representation of women in the managerial and administrative occupational group from 1981 to 1992, but at 32 per cent in 1992 the representation of women is still considerably lower than in the United States and Canada; it is mid-way between the high North American levels and the Australian level of 24 per cent in 1992. Similarly, the increase in the representation of women in the professional and semi-professional occupational groups was exceptionally high, at 15 per cent, and brought the representation of women to the same level as in Australia in 1992. Due to changes in occupational classifications in Australia in the mid-1980s, the base year used is 1986. The representation of women in both the managerial/administrative and professional occupational groups increased in Australia between 1986 and 1992 by 10 per cent. But the former group started from a very low base (22.5 per cent) and reached only 24 per cent in 1992. In contrast, the increase of 10 per cent in the professional and semi-professional occupational groups was higher than the increase in the United States for the whole decade but, starting from a lower base, its 1992 representation of women at 45 per cent is still considerably lower than in the United States and Canada.

The figures outlined above do not differentiate between full- and part-time workers. Evidence from Australia and the United Kingdom indicate that patterns are different for the two groups. For example, Martin Watts and Judith Rich (1992) demonstrate that over the 1978–89 period in Australia there was a modest decline in occupational segregation for total and full-time employment and progress was best for full-time employment. In an earlier work they demonstrated that part-time employment is a structural impediment to the occupational integration of the sexes (M. Watts and Rich 1991). Significantly, part-time employment accounted for 50 per cent of the growth in female employment between 1983 and 1992 (Commonwealth of Australia 1992b). Catherine Hakim (1993b) also demonstrates different patterns for full- and part-time workers in Britain. Over the 1971–91 period the percentages of women in female-dominated occupations – those with more than 55 per cent women – increased for the part-time workforce and declined for the full-time workforce; in contrast, the percentages of women in integrated occupations – those with 25 per cent to 55 per cent women workers – increased within the full-time workforce from 16 to 20 per cent for men and from 17 to 22 per cent for women (Hakim 1993b: 297, Table 2). Hakim argues that these opposing trends explain the slow decline in occupational segregation in Britain despite equal opportunities legislation since the 1970s (Hakim 1993b). It is possible that a breakdown for full-time and part-time workers may reflect a more extensive occupational spread of integration in all four countries but given its higher percentage of part-time workers the effect is likely to be more marked in the United Kingdom.

Occupational segregation by gender has lessened for high status full-time occupations in all the liberal welfare states, most markedly in the United States and Canada but also in the United Kingdom and to a considerably lesser extent for managerial/administrative occupations in Australia. These patterns are consistent with those identified through an index of dissimilarity analysis (which measures the percentage of men and women that would have to change occupations in order to achieve gender equality in occupational distribution), but specify that, even in those countries with sharp decreases in aggregate measures of segregation, increases in the representation of women are confined to a couple of occupational groups at the high end of the occupational spectrum. It must be noted that dissimilarity analyses recently have been the subject of considerable criticism (Hakim 1993b; M. Watts 1993).

These findings raise two questions. First, why are moves towards more equitable gender balance confined to such a narrow range of occupations? Second, why is progress in the managerial/administrative occupations so limited in Australia? Concerning the first question, it is not surprising that overall gains are modest and concentrated in just two major occupational groups, when one considers the characteristics of these jobs and the structure of the labour market within which employment equity/equal employment opportunity/affirmative action was introduced. Managerial/administrative and professional occupations tend to have well-defined career structures and training and promotion opportunities (Dobbin et al. 1993). Many of the women concerned have tertiary qualifications, a strong career orientation, work long hours and would be expected to compete on equal terms with men (M. Watts and Rich 1992). These are also the women who are in the best position to purchase the support services necessary to maintain a full-time commitment to the labour market. The combination of these factors is likely to contribute to a more equitable entry and promotion scenario than characterises other occupational groups. However, numerical integration does not necessarily mean qualitative integration, and we have already mentioned the US Glass Ceiling Commission findings.

It is not surprising that the strategy of employment equity has not been spectacularly successful when one bears in mind that it was introduced at a time when desirable jobs in manufacturing were being lost rather than created. The integration of women into all levels of the occupational spectrum implied by employment equity/equal opportunity legislation was based on the assumption of a growing economy, including a growing manufacturing sector; the sector of the economy that has been growing in all of these countries is the service sector, where the percentage of desirable jobs is relatively low and much of the growth has been in poor quality non-standard jobs – casual, part-time, low skill and low wage jobs. This growth reflects the increasing emphasis on numerical and static 'flexibility' (see Chapter 6) (OECD 1989). This is not confined to the service sector. There is evidence of a dual labour force even within the core sector of the economy. This characterises a division of employees into a mainstream labour force and a contingent labour force comprised of part-time, temporary and other non-standard workers.

Second, concerning the lesser progress in gender integration in the managerial/administrative occupational groups in Australia, it is unfortunate that public and private sector breakdowns are not available. There is considerable evidence that progress in the public service has been relatively good (Australian National Audit Office 1997; Evaluation and Statistical Services Branch, Department of Finance 1993), and widespread recognition that progress at the upper levels of private companies has been very limited; at the very top level the percentage of women declined between 1984 and 1992. While the effectiveness review of the Affirmative Action (Equal Employment Opportunity for Women) Act, published in December 1992, concludes that 'generally speaking, the Act is working well', it points to concern about the quality of affirmative action programs, the lack of consultation with women and unions and 'the so-called glass ceiling inhibiting progress into senior management and board positions' (Affirmative Action Agency 1992: iii). The review found that the rate of 'affirmative action progress is very uneven and it is difficult to attribute identified changes to any one cause', that some organisations are 'still largely untouched by EEO' and that, when 'past discrimination is embedded in an organisation, decisive and sustained affirmative action is required to bring real change' (Affirmative Action Agency 1992: 2). It also points to the fact that high compliance with the Act's reporting requirements has been achieved, but that this 'is not necessarily reflected in widespread quality program development' (Affirmative Action Agency 1992: 3). This, coupled with the fact that, until contract compliance was introduced in 1993, the only sanction was naming in Parliament, is at least a partial explanation of the poor progress.

While it may be argued that the older anti-discrimination and affirmative action legislation in the United States is a probable contributor to the difference between its progress and that of Australia and Britain, it is noteworthy that patterns in the United States and Canada are almost identical, while the timing of the legislative measures in Canada is much closer to that of Australia than of the United States. This points to the importance of labour market structure and location within the international economy. In view of the close economic links between Canada and the United States (O'Connor 1993a: 27, Table 4), one would expect personnel policies to be similar, especially in the multinational companies that operate in both countries, and that practices adopted in the larger US market would dominate. Frank Dobbin et al. (1993) demonstrate that US companies adopted an internal labour market type formal promotion mechanism after 1964 in response to Equal Employment Opportunity law. They found 'that organisations adopt ILM practices less in response to internal imperatives than in response to changes in the general model of organising offered by the environment' (Dobbin et al. 1993: 421) and that managers came to see affirmative action as a force for equity and efficiency (*Harvard Law Review* 1989). Formal selection and promotion mechanisms are viewed by managers not only as ways to protect employee rights but also as ways 'to rationalise the allocation of workers' (Dobbin et al. 1993: 422). Based on analysis of the Comparative Class Structure study data, John Myles and Don Black (1986) demonstrate that in the early 1980s in the Canadian goods sector, which is dominated by US ownership, there was a much higher proportion of labour power in managerial and supervisory positions than in Swedish firms or in the Canadian commercial and state service sectors. They identify the most striking feature of the data as the extent to which Canadian firms have incorporated American practices for organising the class relations in the workplace

> particularly in those sectors where the American branch plant has been dominant. It is the degree to which the Canadian class structure is Americanized that constitutes its most distinctive feature, and, to the extent that the American class structure itself is a curiosity among the advanced capitalist countries that is also its most distinctive 'distortion' (Myles and Black 1986: 177–8).

It is possible that this Americanisation may have become more intense in the intervening period in view of the Canada–US Free Trade Agreement which came into operation in January 1989 and the succeeding North American Free Trade Deal; Americanised managerial practices are likely to have spread at least to the commercial services sector, where American companies are strongly represented, if not to the state sector.

The dramatic increase in the representation of women in management in the United Kingdom throughout the 1980s has occurred without legislated affirmative action although there is government encouragement for voluntary action and there is considerable evidence of this in relation to women in managerial positions. This reflects, at least in part, a preoccupation with the smaller cohort of young people entering the labour market in the mid-1990s and the desire to retain highly skilled and expensively trained personnel (*Labour Research* March 1993: 12).

Pay Equity Versus Employment Equity

The patterns identified indicate that the ranking of countries on aggregate measures of segregation is the reverse of the ranking of countries on aggregate female–male wage differentials. Why is there an apparent incompatibility between success on pay equity and employment equity strategies? The most important point is that the integration of women into higher level occupations has been relatively modest and there are indications that this integration is not always on the same terms as men, that is, there is the persistence of considerable levels of internal segregation. Detailed analysis of occupations which had above average integration in the 1970–88 period in the United States demonstrates that numerical integration may hide significant segregation within occupations. Barbara Reskin and Patricia Roos point out that occupational integration is likely to lessen gender pay differentials only if the occupations 'become and remain genuinely integrated'; they conclude that the substantial segregation evident within desegregating occupations 'has bleak implications for women's prospects of achieving economic equity with men' (Reskin and Roos 1990: 307; detailed case studies were carried out on pharmacy, public relations, typesetters and compositors, bank managers, insurance sales and insurance adjusters and examiners, residential real estate, systems analysts, bartenders, bakers; partial case studies were carried out on accountants and auditors, reporters and bus drivers. Reskin and Roos found that two occupations – insurance adjusting/examining and compositing/typesetting – had become resegregated as predominantly female and a few occupational specialities had been relabelled as women's work). In occupations where the earnings gap declined it did so mostly through an erosion of men's earnings during the 1970s. However, despite the decline in real earnings there were real gains for women relative to traditionally female occupations.

Two reports on the gender pay differential for the British Equal Opportunities Commission in the early 1990s demonstrate that aggregate indicators mask divergent trends for different sectors of the labour force. Based on case studies of twenty organisations the Commission identified two trends which push the national gender pay differential in different directions: the movement of a minority of women into higher paid jobs formerly held predominantly by men is associated with a narrowing of gender differences in pay; in contrast, 'Employers' increasing use of flexible and market-based pay systems has tended to widen the differential' (Equal Opportunities Commission 1992: 4). The case studies indicate that an organisation may use different approaches to the pay of different groups of employees depending on the perceived relative importance of market pay rates. This selectivity has the potential for gender bias. This may become increasingly difficult to detect since the survey evidence indicates that the growth of flexibility is associated with less openness about pay matters in the public sector, which traditionally had transparent structures, and very little monitoring of the differential impact of pay practices in the private sector (Equal Opportunities Commission 1991: 78).

We have already discussed reasons for the poor success of the legislative approaches to pay equity in the United States, the United Kingdom and Canada – the complaint-based approach, the absence of a collective approach to implementation, weak government support, weak trade union support in the early stages and narrow coverage. Conversely, the individualistic legalistic approach to integration, pursued most strongly in the United States, works well at the upper end of the occupational spectrum where internal labour markets and the merit principle can be demonstrated to make good business sense. Yet, it is important to remember that the 'upper end' of the occupational spectrum does not usually include the top management positions (Glass Ceiling Commission 1995).

It is noteworthy that the pay equity/employment equity pattern evident in Australia is similar to that evident in Sweden, an exemplar of the social democratic welfare state. It has even lower female–male pay differentials than Australia but relatively high gender-based occupational segregation. This raises the issue of a conflict between mass and élite equality strategies or at least the possibility of different policy legacies and political configurations being favourable to one strategy rather than the other (O'Connor 1996: 78–100).

Unfortunately, the centralised bargaining system, which has been instrumental in narrowing the gender wage gap in Australia since the principle of equal pay for work of equal value was accepted, is now under threat with the introduction of enterprise bargaining. The evidence on the outcome of enterprise bargaining to date is not encouraging (Hall and Fruin 1993) and the indications are that gender wage differentials have not lessened between 1992 and 1996 (see Table 3.6). The Industrial Relations Reform Act, which came into effect in May 1994, has created a floor of minimum entitlements which are progressive when considered relative to the other three countries: relating to minimum wages; unpaid parental leave; termination of employment, including unfair dismissal; and equal remuneration for work of equal value, which covers basic pay, over-award and other work-related benefits. But the objective of this Act is to facilitate enterprise bargaining, which has been demonstrated to militate against women and probably other weakly organised groups in the labour force. This is a good illustration of the contradictory forces at work in all countries in the movement towards gender equality in employment.

Several often contradictory factors affect, and condition the outcome of, the equality strategies chosen in each of the countries. One that is common to all four is economic restructuring; this is likely to result in the exclusion of larger and larger proportions of the increasing female labour force from the benefits of the equality strategies pursued to date and to limit the possibilities for independence and autonomy potentially associated with labour market participation (discussed further in Chapters 6 and 7).

Earner-carer Labour Market Participation Without Earner-carer Social Policy Frameworks

Labour force participation figures indicate convergence in male and female levels of participation over the 1960 to mid-1990s period in Australia, Canada, Great Britain and the United States but the characteristics of participation indicate the persistence of marked gender-based stratification. This is evident not only in participation by family type and continuity of employment over the life cycle but also in part-time work, which is predominantly female, and in occupational location and pay. But there is considerable cross-national variation particularly in continuity of employment and part-time work, with Australia and Great Britain demonstrating higher levels of gender stratification than the United States and Canada. While the labour force participation pattern indicates a trend towards earner-carer labour market participants, reflected in the increase in dual-earning units and participation by sole parents in all of these countries, location on this trajectory varies. The constant is that this change is occurring in the absence of a social policy framework that is attuned to the needs of dual-earning and sole parent units.

None of these countries has a comprehensive strategy directed to responding to labour market stratification but there are two broad sets of policies that are relevant: policies to facilitate participation for those with caring responsibilities; and policies directed to enhancing the quality of participation. The key policies which can facilitate labour force participation are child care and maternity and/or care leave. Despite political pressure over the past decade child care has not achieved the status of a social citizenship right in any of these countries. Maternity leave in Australia, Canada and Great Britain and the relatively recently introduced care leave in the United States have a stronger social rights connotation than child care but eligibility criteria and/or coverage may limit scope and/or duration. The absence of care benefit in the United States is likely to build in class stratification in leave take up, as are the stringent eligibility criteria for maternity benefit in Britain and the narrow range of workers eligible for benefits in Australia. Despite shorter maternity leave duration in Canada than in Britain and Australia it is less class stratifying in terms of benefit access criteria, although some workers have enhanced leave and/or benefits through occupational provision.

All four countries have implemented a range of employment equality strategies, based on similar principles. Equal pay for equal work was followed by policies relating to comparable worth in all countries, although the commitment, strategy of implementation and success vary cross-nationally and within countries depending on the category of workers. A similar pattern is evident in relation to employment equity policies. Anti-discrimination policies gave way to affirmative action/ employment equity policies and some focus on expanding opportunities through child care and training. While gender-based pay differentials and gender-based occupational segregation are still pervasive in all these countries, both have lessened over the past couple of decades although to varying degrees across the countries and across the labour force within all countries. While the United States and Canada have been most successful in terms of lessening gender-based occupational segregation, Australia and to a lesser extent Britain have been most successful in lessening gender-based pay differences.

Despite variation among them, social policy relating to labour market support services in all of these countries broadly fits a liberal framework in which state intervention is clearly subordinate to private provision. A market orientation is evident even when public funding is involved, as is evidenced by the increasing move towards commercial provision of child care in Australia. While all four countries support private responsibility over public responsibility for service provision, the extent of the support for public provision varies not only cross-nationally but over time in individual countries and across sub-national units. The form of private responsibility supported – market or family – also varies cross-nationally. There is also an important cross-national difference in relation to which element of the private dimension is relied on for service provision. There is a clear division between the United States, on the one hand, where there is a strong commitment to gender sameness and reliance on the market for provision of services, and Britain, on the other hand, where a gender difference orientation is still relatively pervasive and provision by the family is assumed by public policy. The gender sameness market strategy, pursued most strongly in the United States and to a somewhat lesser extent in Canada, is potentially positive in terms of gender equality, although strongly market reinforcing. It facilitates labour market participation for men and women with caring responsibilities, provided their market return is sufficient to meet care costs. The problem is that location in the labour market may constrain one's ability in the care market with the consequence that a gender sameness orientation ends up reinforcing differences according to occupational location including differences among women. The US, and to a lesser extent the Canadian, pattern reflects the application of the universal breadwinner approach, but without acknowledging the family status–market status links. To use Nancy Fraser's terminology, it is the universalisation 'of the male half of the old breadwinner/homemaker couple' to everyone (Fraser 1994: 605). Unless the family status–market status interaction is recognised in public policy the resolution to the associated caregiving crisis in the context of a gender sameness commitment is increasingly likely to be a perpetuation of the transfer of responsibility by those who are strong in labour market terms to those who are weak in these terms. The alternative solution, identified by Nancy Folbre (1994: 102–3), would be a more equal sharing of paid work and caring between men and women. This is more difficult to achieve only because of its remove from the present pattern.

The failure to acknowledge family–market links means that class differences are not taken into account and this is equally a problem in the strong family-oriented approach adopted most forcefully in Britain. There is evidence of differences in patterns of work which suggest differences in gender ideology within classes and across educational groups with a stronger commitment to continuous labour market participation among those with higher levels of education in all four countries. What differs among labour force participants across classes is the range of solutions to their care requirements which they can afford to purchase through the market or afford to provide within their families.

In addition to the specific conclusions, a general conclusion can be reached from this analysis: there is consistent evidence of differences in labour market experience and the ability to exercise citizenship rights among women depending on occupational sector. Differences are evident in relation to the extent of female–male pay differentials, the characteristics of part-time work, access to child care and the ability to exercise rights to maternity and parental leave. Furthermore, there is evidence that polarisation may be increasing rather than lessening. This analysis strongly indicates that welfare states are structured by gender and not only by class and, in these societies, by race. It points to the need for a twofold research strategy, focusing on the implications of gender divisions in paid and unpaid work as well as other divisions which cross gender lines. Failure to recognise in policy analysis the three-way linkages and reciprocal relations between the organisation of paid work, and in particular labour market segmentation, the organisation of unpaid work and public policy means that significant limitations of public policy from a gender equality point of view are masked.

Our focus on labour market participation and associated programs and outcomes in this chapter reverses the concern with decommodification, or protection from dependence on the labour market for survival, that characterises much comparative work on social citizenship rights. This protection from forced participation, irrespective of age, health conditions, family status and availability of suitable employment, is obviously of major importance to both men and women (O'Connor 1993c: 513) although the associated benefits affect them in different ways because of their different patterns of paid and unpaid work (Orloff 1993b: 317). However, before employment-linked protection becomes an issue for individuals a crucial first step is access to the labour market. We have considerable evidence that some categories of labour force aspirants have greater barriers to overcome than others; in particular, work performed outside the labour force – work on which the paid labour force is dependent – may constrain labour force participation. The two types of labour are relevant to citizenship rights and their exercise. But the two types of labour cannot be adequately analysed unless the complex interactions between state, market and family are recognised.

CHAPTER 4

Social Rights Versus Gender Stratification and Gender Power?

Cash transfers for income maintenance have been central to all systems of public social protection in the industrialised west, and have been of particular significance to women because of their economic vulnerability. Programs differ in criteria for initial and ongoing eligibility, levels of benefits and duration, and, in the context of distinctive labour markets and gender divisions of labour, contribute to the varying gender effects of policy regimes. In this chapter, we assess these effects of the main income maintenance programs on gender relations in the four countries using our analytic framework. The dimension of social organisation of income and services considers the ways countries organise the provision of welfare and income through families as well as through states and markets; the stratification dimension considers the effects of social provision on gender inequality through evaluating the treatment of paid and unpaid labour and of men and women (and subgroups of men and women), and also its effects on the extent to which gender differentiation is affected by processes of claiming benefits and by the existence of different programs for family and labour market needs; the social citizenship rights dimension assesses the quality of social rights as this contributes to decommodification, or protection vis-à-vis the labour market, and to the capacity to form and maintain an autonomous household.

Following are profiles of the income maintenance systems in each of the four countries based on data from the 1990s. These profiles are not intended as comprehensive descriptions of the welfare states of the four countries, but rather as sketches of the features of social provision relevant for assessing policy effects on gender stratification and power relations. The analytic dimensions do not correspond neatly to specific features or programs of income maintenance. To determine the ways in which states affect power relations, we assess the character of social rights as they undermine or reinforce citizens' dependencies in markets and families. The extent to which citizens have individual access to benefits is important, for so-called 'derived' rights – those mediated by one's relations to others through marriage or familial relationship – have less potential to undermine existing power relations than do individually based rights. We also examine relative benefit levels, time limits on benefits, and the character of ongoing requirements to get a sense of how (or if) welfare state programs function as counterweights to dominant forces in markets and families. To see how states stratify, we look at the extent to which the overall system is divided between programs based on caregiving or family status and those based on paid work, and at the proportion of men and women (and subgroups of men and women) making claims based on participation in the paid workforce, financial contribution, citizenship, need, family or marital status, and the distribution of men and women (and subgroups) across different kinds of programs. To understand the relationships among states, markets and families, we examine the sources of provision called upon by citizens facing different risks and needs.

As one measure of stratification and of the extent to which states provide safety nets, in Table 4.1 we report poverty rates for particular vulnerable groups in the United States, Britain, Canada, Australia and several European countries, using Luxembourg Income Study data from the late 1980s and early 1990s reported by Smeeding (1997) and associates. The measure of poverty used is less than half the median income, adjusting for family size. (The US poverty line, derived by a different methodology, is the equivalent of about 40 per cent of median income.) There is debate among experts about how properly to measure poverty, for example, whether to include in-kind benefits, and how to factor differences in family size (see, for example, Blank 1997; Smeeding, O'Higgins and Rainwater 1990). We note that while poverty rates may vary somewhat using different measures, the ranking of these countries and of poverty rates among specific groups – notably single mother families – within them remains rather consistent (Shaver 1997). There is one important exception, however: elderly women living alone. Because the incomes of elderly people, especially women, depend heavily on public pensions, and these are close to half the median income, the poverty rates of elderly women and the rankings of these countries do fluctuate depending on which equivalence scale is used, and at what proportion of median income the poverty line is set.

From its origins in the first part of this century, through to the 1960s and 1970s, social provision in Britain, the United States, Canada, and Australia institutionalised the traditional gender division of labour. Most

Table 4.1: Poverty Rates for Sole Mothers and the Elderly in the Mid-1980s[1]

	Overall Population	Sole Mothers	Elderly[2]	Single Elderly Women[3]
Australia (1985)	11.1	61.1	28.6	62.1
Canada (1987)	12.9	51.0	7.1	16.2
United Kingdom (1986)	7.0	16.5	30.5	50.1
USA (1986)	19.1	57.9	22.7	43.1
Germany (1984)	7.1	39.1	8.1	12.7
Netherlands (1987)	6.3	7.9	4.4	3.4
Sweden (1987)	8.3	6.5	6.4	14.7

Notes: [1] Poverty rates reflect the percentage of each category of persons whose disposable after tax income is below 50 per cent of adjusted median income.
[2] Elderly refers to both women and men over 65 years.
[3] Elderly women living alone.

Sources: Rates for overall population: Smeeding, Torrey and Rainwater 1993: Table 5; for sole mothers: Rainwater 1993: Table 3; for elderly and single elderly women: Smeeding 1997: Table 1. All are analyses of Luxembourg Income Study data.

women's and working-class organisations in the four countries accepted the goals of a 'family wage' for men and stay-at-home, full-time motherhood for women, although at first this was limited to members of the dominant racial/ethnic groups. (Indigenous peoples were clients of separate governmental agencies which combined regulatory and welfare functions, while they and other people of colour were excluded in various ways from mainstream programs; see, for example, Wennemo 1997 on family allowances.) Income security systems were marked by a (paid) work/family dualism, and inequality in the benefits available to men and women, wage earners and caregivers, was the concomitant of gender-differentiated programs. Maternalist discourses were important among reformers in all four, and women who were single mothers through no choice of their own – widows – received support that allowed them to keep their children and to forgo full-time waged work. However, women of colour in the United States were often expected to work for pay (Glenn 1992), and the cultural specificity of motherhood models meant that some women of colour as well as women who defied conventional sexual morality ('unwed mothers') would be declared 'unfit' mothers and therefore ineligible for income support; indigenous women were often deprived of the right to a family when children were removed under policies of forced assimilation (see, for example, McGrath 1993).

In the 1960s and 1970s, western welfare states were expanded, and legislation and court decisions, spurred in part by feminist-led legal challenges, shifted social provision towards formal gender (and racial) neutrality. Almost all programs were opened to both men and women, but there continued to be a split between programs based on employment and those based on family. In this period also, single mothers' right to benefits that provided the capacity to form and maintain autonomous households without working for pay – that is, benefits for being a full-time mother – expanded from widowed women of the dominant racial group to almost all women, as de jure exclusions (for example, of indigenous women) and de facto discrimination (for example, excluding African-American women as 'employable mothers' – see Bell 1965) were challenged. But rules in some jurisdictions were also changed to allow combining employment and welfare. Women's movements in these four countries were reaching a peak of mobilisation at about the same time, but concentrated on the liberalisation of reproductive policies, family law reforms and the initiation of anti-discrimination and employment equity programs in the workplace. Yet women's movements also comprised groups of welfare workers and welfare clients who demanded the liberalisation of social provision (such as the US National Welfare Rights Organization; see Piven and Cloward 1993; Gordon 1988).

Changes across the four countries in the 1980s and 1990s have been understood variously as cutbacks, reforms, retrenchment and restructuring. New right governments announced their intention to cut the welfare state, but, with some important exceptions, they have not been successful in entirely eliminating protections against well-recognised social risks or in cutting back the overall levels of social expenditures (Weaver 1998; Myles and Pierson 1997; P. Pierson 1994; Battle 1997; D. Mitchell 1997), though they may well have slowed rates of growth. Liberal thinking has also influenced centre and centre-left parties and governments, leading to other variants of welfare reform. Some figures associated with the women's movements or influenced by feminist intellectual currents have been involved in carrying through these changes under centre or left governments, while others have opposed market-strengthening changes whether proposed by left or right. In part, this reflects continuing questions about the proper strategy for improving women's situations – by opening employment opportunities or better recognising and compensating care. Yet it is hard to deny that changes in women's patterns of labour force participation and in the character of employment and the economy more broadly (as we outlined in the last chapter) have helped to change the context within which social provision has developed. From a policy legacy of family/employment dualism and in the context of a continuing gender division of household labour, politicians and administrators of the welfare states in all four countries have been challenged by issues associated with women's employment in making social provision compatible with new labour market conditions.

In all four countries, work incentives within social assistance have been strengthened, and obligations – to be 'active' in seeking training, to identify and help locate absent parents, and so on – have been increased. There is greater targeting and social insurance eligibility has been tightened and more closely linked with labour force participation. Moreover, increasing numbers of jobs – particularly those that are part-time and/or precarious, disproportionately held by women – no longer bring entitlement to labour market-based programs. Private forms of retirement financing have been promoted by some élites but these have (as yet) made less headway than have changes in programs for the working-aged population. Thus, while retrenchment has occurred, restructuring is perhaps a better overall description of the social policy changes of the last two decades. Despite these similarities, there continue to be differences between the United States and Canada on the one hand and Britain and Australia on the other, most notably in terms of whether or not mothers are expected to enter the labour force.

Contemporary Policy Regimes

We have organised these profiles around the different politically recognised risks of income interruption and needs for extra income that are addressed by social provision. We acknowledge that both 'risk' and 'need' are culturally constructed and politically contested (Baldwin 1990; Beck 1992; Fraser 1989). We describe the programs addressing each risk in each country. State social provision protects against the failures of the market, especially unemployment and retirement, and also 'failures' of the family, particularly the break-up of marriages. What is commonly understood as the 'risk' of old age is in reality two separate – and distinctively gendered – risks: of losing income due to retirement; or of losing income because of being economically dependent on someone who retires or dies. Single parenthood is principally a risk to income security for women who, when they divorce or remain unmarried, usually lose access to a family-supporting male wage even as they typically retain custody of the children. However, all single parents – even single fathers or women earning (atypically) high wages – must be both nurturers and breadwinners, and lack the labour and/or wages provided by a second parent. States also offer support to families, principally to help with the costs of child-rearing. Public support of reproduction – a key form of what Foucault (1980) called biopolitics – has reflected many different political agendas: wage restraint, nationalism, eugenics, or religious beliefs (Pedersen 1993; Macnicol 1980; Cass 1983). It is in the support of reproduction – or withholding such support – that racial, ethnic and other exclusions were often expressed, although this now takes less explicit forms than in the past (Bock and Thane 1991). Economic dependency may also result from caring for the needs of others, while those who require care are also often dependent; states have sometimes provided caregivers' allowances or benefits to allow the purchase of care services. Finally, low income may be understood as a social problem requiring a public solution because it hinders effective social and democratic participation.

The United States

The welfare state in the United States has a very distinctive form: coverage is concentrated on the elderly, while the majority of the working-aged population depends mainly on employment or marriage with very little public safety net (Myles 1989). Education is the one universal public program, in keeping with America's emphasis on equality of opportunity. The 'private welfare state' looms large in Americans' security and standard of living. While public provision does fairly well in protecting elderly men and couples, it is comparatively ineffective against poverty among non-elderly groups and single older women (Ellwood 1988; Smeeding, Torrey and Rainwater 1993; Smeeding 1997) (see Table 4.1). There are no guarantees of employment or training for men or women, nor is there a citizenship entitlement to health coverage or housing (although these are provided to some of the needy). There is now no entitlement to social assistance after the passage in 1996 of the Personal Responsibility Act (PRA) and the elimination of the main US assistance program, Aid to Families with Dependent Children (AFDC), which went primarily to women-maintained families. Welfare – social assistance, primarily for single mothers – is now implicitly rather than formally racialised (that is, welfare politics are in large part racial politics). Almost all public help is now linked to employment (or workfare), while caregiving is relegated to the status of a barrier to labour force participation.

Old Age

Old-Age, Survivors' and Disability Insurance (OASDI) – what Americans call 'Social Security' (and not the 'welfare state') – insures against the loss of income due to retirement and the loss of income suffered by those who depend economically upon a retired wage earner (United States Social Security Administration 1993: 7–50). Entitlement is established in two distinctly gendered ways (Burkhauser and Holden 1982). First, retired workers claim benefits by working for a minimum number of years (ten) in a covered occupation and making contributions; full benefits require forty years' contributions (Myles 1989: 61). Second, one can also claim an auxiliary entitlement to benefits by being married to such a person or having once been married to such a person. Divorcees, if married for at least ten years, retain pension rights unless they remarry before reaching the age of sixty (making clear that marriage to a wage earner rather than caregiving brings the entitlement). The system is now formally gender-neutral, in that both retired worker and dependent spouse claims are open to men and women. Many women – about one-quarter of all female beneficiaries – are dually entitled: they have established an individual entitlement through employment but also have an auxiliary entitlement through marriage. Since their individual benefits would be lower than the dependants' benefits, they receive a 'partial wife's benefit' combined with their own retired worker benefit – but this is no more than what they would have received based on their marriage even if they had not worked (Meyer 1996; McCaffery 1997).

The vast majority of elderly people do receive OASDI, but the system leaves vulnerable those who had a marginal attachment to the labour force and who lack secure marital ties to workers. (Provisions initially excluded most African-American and Latino workers, and some women of all races – see Orloff 1993a: ch. 9 – but today, few workers are outside of Social Security.) These people – a distinct minority of the elderly (about 5 per cent) and predominantly women – must depend on the income-tested Supplemental Security Income (Bolderson and Mabbett 1991: 152).

Over 99 per cent of male Social Security beneficiaries make claims as worker-contributors, while almost 60 per cent of women are entitled to retired-worker benefits (many of these with a dual entitlement). The majority of retired workers, 52 per cent, are men, but women make up almost half of all retired workers (with about 40 per cent of these also relying on spousal benefits). The proportion of women with only an auxiliary entitlement has been declining, but women's growing propensity to engage in paid labour is not yet reflected in individual entitlement to benefits; rather, the legacy of women's low pay and intermittent work histories is reflected in the large and growing proportion of women with dual entitlement. In total, almost two-thirds of all women who are Social Security beneficiaries are receiving benefits based on their status as wives or widows of male workers. Of course, this reflects the labour force experiences of older women; women born after the 1950s will be more likely to claim benefits on the basis of their own employment. Men are not entering family statuses in parallel with women's entry to labour market statuses, however. Among spouses and survivors, men make up a minuscule proportion of claimants – about 1 per cent in each category; since Americans can claim only one social security benefit, they take survivors' benefits only if they are higher than their own retired-worker benefits.

Benefits are income-related, but a minimum benefit for those with low wages or intermittent work histories was abolished in the 1980s (Williamson and Pampel 1993: 101). The dependants' benefit is set at 50 per cent of the contributors' benefit, while survivors receive 100 per cent. The system does a better job of ensuring income security for the non-poor than of providing basic security for the poorest elderly – minimum benefits are lower in the United States than in Canada or Australia (Myles 1989; Whiteford 1995). Wage replacement rates are low in comparison with other countries, and low enough that there is still plenty of scope for private occupational pension coverage for higher income workers (Palme 1997). Because of men's economic advantages, their overall average and work-related benefits tend to be higher than women's. Poverty levels among the elderly have fallen to below the rate for the population as a whole since the 1970s (Myles 1989), but single elderly men and elderly married couples were more likely than single older women to receive a benefit sufficient to keep them above poverty (see Table 4.1). Single elderly women are still quite vulnerable to poverty – their rates are higher than for the population as a whole, and higher than for elderly couples and single elderly men – and the United States does less than Canada, Britain and other countries to protect this group (Smeeding, Torrey and Rainwater 1993; Smeeding 1997).

Unemployment

While OASDI conforms to the picture of a relatively effective and generous top tier of the US welfare state, Unemployment Compensation looks somewhat different. The proportion of unemployed American workers – both male and female – with coverage under Unemployment Compensation has declined over the last decade or two to about 40 per cent in 1995 while benefit duration has also been cut (US CWM 1996: 331, 340–3). The eligibility criterion of a recent and fairly stable work history precludes benefits for new entrants to the workforce, the erratically employed, and the chronically under-employed (Burtless 1986: 29). Explicit disentitlement from tightening of eligibility is accompanied by 'implicit disentitlement', as many workers shift to jobs unlikely to allow them to build up eligibility (US CWM 1996: 331). Still, men (and whites) are over-represented among the insured unemployed (Blank and Blinder 1986: 192–3). Unemployment insurance benefits are income-related (and taxable), although offering a fairly low wage replacement rate (about 36 per cent on average in 1995 – about the same level as average benefits for single parents; see US CWM 1996: 1168; Kamerman 1986). Men's benefits on average are higher than women's, and are more likely to be sufficient to lift their families out of poverty (Pearce 1986: 158). Still, unemployment among men (either with or without children), especially long-term, is associated with high poverty rates since little social protection goes to this group (Ellwood 1988; Blank 1997).

Unemployed women and men who cannot qualify for coverage under Unemployment Compensation, or who have exhausted their benefits, must rely on other, income-tested sources of support; if they have children they might be eligible for income-tested family assistance, but if childless, they have fewer options. Some, but not all, states and municipalities have General Assistance, the true descendant of poor relief, retaining all its administrative discretion and lack of entitlement. The long-term unemployed, disproportionately people of colour, are not given much support for maintaining households. The Food Stamps program was the only federal program available to any poor person who met the criteria – a very low income and limited assets, but the Personal Responsibility Act increased work requirements so that childless people out of work for more than a short time cannot get them unless they are involved in work programs (US CWM 1996: 1386–7).

Single parenthood

Survivors' Insurance is available to the widowed spouses of wage earners covered under Social Security, if caring for children under the age of sixteen (paid employment is not precluded or mandated) (Garfinkel and McLanahan 1986: 18–21, 26). Survivors' Insurance benefits are higher than welfare benefits, and are reduced by earnings at a lower rate than welfare benefits had been; widowed mothers are less likely to be poor than other single mothers (29 per cent versus 35 per cent for divorced mothers and 58 per cent for never-married) (1994 figures from US CWM 1996: 1187). Today, however, most (adult) single parents in the United States are divorced (38 per cent), separated (42 per cent) or never-married (35 per cent), rather than widowed (4 per cent) (1995 figures from US CWM 1996: 1182).

Prior to the demise of AFDC in 1996, the federal government had given very poor single parents and their children an entitlement to assistance, offering matching funds to state-administered programs that meet federally set criteria. AFDC was available to divorced, deserted, or never-married single parents (or other caregivers) of children under eighteen with very low incomes and few assets. By the 1970s, AFDC partially assumed the character of an income-tested entitlement, and the addition of Medicaid benefits in 1965 – income-tested medical coverage – was an advantage welfare families had over other groups of the poor and near-poor (the United States as yet has no universal health insurance). But income limits decreased and coverage contracted through the 1980s, despite increases in the numbers of single mother families and their proportion in the population (Blank et al. 1995). This trend was bolstered by new restrictions, mainly against combining paid work and welfare, brought in during the early Reagan administration (Blank 1997: 137). AFDC lacked limits on duration beyond the age of the youngest child. For most women, AFDC served as a transitional safety net or as a kind of unemployment assistance in a labour market where jobs and child care arrangements were precarious, particularly for women of colour (see, for example, Spalter-Roth and Hartmann 1994; Bane 1988; Blank 1997: 153). The model of motherhood formally institutionalised in AFDC was sharply at odds with the predominant thrust of policy relevant for gender relations and with dominant patterns of women's employment. AFDC regulations made it difficult to combine employment and welfare, but most women did informally combine work and welfare, depending on combinations of welfare benefits and unreported income from family, boyfriends or work (Edin and Lein 1997). Indeed, the clamour for reform intensified despite the fact that US single mothers exhibit relatively high rates of labour force participation, comparable to rates of married mothers (see Table 3.2, p. 70). Only about two-fifths of single mothers received AFDC in the 1980s and 1990s – a much lower proportion than received social assistance in Australia or Britain (Millar and Whiteford 1993), and slightly less than in Canada (Hanratty and Blank 1992).

AFDC has been replaced with a block grant, Temporary Assistance to Needy Families (TANF), for new state-run welfare programs; it is accompanied by a child care block grant. The new law mandates that adults receiving assistance engage in work activities (paid or subsidised employment, community service employment, or approved training) after two years (less at state option) and that there be a five-year lifetime limit on cash benefits (less at state option); states must also have increasing proportions of their caseloads engaged in work activities over several years after the law's passage (US CWM 1996: 1334–5). States decide other eligibility criteria, benefit levels and specific work require-ments, but there is no guarantee of assistance even if these criteria are met. A 'Domestic Violence Option', adopted at the urging of women's organisation activists, allows but does not mandate states to exempt some victims of domestic violence from work requirements; as of late 1997, twenty-eight states had adopted it (DeParle 1997c). Because of good economic conditions, caseloads have fallen in the 1990s, while block grant amounts were set for earlier, higher levels of coverage; thus, states have had something of a windfall to pay for experimentation, and states are spending more per capita on welfare recipients (DeParle 1997d). But, unlike federal funds for AFDC, block grants for TANF will not automatically expand in the event of an economic downturn.

TANF makes few concessions to caregiving in imposing work requirements. The original AFDC program was designed to allow single mothers to stay at home to care for minor children, but work incentives began to appear in the mid-1960s, coincident with increasing proportions of married mothers of all races entering the labour force and increasing proportions of women of colour successfully claiming the benefits. With the 1988 Family Support Act, all AFDC parents with children aged three and above (aged one or above at state option) were required to work or undergo training. The age limit is now twelve weeks (one year at state option). Parents of pre-school children who cannot find child care are exempted from work requirements (although determinations of 'acceptable' child care may be at issue). In the early phases of the new law, many states are experimenting with expanded casework, training and child care services alongside greater efforts to place recipients in jobs or to divert potential recipients by requiring work searches before granting aid, but there is no mandate that they do so; they are also experimenting with penalties (Pear 1997; DeParle 1997a, 1997b).

The vast majority of adult recipients of AFDC and TANF were and are women. Of the approximately one-fifth of all US families with children headed by a single parent, over one in ten are headed by fathers (Rainwater 1993: 26). However, few single fathers received AFDC (nor did many married men get AFDC-Unemployed Parent – AFDC-UP); about 90 per cent of all adult recipients of AFDC, and a higher proportion of sole parent beneficiaries, were women (unpublished data on AFDC supplied by US Department of Health and Human Services).

Child support enforcement and paternity establishment, significant components of welfare reforms for the last three decades, enforce income sharing on non-custodial parents. Mothers and fathers are required to co-operate with efforts to establish and enforce child support obligations, and, if necessary, paternity (Monson 1997). Formulas for establishing levels of child support awards reflect the number of children and the non-custodial parent's income; they do not include support for the custodial parent. Under AFDC regulations, all child support collected, save for a small amount (about a sixth to a tenth of the value of cash benefits, depending on the state), went to the state to offset benefits paid to the custodial parent and her children. Many poorer men and women see little gain for their children's well-being from co-operating with authorities, while informal support to mothers from children's fathers has often been an important component of their income (Edin and Lein 1997). Under TANF, states are free to pass along larger or smaller amounts of child support collected.

The relative stinginess of America's provision for non-widowed single parents is well-known in academic circles, though not among the public; yet even at low levels these benefits were sufficient (albeit barely) to establish an independent household and have been a significant help to women leaving domestic violence (Blank et al. 1995: 70). AFDC benefits – though increased somewhat in the late 1960s and 1970s – fell in real value through the 1980s and 1990s, as they were not indexed to inflation (Ellwood 1988: 58). Benefits have varied across states, and will continue to do so under TANF. But benefits did not bring recipients up to the US poverty level, although in some states, in combination with Food Stamps, they have come closer than in others. Poverty rates (at the 50 per cent of median level) for single mothers with no earnings – that is, mostly dependent on benefits – were around 90 per cent in the mid-1980s, somewhat worse than Canada and Australia, and considerably worse than Britain (Rainwater 1993). State-run programs under TANF can vary more widely, and it is possible that some states' initiatives allowing parents to combine employment, assistance, child support and services will bring them above the poverty level. If parents can get private employment, they will be eligible for the Earned Income Tax Credit (EITC), which in combination with even minimum-wage earnings will bring many recipients above the US poverty line.

Family Needs

The United States has had no universal family allowances, which have been a common way for governments to support child-rearing. Family allowances in a number of countries have recently become income-tested, and/or supplemented by tax credits for the working or non-working poor (Myles and Pierson 1997). Here, there is an important American parallel: the EITC. Parents who have (low) earnings – the working poor, male or female – are eligible for a modest benefit, claimed through the tax system (operating along lines similar to Negative Income Tax proposals). The EITC, unlike other elements of US social provision, has been expanded several times in the 1980s and 1990s, most recently and significantly in Clinton's 1993 budget package

(Myles and Pierson 1997; Weaver 1998). Indeed, federal spending on EITC surpassed AFDC in 1992 ($US12.4 billion versus $US12.3 billion); for 1996, it was projected to be almost twice as much ($US25.1 billion versus $US13.2 billion) (Myles and Pierson 1997: 450, Table 2). The EITC bolsters the incomes of those parents in the paid labour force, bringing many above the US poverty line. Poverty rates (at the 50 per cent of median level) in the mid-1980s for single mothers and two-parent families were high – about 40 per cent – even if they had some earnings; this is considerably more than in the other three countries (Rainwater 1993). The EITC has expanded since then, and it should improve the position of households with earnings. It complements recent policies to push (poor) mothers into employment, but unlike AFDC/TANF does not feature bureaucratic surveillance of clients' behaviour. It represents something of a departure vis-à-vis fathers and two-parent families, who had been basically excluded from state assistance under earlier policies.

Support to Caregiving

The US system offers little explicit public recognition to care work, and no entitlements to income support when citizens need to care for children or disabled or elderly relatives or friends. As we noted in the last chapter, family and medical leave was late in coming, is limited in coverage and offers no income replacement. Married parents' care responsibilities are supported only through tax deductions for dependent care expenses, of greatest use to better-off segments of the population. Single parents' caregiving was supported as an entitlement, albeit meagrely, under AFDC, but is no longer. Rather, the need of children for care is understood as a barrier to their parents' labour force participation, to be overcome by the provision of child care subsidies or allowances. Some analysts have tried to portray spousal and survivors' provisions in Social Security as rewarding care work, but there are no requirements relating to the actual performance of care work, as in countries which offer pension credits for periods of caregiving. In addition, the United States provides vouchers to some people with disabilities (for example, veterans) for purchasing care services, and also has a patchwork of support to care service providers (Keigher and Stone 1994). Thus, most care work remains unpaid and dependent on 'private' support.

Great Britain

Britain's system is similar to that of the United States in that it is bifurcated between contributory social insurance, National Insurance, and income-tested social assistance, Income Support. But in contrast to the United States, Britain's system is more comprehensive and, despite attacks under Thatcher, retains a strong element of universalism in the flat-rate benefits of the basic old-age pension, in universal children's allowances and, most famously, in the National Health Service. In the 1980s, state provision was cut back, opening greater space for private provision, especially in retirement provision. Income Support was restructured and retrenched in various ways, and work incentives within social assistance and unemployment insurance were strengthened, while Family Benefits for the working poor were expanded. British provision was and continues to be shaped by the logic of the male breadwinner and female caregiver family, and offers support for caregivers at levels greater than offered in the other three countries. (Support of reproduction in Britain was less fraught with the politics of internal racial and ethnic divisions than the other three until the last few decades.)

Old age

In the wake of World War II, National Insurance (NI) was established, replacing earlier pension programs. It provides a flat-rate benefit to contributors over the age of sixty for women (now being raised to sixty-five), and sixty-five for men (Walker 1992: 187), along with a dependants' benefit for spouses of contributors. Thus, as in the United States, the old-age portion of National Insurance is internally dualised along gender lines. Entitlement depends on long years of employment and contribution (thirty-nine years for a full pension), or on being married to someone who worked for pay and contributed. Women divorced after relatively long unions are also afforded access to benefits. Spouses receive benefits equal to 60 per cent of a single person's pension. Those with non-standard work are disadvantaged by the earnings threshold for paying National Insurance contributions, which excludes many low-wage and part-time jobs from coverage; in the late 1980s, almost one-fifth of employed women but only 3 per cent of men had earnings below the minimum (Callendar 1992: 136).

   The basic old-age pension, despite its universalistic tendencies, was not meant to undercut the market. Rather, it was designed to allow all to live decently while encouraging supplementation with private provision. In 1975, an earnings-related second tier of pensions – the State Earnings-Related Pension Scheme, or SERPS – was introduced. From the beginning, employers were allowed to contract whole occupational groups out of SERPS and into private employers' provision (Groves 1992: 202). The Thatcher administration succeeded in reducing the Basic Pension, and although it failed in its attempt to eliminate SERPS, the scheme was scaled back, with reductions in survivors' benefits (P. Pierson 1994: ch. 3; Walker 1992: 188–9). Privatisation was encouraged: for example, employees can opt out of SERPS in favour of Appropriate Personal Pensions (APPs), which depend upon investment performance (Groves 1992: 204). Given the relatively low replacement rates of the basic pension and of SERPS benefits (Palme 1990: 64; Palme 1997), occupational pensions are important, but access goes disproportionately to those in advantaged positions in the labour market. In the mid-1980s, only 26 per cent of women, but 62 per cent of men, had income from their own or a survivors' occupational pension; among current employees, full-time workers have greater coverage than part-time workers, and men have greater occupational pension coverage than do women (Groves 1992: 199–200). The reduction in the Basic Pension, which will be felt increasingly over time, spurs private provision for those who can afford it and leaves those with no other protection to 'top up' with means-tested Income Support – which in the last years of Conservative government was giving higher rates of benefit than the Basic Pension (Commission on Social Justice 1994: 271).

In 1995, just under three-fifths of women receiving a retirement pension qualified on the basis of their partner's contribution; in contrast, all men made claims on the basis of their own contributions as workers (UK DSS 1996: 15–23). As in the United States, the proportion of women making claims on the basis of their own earnings is rising slowly (UK DSS 1992: 105). But because of women's continuing labour market disadvantages and the expansion of non-standard employment, particularly among women, the number of working women whose own work-based pension 'would be less than the standard rate payable to a married woman on her husband's insurance' is also likely to increase (British data do not permit the disaggregation of the dependent pensioner group to see the proportion of what are called in the United States 'dually entitled'). Indeed, because more British women are in precarious employment, this group may be larger in Britain than in the United States.

The gender breakdown within National Insurance categories of 'worker', 'spouse' and 'survivor' is similar to that observed in the United States. About three-fifths of retired workers are men; two-fifths are women. No men claim benefits as spouses and survivors. The aged make up a substantial proportion, a little under one-third, of all Income Support recipients, and women predominate among the elderly – over a quarter of all Income Support recipients are women of sixty and older, while only about 10 per cent are older men (UK DSS 1996: 22–3).

Benefit inequality among contributors is precluded by the flat rate of the Basic Pension, but gender inequality (and perhaps also assumptions about 'economies of scale') is built into the formula by which married women on their husband's insurance get 60 per cent of the Basic Pension (UK DSS 1996: 89, 110). Where benefits are income-related, as in the United States and Canada, women's labour market disadvantages are reflected in lower average benefits. In Britain, women who make full contributions will get a full National Insurance benefit, although if that is all they get, they will be quite poor (and eligible for Income Support). The problem for many British women is making sufficient contributions to qualify. Even with the addition of credits for periods of time spent in caregiving, women on their own insurance have slightly lower average benefits. To the extent that earnings-related pensions become more important, women's disadvantage in the labour market will be reflected in their benefits, as it already is in SERPS (UK DSS 1992: 118). By US standards (a poverty line at 40 per cent of median income), relatively fewer older people, including older women, are poor, but many are just above that poverty line (Smeeding, Torrey and Rainwater 1993; Smeeding 1997). At the 50 per cent of median income standard (see Table 4.1), there are more British than American elderly (men and women) in poverty (though it is likely that exact proportions are influenced by the methods of measurement used). The Basic Pension does not alone bring elderly recipients to the level of Income Support, and more women than men have to resort to the income-tested social assistance program to reach that very modest standard of living.

Unemployment

Contributory unemployment insurance is part of National Insurance, and has been targeted on the 'standard' worker (Callendar 1992). Unemployment Benefit goes to covered individuals, who could then get Income Support if they were still unemployed when their insurance entitlement was exhausted. In 1996, Unemployment Benefit was replaced with Jobseeker's Allowance, which also goes – although at a different benefit level – to unemployed people who were formerly collecting Income Support. Both the income-based and the contribution-based Jobseeker's Allowance feature a 'Jobseeker's Agreement', part of the Conservative Government's strategy to increase work incentives and emphasise job search while increasing sanctions and surveillance (Eardley and Thompson 1997: 21; P. Pierson 1994: ch. 5).

Changes made during the 1980s tightened eligibility, shifted more of the unemployed to means-tested programs, reduced young people's access to coverage, and made it more difficult for non-standard workers, disproportionately women, to gain coverage under the contributory system (P. Pierson 1994: 107; Lister 1992). For example, after thirteen weeks, claimants must be available to accept full-time employment, must demonstrate adequate child care arrangements, and 'can neither impose restrictions on the nature, hours, rate of pay or location of work for which they are available, nor refuse a job handled by the Employment Service for those reasons' (Callendar 1992: 136). The duration of unemployment insurance coverage has also been reduced from a maximum of one year to six months (UK DSS 1996: 119).

Unemployed people without eligibility for full benefits, or whose eligibility has run out, must rely on income-tested assistance or their partners. In contrast to the United States, the long-term unemployed and new entrants to the workforce in Britain have had access to nationally administered social assistance, the Income Support program; indeed, in recent years, more of the unemployed have received Income Support rather than Unemployment Benefit. Eligibility for Income Support has been based on a household test of means and on the employment status of the spouse. These rules remain under the new system; one is disqualified for income-tested Jobseeker's Allowance if one's spouse works more than twenty-four hours per week (UK DSS 1996: 120) – this makes it difficult for unemployed second earners to qualify for the income-tested benefit.

Men made up over two-thirds of those claiming Unemployment Benefit and over four-fifths of unemployed claimants of Income Support (UK DSS 1996: 18, 22–3, 122). It seems likely that they will predominate among recipients of the Jobseeker's Allowance as well, as eligibility requirements pertinent for gender differences remain similar. Because of the household means test, fewer married women have been Income Support beneficiaries than either men or single women; married women tend to rely on their own contribution-based benefits or go without any coverage at all (Callendar 1992: 138; Lister 1992). Indeed, among those losing the contribution-based unemployment benefit, fewer women than men are expected to qualify for an independent social assistance benefit (Lister 1996: 25, 29).

Single parenthood

National Insurance covers widows with children at home as well as elderly wives and widows. Poor, non-widowed sole parents rely on Income Support if they are not working outside the home, or on Family Credit and other programs if they are employed. Thus, as in the United States, there is a split between widowed and other single mothers in policy treatment, but no gap in benefits. All poor and 'unemployable' people over seventeen years of age, including non-employed single mothers, have access to Income Support, but they are separated from the working poor – who have access to Family Benefit, and, from 1996 on, from the unemployed, who receive Jobseeker's Allowance. In 1995, single mothers made up less than one-fifth of the Income Support caseload, while the unemployed made up a little under one-third (the balance made up by the aged and disabled).

The treatment of single parent families on social assistance was slightly more generous than that of two-parent families until recent benefit cuts carried out by New Labour (*Economist* 1997: 59); single parents are still not required to take employment (Millar 1989: 149; Millar 1992). Income Support is income-tested on aggregate household income, and if one partner is employed full-time – defined at the low level of sixteen hours per week or more, the other cannot get Income Support (Callendar 1992: 137). Income Support may be received for an indefinite period as long as conditions are met. However, with employment rates for single mothers far below those of married mothers (see Table 3.2, p. 70), the Conservative Government attempted to find ways to encourage, in particular, part-time employment, for example by reducing to sixteen the number of hours necessary to qualify for the employment-linked Family Benefit. New Labour has followed the policy of encouraging but not mandating employment for single mothers; the Blair administration has targeted both the social exclusion and the 'worklessness' of single mothers, but pilot programs to get mothers on Income Support into employment or employment counselling, unlike in the United States, are not compulsory (T. Baldwin 1997; G. Jones 1997). Mothers have long been expected to stay out of the labour force to look after their children, although part-time work when children are older is now accepted, indeed expected, and this new expectation is beginning to be institutionalised in social provision (Millar 1996). New Labour 'welfare-to-work' schemes are to be complemented by an expanded family tax credit, which is expected to add to work incentives.

While policy-makers still seem inclined to leave women's employment as a matter of individual choice, there is no choice about seeking child support and maintenance if one is receiving Income Support or Family Benefit. Substantial changes to Britain's child support system were introduced in the 1991 Child Support Act, requiring that mothers claiming income-tested benefits co-operate in tracing absent parents, regularising and increasing child support awards, increasing compliance, and enhancing the state's collection capacities (Lister 1994b). These features are similar to those adopted in the United States and Australia. The British approach is distinctive in including an allowance for the caring parent (Lister 1994b: 219; Millar 1994). Until awards, which depend on the ex-partner's income, are large enough to get women off Income Support, their families get no benefit from the child support collected;

the state does, as amounts collected are set against benefits paid. In contrast, women collecting Family Benefit may keep a portion of the child support collected – this is intended as an incentive to work at least part-time (Millar 1996: 53–60). Meanwhile, single mothers remain at least partially economically dependent on their former spouses (Wasoff and Morris 1996).

About three-quarters of single mothers receive Income Support, and another 15 per cent Family Benefit (Wasoff and Morris 1996: 68). Ninety-five per cent of the single parents receiving assistance are women, but they are not the only constituency served by the program. Compared with the United States, Canada and Australia, British single mothers are less likely to be below the (50 per cent of median income) poverty line (see Table 4.1); even when they are not employed and are dependent on benefits, only about 20 per cent are poor, compared with around 90 per cent in the other three countries (Rainwater 1993). And, compared with the other three countries, single mothers in Britain are not especially more likely than other groups to be poor (D. Mitchell 1993). Single mothers' benefits are no worse than those of the un-employed and aged poor, but none of these benefits raises recipients very far above the poverty level.

Family Needs

Universal family allowances, paid to mothers, have featured in British social provision since World War II; the Child Benefit goes to all children up to sixteen years of age. The Thatcher administration advertised its hostility to the universal benefit, but it survived, although its value was allowed to fall (P. Pierson 1994: 107–9). It is now a less significant portion of a family's income package than it was in the late 1970s, when it provided over one-quarter of the income of a non-employed single mother with two children (compared with less than 10 per cent in Canada and Australia) (Millar 1989: 155); however, the modest Child Benefit still helps to make up for women's low wages by contributing to a 'package' of family support of about medium generosity (Bradshaw et al. 1993). Universal benefits have been replaced in importance by the income-tested benefits for families. All families in Britain, even those without earnings, are given better protection against poverty than are families in any of the other three countries (Rainwater 1993).

Support to Caregiving

Britain is unusual cross-nationally in having a benefit specifically tar-geted on informal carers of people with disabilities, the Invalid Care

Allowance (ICA), designed to replace partially the lost earnings of care providers. It is also a prime example of the assumptions about the gender division of labour which were embedded in social provision until changes forced by the European Community in 1986 – before that date, married women were simply ineligible for the ICA on the grounds that 'they might be at home in any event' (Department of Health and Social Security 1974, quoted in Glendinning 1992: 172; see also Joshi 1992). Britain's treatment of caregivers is a good example of the 'Janus-faced' character of the welfare state (Lewis 1997). Social provision in various ways enables and even rewards (albeit minimally) caregiving, as in the treatment of single parents, the availability of ICA and pension credits for periods of caregiving. A gender-neutral rule initiated in 1978 gives 'Home Responsibility Protection' (credits toward a pension) to those who are caring for children, or disabled or elderly people; twenty years of such credits are needed for a full pension (to claim these credits, a person had to have been a full contributor before leaving the labour market for unpaid caring work; Sainsbury 1993: 74). But there is also an obligation to care, seen in recent legislation about community care, which assumes that relatives – usually female – will be available to care for the elderly and disabled 'in the community'. It is also seen in the assumption that mothers will subordinate employment prospects to child care (H. Jones and Millar 1996; Glendinning 1992; Ungerson 1990).

Canada

In the comparative literature on welfare states, Canada is supposed to be most similar to the United States. Like the United States, Canada is a low spender, and its system of social provision is structurally similar to those of the United States and Britain in that it is split between social insurance and social assistance programs. But, like Britain, and unlike the United States, Canada has a history of universal citizenship programs, family allowances, old-age pensions and health insurance. However, there has been an important shift in all social programs save health insurance away from universalism and towards selectivity of a new kind. Canada is not rehabilitating poor relief-style means-testing, but moving towards a negative income tax-style income-tested benefit system (Myles and Pierson 1997). Much of the change has been 'policy by stealth' (Battle 1997), but more dramatic efforts to cut social assistance have also characterised Canadian social politics. Provincial conservative governments have cut social assistance for the non-working poor, and in 1995, the Canada Assistance Plan was replaced with the Canada Health and Social Transfer (CHST), which gives funds to the provinces to run their own welfare plans with fewer federal mandates and no guarantee of assistance.

Old age

Old-age provision had been in the form of a universal 'demogrant' – Old Age Security (OAS) – since World War II, but the program's universality ended in 1989 with the introduction of a 'clawback' of benefits from higher income seniors, heralding an overall shift in the system to greater selectivity (Battle 1997: 25–6). In the mid-1960s, concerns about income security and adequacy helped to usher in an earnings-related pension plan, the Quebec/Canada Pension Plan (Q/CPP), and a new income-tested supplement to OAS benefits, the Guaranteed Income Supplement (GIS) (Bryden 1974: 130–3). A new, income-tested program, the Seniors Benefit, will replace OAS, GIS and some other credits in 2001 (Battle 1997: 27).

The eligibility requirements for the different programs of old-age protection represent four of the major bases for making claims on the state: citizenship, contributions, marital status (widow or widower) and need. Both the income-tested and the universal pensions are gender-neutral: men and women qualify on the same basis – need, for the income-tested pension, and citizenship, along with forty years' residence after age eighteen, for the universal pension. Couples received two OAS pensions, but the more tightly targeted Seniors Benefit (like the GIS before it) is based on household income (Battle 1997: 27–8). Eligibility for benefits under the Q/CPP is established through contributions based on paid work; survivors inherit part of the pension.

The Q/CPP is formally gender-neutral, but favours workers with typically male work careers (Statistics Canada 1990: 123). There is no provision for credits for periods of unpaid caregiving as in Britain, although years with no or low earnings spent caring for a child under seven years old may be excluded from benefit calculations (Health and Welfare Canada 1991: 163). And the period of contributions required for a full benefit is relatively long – forty years – a plateau difficult to reach for those who have had intermittent work careers (Myles 1989: 61). Unlike the British and US systems of contributory insurance, there is no dependants' benefit for non-working spouses (usually wives), but survivors inherit 60 per cent of their spouses' pensions (Bryden 1974: 155). Indeed, proposals in the mid-1980s to expand the plan by increasing earnings replacement capacity and adding benefits for homemaker spouses – in effect, to make the Q/CPP more like US Social Security – failed; divorced spouses split pension credits (if married at least three years), and divorced and remarried survivors remain eligible for benefits (Battle 1997: 29).

For the impoverished or income-poor elderly, the income-tested GIS, seen as an interim measure until the Q/CPP matured, was available to OAS recipients with insufficient incomes (Statistics Canada 1990: 109 n. 5; Myles and Teichroew 1991: 89). Progressive Conservative policy-makers preferred to expand the GIS rather than the universal demo-grant (OAS), the largest source of rising social spending, to address the problem of old-age poverty, particularly among widows (Myles and Teichroew 1991; Battle 1997: 28). The logic of expanding income-tested programs has found fruition in the initiation of the new Seniors Benefit, launched in the Liberals' 1996 Budget.

Canada provides better protection against poverty among elderly people – particularly among elderly single women – than do the other three countries (see Table 4.1) (Smeeding, Torrey and Rainwater 1993; Smeeding 1997). However, it does less well at maintaining income differentials important for the standards of living of better-off workers, disproportionately men (Palme 1990: 89; Palme 1997). As Myles and Teichroew (1991: 91, 99) put it, 'the public system was meant to provide a base that would be completed by occupational pensions ... [and] private savings for retirement'. But this dualistic design has important gender implications. It results in two spheres of public provision for the aged – a public, but income-tested, domain, which is 'predominantly a welfare state for women', and a tax-subsidised and government-regulated 'semiprivate welfare state of occupational pensions and RRSPs [Registered Retirement Savings Plans] [which] is mainly, if not exclusively, a welfare state for men – organized workers and the predominantly male occupations of employed professionals and managers'. In the absence of well-developed earnings-related public provision, private provision is relatively more important to the well-being of the elderly in Canada. But 37 per cent of the female workforce – as contrasted to 52 per cent of the male workforce – has occupational pension coverage (National Council of Welfare (Canada) 1989: 42).

Old Age Security has been about evenly split between the sexes while the income-tested GIS is utilised more heavily by women than by men (Health and Welfare Canada 1991: 174). The new Seniors Benefit, too, will serve more women than men. The contributory Q/CPP, in contrast, gives the greatest benefits to those with the best labour market histories, which tend to be men, although survivors do inherit part of the pension. Men make up 58 per cent of retired worker beneficiaries, but women predominate among those receiving survivors' benefits (91 per cent) and among those receiving both survivors' and workers' benefits (85 per cent). Almost all men are claiming their benefits as workers (93 per cent), while 4 per cent receive survivors' benefits and 3 per cent get both. (Unlike the situation in the United States, Canadians do not have to choose between survivors' benefits and retired worker benefits.) The majority of women – 51 per cent – claim as workers, and another 22 per cent get both worker and survivors' benefits, but a significant proportion, 37 per cent, get only the survivors' benefit (unpublished data on the Q/CPP was provided by Health and Welfare Canada).

Unemployment

Contributory Employment Insurance gives income-graded benefits along with a small supplement to cover the dependants of married claimants (Guest 1997: 105–7, 184–5). In the last decade, eligibility requirements for unemployment insurance have been tightened, a clawback of benefits for upper income recipients has been instituted, and benefits have been cut; the measures have been partially softened by the provision of more assistance in the form of a Family Income Supplement to lower income parents with dependants (Battle 1997: 19–23). Finally, underlining the shift to 'active' employment rhetoric, in 1996, the program was renamed Employment Insurance (Guest 1997: 279). The program gives short-term protection for the unemployed who have worked recently and are available to take new jobs. Parental and maternity leave is part of the unemployment insurance system, with similar qualifying conditions. There are no explicitly gendered provisions. Men are the majority of beneficiaries under the regular Employment Insurance program, while women make up over 99 per cent of those taking parental leave (Health and Welfare Canada 1991: 184–6).

For the unemployed without insurance coverage, Canada has provided various forms of social assistance. In 1966, the Canada Assistance Plan (CAP) was initiated, under which provinces were free to consolidate all need- and means-tested categorical programs, including employment assistance, mothers' allowances and general public assistance (that is, poor relief) with the federal government providing partial, but unlimited, funding and mandating that welfare would be available to all people in need, including Native Canadians, who earlier had been excluded from some provincial programs (Guest 1997: 145, 323 n. 39). CAP provided a guaranteed safety net for all, but distinctions were made between long-term recipients ('unemployables') and those considered employable, with the former – including single mothers – receiving higher benefits (National Council of Welfare (Canada) 1987: 4–6). CAP benefits were subject to a household means test, meaning that secondary workers in two-parent households, disproportionately women, were unlikely to get any unemployment benefits unless their spouses were unemployed, too.

In 1995, CAP was replaced by the Canada Health and Social Transfer (CHST), a block grant to the provinces to run their own welfare programs, accompanied by severe cuts in federal spending. With the withdrawal of unlimited federal matching funds, federal mandates have been withdrawn as well, and social assistance is no longer available to all needy Canadians (Battle 1997: 11–14). Rather, provinces can decide on which categories of the poor to assist, with what requirements and at what level. Most provinces, led by those with new conservative administrations, have introduced benefit cuts and various forms of 'workfare', that is, welfare benefits for the unemployed (sometimes including single parents) are made conditional on the performance of work or work-related training (Shragge 1997b).

Single Parenthood

Until the initiation of the Q/CPP in the 1960s, widows, like divorcees and never-married mothers, relied exclusively on mothers' allowances. Now widows (and widowers) do get a survivors' benefit through their spouses' contributions under the Q/CPP, while other types of single parents have relied on CAP and now must rely on provincial welfare without any entitlement. Since the late 1970s, some of the provinces have explicitly defined single mothers as employable with concomitant work requirements, but workforce schemes were understood to be excluded from cost-sharing under the CAP (P. Evans and McIntyre 1987; P. Evans 1992, 1993). This is no longer the case with provincially run programs under CHST. But while workfare programs have proliferated in the wake of CAP's end in 1995, single mothers with young children remain exempt from work requirements (Lightman 1997; Shragge 1997a: 23), although there is no guarantee that this will remain the case.

Child support enforcement in Canada is most similar to the US situation. That is, while there have been initiatives to standardise and increase awards and to improve collection rates, there is still considerable interprovincial variation, and responsibility for collection also remains at the sub-national level (although, as in the United States, there is some move to involve federal tax authorities). Moreover, awards do not include an amount for the parent caring for the children. Unlike the United States, child support is taxable income for the custodial parent, thus affecting eligibility for social assistance, and a tax deduction for the absent parent (Baker 1995: 311).

National data is lacking on how many single parents rely on welfare, but analysts estimate that about two-fifths get benefits and that single mothers made up 20–30 per cent of the CAP caseload (National Council of Welfare (Canada) 1990: 78). There is no published breakdown of sole parent recipients by sex, but a government inquiry into sole parents and welfare in Ontario (Ontario Social Assistance Review Committee 1988) assumes women were the parents in 95 per cent of sole parent families on welfare. Women made up 90 per cent of those receiving surviving spouses' pensions (a pension for those under forty-five years of age, most of whom would be caring for children) (Health and Welfare Canada 1991: 174).

In cross-national perspective, Canada's poverty rates for single mothers do not look considerably better than US or Australian rates, and are considerably worse than poverty rates among older Canadians (see Table 4.1). However, closer comparisons of the United States and Canada suggest that Canadian sole mothers are somewhat better off than their US counterparts despite very similar patterns of employment and benefit utilisation (see, for example, Hanratty and Blank 1992), paralleling findings that, overall, Canada has less income inequality and deep poverty than does the United States (Myles and Pierson 1997). However, sharpening welfare politics may mean that in some provinces, radical conservative administrations will cut benefits, as did Premier Mike Harris in Ontario, which could decrease the differences between the North American countries.

Family Needs

Family allowances were an important token of Canada's commitment to universalism. However, in the mid-1980s, family allowances were de-indexed, benefits for upper income Canadians were made subject to a clawback, and a children's tax exemption was converted to a refundable credit (National Council of Welfare (Canada) 1992: 52–4; Goldberg 1990: 74). In 1993, these programs were replaced by a single income-tested Child Tax Benefit (CTB), paid monthly, like the old family allowances, to more than 80 per cent of families with children (Myles and Pierson 1997; Battle 1997: 32). Current debates centre on how to achieve equity between poor families with employed parents (who get only the CTB and a modest supplement for the working poor) and those families with parents on welfare (who get the CTB as well as welfare) (Battle 1997: 32–4).

Support to Caregiving

The Canadian system offers somewhat more public support for care work than does the United States, but gives no citizenship entitlements to income support when citizens need to care for children, relatives or others, although workers with coverage under Employment Insurance get a short paid maternity and parental leave. Parents' financial responsibilities for children are supported through the CTB, which, in contrast to the United States, offers greater assistance to less affluent segments of the populace. Single parents' caregiving work was supported, albeit meagrely, under CAP, and provincial welfare programs will probably continue to allow some single parents (or married parents, if both partners are unemployed) to stay at home to care for young children, though perhaps with more onerous requirements than under CAP. Some provinces give direct payments to the disabled to pay for care services (Stryckman and Nahmiash 1994). Again, caregiving remains largely unpaid and dependent on 'private' arrangements.

Australia

Australia is cross-nationally unusual in that contributory social insurance is virtually undeveloped, while all other social programs – family allowances, benefits for the elderly, sole parents, the unemployed, and others – are income-tested. Thus, according to Shaver (1989b: 160), the Australian system is

> more unitary than contributory systems, in which gaps and shortfalls in contributory coverage typically have to be filled by means-tested supplements ... The two-tier [that is, social insurance and social assistance] basis creates social and political distinctions between entitlements paid for through contributions, and welfare conceded to the poor. Australia's tax-transfer framework defines access and equity within a single system of revenue and eligibility. While it makes comparatively few distinctions among claimants, the rights of all claims carry the welfarist connotations of means-testing.

Income tests function more to keep out the affluent than to make social provision residual, but while the system in Australia is more effective in preventing deep poverty than the one in the United States, benefit levels are still quite low, leaving much scope for private provision. There has also been a division between programs aimed at family needs and those serving labour market needs (Bryson 1992).

The foundation of Australian social provision – until quite recently – was a unique system of 'social protection by other means' (mainly tariff protection, immigration control and wage arbitration) which has kept the 'private' wages of male workers at a breadwinner level (that is, sufficient to support a dependent wife and children) (Castles 1985). But the features of this (male) 'wage earners' welfare state' (Castles 1994) have been eroding since the 1980s.

Old age

Public provision for the elderly has been a means-tested and flat-rate system, offering men and women individual entitlement, conditional on need and a household means test. Debates have tended to focus on the restrictiveness of the means and assets tests, with bipartisan changes to weaken the means and assets tests through the 1970s and similarly bipartisan efforts to increase selectivity in the 1980s (Shaver 1991). Men and women became eligible for pensions at different ages, women at sixty, men at sixty-five, though women's age of eligibility is being raised. With pension entitlement not based on labour force participation, there is no privileging of male workers over unpaid female carers. However, 'housewife-maintaining' households have received some advantage in this system in that there has been a wife pension for the spouses of male aged and invalid pensioners who do not qualify on their own, but none for husbands (Bryson 1983: 138). After 1995, reflecting a larger trend of replacing support for women as wives with direct support for caring, these pensions are being phased out (D. Mitchell 1997). Women caring for husbands or anyone caring for a disabled or elderly pensioner will still be eligible for the Carer Pension (Shaver 1995).

Shifting levels of coverage reflect the shifting means test. In 1960, about half the aged population received pensions; this rose to two-thirds in 1972, and by 1981 the pension was virtually universal (with some receiving partial pensions). The selectivist turn was evidenced by the end of the decade in falling coverage; in 1994, about 70 per cent of pension-age women received age pensions, as compared with a little under 60 per cent of men (Shaver 1991: 113–14; AOSW 1995: 148). Women predominate among pensioners because of their longer lives, lower age of eligibility and greater economic need (especially when widowed); about 30 per cent of all age pensioners were male, while 70 per cent were female (AOSW 1995: 148).

Given the relatively low wage replacement rate of the age pension (Palme 1990: 60; Palme 1997), private provision for retirement is quite important. In the early 1990s, private pension funds were made compulsory under the Accord; this measure has extended coverage to women, widely and rapidly: in 1993, 86 per cent of female workers – and 91 per cent of male workers – had superannuation coverage (AOSW 1995: 150). However, many of the actual entitlements are quite small (Sharp 1995).

At the US poverty line, fewer Australian than American elderly women are poor, while Timothy Smeeding (1997) reports higher rates for Australia than the United States at the 50 per cent of median line (shown in Table 4.1). However, Sheila Shaver (1997) demonstrates that these proportions are quite sensitive to the equivalence measures used, partly because those with incomes based mainly on pensions cluster close to 50 per cent of median income. The pension for lower income people is more generous than the US analogue (Whiteford 1995: 26), leading to lower poverty rates at the lower poverty lines. But the lower benefits and income-testing mean both that those with only a pension have fairly low incomes, and that better-off Australians are less well-protected by public benefits.

Unemployment

Unemployment benefits are non-contributory and tested on household income. As is the case in both Britain and Canada with means-tested (though non-categorical) social assistance for the unemployed, this rule disqualifies second earners – usually women – in couples where the primary earner is employed. Unemployment benefits are more likely to be claimed by men than by women (AOSW 1991: 146–7). Unemployment benefits also offered dependants' allowances for spouses and children (Bryson 1983: 138). Important changes leading to a greater degree of individual entitlement were introduced in association with the ALP's 1994 'Working Nation' White Paper on Unemployment (Saunders 1995; D. Mitchell 1997; Bradbury 1994). Although still conditional on a household test of means, the spouse of an unemployed person must establish individual eligibility for either an allowance for carers of children under sixteen or for their own unemployment benefits, also being subject to work tests (partners aged forty and over and lacking recent employment experience can get a 'Partner Allowance', and are exempt from work requirements, but this exemption will not apply to those coming after the currently eligible cohorts) (McHugh and Millar 1997).

Reflecting the tenor of restructuring, unemployment assistance is now called Job Search Allowance. The long-term unemployed (and single mothers) were to be targeted for case management, special training programs and assistance in re-entering the labour market as part of 'Working Nation' (Eardley and Thompson 1997). There has been no definite limit on the duration of unemployment benefits, but in the recent reforms, as across the other three countries, work incentives have been strengthened and training and job search assistance enhanced (Saunders 1995). And, as in Britain, young people have been deprived of entitlement to unemployment support. However, many of the 'Working Nation' reforms have been eliminated, or had their funding severely cut, by the Liberal–National Coalition Government.

Single Parenthood

Non-contributory widows' pensions were initiated during Labor's wartime extension of social provision, allowing widowed and deserted (de jure and de facto) wives to stay at home to care for their children. In 1972, the supporting mothers' allowance extended these benefits to never-married mothers, and, in 1977, the supporting mothers' allowance was extended to male sole parents, becoming the Supporting Parents' Benefit (Shaver 1989b: 165–6). In a final change, in 1989, it was combined with the Widows' Pension for widows with children. A second category of widows' pensions went to childless widows aged fifty or more, and to women whose children had grown up (Bryson 1983: 139); these are now being phased out as part of a move towards gender neutrality and away from recognising 'difference'. With changes made as part of the comprehensive mid-1980s Social Security Review, the Supporting Parents' Benefit is to end once the youngest child turns sixteen, and the expectation is that sole parents will return to the paid labour force at this time (if not sooner) (Cass 1993: 10). Shaver (1995: 149) notes that this ensemble of changes means that 'the provisions for a distinctive life cycle pattern shaped by motherhood has been effectively removed from the social security system'.

Sole parent pensioners are encouraged, but not required, to seek paid employment before their children reach sixteen years of age (Cass 1994); as in Britain, the official stance on mothers' employment is neutral, respecting 'choice'. Yet there are concerns about low activity rates (D. Mitchell 1993); indeed, single mothers are employed at lower rates than are married mothers (see Table 3.2, p. 70). In the wake of the Social Security Review, the voluntary Jobs, Education and Training (JET) scheme was established to give support and training to single mothers who wanted to enter paid employment, although this program is slated to receive less help under the Coalition Government (McHugh and Millar 1997).

As in the United States and Britain (and to a somewhat lesser extent in Canada), child support enforcement was significantly enhanced in the 1980s, and co-operation with authorities in identifying and locating absent parents made a condition of receiving social assistance (McHugh and Millar 1997). Child support collection has been turned over to the Commonwealth Tax Office, which seems to have made it more efficient than it is in the other three countries. And, in contrast to the British scheme, Australian sole parents on Supporting Parents' Benefit keep a portion of the award (more than in the United States), and the award does not include maintenance for the caregiver.

Despite the formally gender-neutral eligibility, women are disproportionately represented among sole parent pensioners. Mothers are the heads of the vast majority of sole parent families (89 per cent in 1986; Millar and Whiteford 1993: 61), but in the early 1980s only about one in ten male sole parents received a pension compared with 80 per cent of female sole parents (Bryson 1983: 136, 145). Single mothers make up almost all (94 per cent) the sole parent pensioners; but the proportion in receipt of benefits has been declining since the mid-1980s, as more have taken up paid employment in the 1980s (in 1994, about 72 per cent of all sole parents received a pension) (Millar and Whiteford 1993: 61; McHugh and Millar 1997; D. Mitchell 1997).

Benefits for sole parents have been set at the same level as those for other social security recipients – the Australian welfare state does not create much gender inequality in benefits. But benefits (for all) have been rather modest. The relatively high poverty of single mother families (see Table 4.1), the majority of whom were without earnings and dependent on welfare (Rainwater 1993) – internationally and as compared to other families – was spotlighted by researchers in the 1980s. Although there were disagreements about methods and measures, all showed high rates of poverty – between about a half and three-fifths (depending on the measure) – among families maintained by single parents (D. Mitchell and Harding 1993; Saunders and Matheson 1991; Shaver 1997). Moreover, these rates were higher than rates for other groups of Australian citizens substantially reliant on the welfare state, such as elderly people (D. Mitchell 1993: 59, Table 3). Several initiatives were undertaken by the ALP Government to improve their situation, including increases in targeted cash transfers such as the Additional Family Payment (earlier the Family Income Supplement) (D. Mitchell 1997).

Family Needs

In the 1970s, near-universal child endowments were expanded and renamed family allowances; in the 1980s and 1990s, the renamed program – the Basic Family Payment – featured income-testing that excluded affluent families (D. Mitchell 1997). In 1982 family allowances were supplemented by a special payment for low-income workers' families, the Family Income Supplement, renamed the Additional Family Payment in 1992. This was partly as a way to avoid 'poverty traps' and work disincentives for larger families (whose benefits if the earner was unemployed could exceed market wages). Spending on this program has expanded relative to the broader family payments, but it targets a narrower range of families (D. Mitchell 1997). The Accord brought wage restraint and the Family Income Supplement served as a trade-off, with an increasing number of eligible families. Prime Minister Bob Hawke's 1987 election campaign promised that 'no child will need to live in poverty' by 1990 (quoted in Millar and Whiteford 1993: 62). All families with children, including those headed by single parents, benefited from a number of initiatives to direct resources towards children, even as targeting within these programs increased (D. Mitchell

1997). Yet, while poverty among children may have declined slightly, overall rates of poverty among single parent families with children remain quite high.

Aboriginal people and Torres Strait Islanders historically were excluded from welfare state programs such as family allowances (Beckett 1987; Altman and Sanders 1992) and women were 'disenfranchised as mothers' (McGrath 1993). Today, this is no longer the case, but poverty, unemployment and family disruption plague Aboriginal communities; while welfare prevents worse destitution, levels of dependency are quite high. In an attempt to deal with these problems, Community Development Employment Projects allow Aboriginals to forgo individual welfare payments to work for community projects; this has offered work to many men, but since women on sole parents' benefits are not expected to work, it does less to improve their more limited employment prospects (A. E. Daly 1991).

Support to caregiving

Historically, Australia supported caregiving principally through the support given to male breadwinners, whose wages were kept relatively high by protectionist policies and wage arbitration. Support for dependent spouses was being phased out of the system by the ALP as part of the 'Working Nation' and other reforms, and it has largely been replaced by direct support to caregivers. Indeed, there is also a tradition of supporting caregivers directly, with widows' and supporting parents' pensions, when male breadwinners were not present. Full-time caregiving was assumed to be women's responsibility, and the state's responsibility was to enable it. The new approach supports caregiving inside and outside marriage, marking a departure from the logic of the male breadwinner model. Until very recently, taxpayers – mainly male wage earners – received a Dependent Spouse Rebate if they supported a non-employed spouse. In 1994, this was cashed out to give a direct payment to mothers at home with children – the Home Child Care Allowance (HCCA), means-tested on the claimant's income but not her partner's (leaving the Dependent Spouse Rebate as a much smaller tax credit for wage earners with non-working spouses without children at home – mainly a cohort of older couples) (D. Mitchell 1997). A Parenting Allowance was introduced in 1995, incorporating the HCCA; it is a payment for any parent with children at home and a low personal income (McHugh and Millar 1997). Replacing the arrangements in unemployment assistance under which beneficiaries with dependent spouses claimed additional benefits, there is an additional payment to the Parenting Allowance (Additional Parenting Allowance) paid directly

to the partners (mainly wives) of unemployed workers (mainly husbands) who are caring for children – so their caregiving establishes
eligibility for individual benefits rather than their husbands being given
a bonus for supporting dependants (McHugh and Millar 1997). Others
will be expected to establish their own eligibility for benefits, and are
thus subject to work requirements. A Carer Pension – drawn on by both
men and women, elderly and not – was introduced in 1985 to give
support to providers of long-term care to someone receiving income
support, and not otherwise eligible for assistance (Bradbury 1996: 6).
Thus, Australia has developed a modest and gender-neutral system of
support to caregivers.

The Social Organisation of Income and Services

As we have seen, the United States, Australia, Canada and Britain
feature a strong emphasis on private sources of services and income –
markets and families, as opposed to states – for most individuals and
households. Households with men present gain more income from the
market than do households maintained by women. Yet we also see
variation across the four in the extent to which the state offers a safety
net and in the balance between 'private' institutions, families and labour
markets. Luxembourg Income Study data on income sources confirm
that Britain and Australia give more public resources to families with
children than do the United States and Canada, where families of all
types are more market-reliant (Rainwater 1993; D. Mitchell 1993).
Differences across the four are especially notable among single mother
families. Deborah Mitchell (1993) found (in the mid-1980s) that on
average the proportion of their income derived from earnings ranges
from a low of 21.3 per cent in Britain to a high of 54.7 per cent in the
United States. Single mother families in Australia are closest to those in
Britain in the proportion of their income derived from earnings –
30 per cent – while those in Canada, at 49.2 per cent, are closer to those
in the United States. This clustering is replicated in reliance on public
transfers. Fewer single mother families in Australia and Britain than in
Canada and the United States have any earnings (Rainwater 1993), and
higher proportions of them rely on public sole parent benefits. Of
course, these patterns reflect the patterns of labour force participation
described in the last chapter.

The United States has the strongest emphasis on employment; both
unemployment and retirement insurance are conditional on steady
work and contributions, while work requirements have been enhanced
for social assistance programs, seen in the recent shift from Aid to
Families with Dependent Children to Temporary Assistance to Needy

Families. Assistance linked to employment is also seen in the Earned Income Tax Credit. Market-based services and private arrangements in families – supported by tax policy – are to allow all adults to participate in the market. Canada features similar emphases, but offers greater public assistance to workers and the non-employed and makes greater concessions to the demands of caregiving. But both North American countries have intensified citizens' dependence on private sources of support by ending entitlement to social assistance. Australia and Britain follow the United States and Canada in emphasising employment, but limit this to men and childless women, and they feature a stronger safety net for the unemployed, single mothers and elderly women than does the United States. Mothers are not expected to be commodified to the same extent as are men, as reflected in programs which allow them to depend on state sources of support – when outside relationships with men – which reveals the extent to which women, too, are expected to rely on 'private' sources of support: husbands (or partners). Moreover, in Britain, families are expected to be the principal sources of caregiving; in Australia under the ALP such an expectation was tempered by expanded child care, but is being reversed by Coalition social policies emphasising support for caregiving within the context of traditional families. Thus, family – marriage – plays a larger role in these two countries than it does in North America.

Gender Stratification

The four countries have had high poverty rates as compared with other western nations. This is notable for households maintained by women of all ages, especially – but not only – those headed by women of colour, whose economic vulnerability is more exposed without the protection of either marriage or 'good' jobs (see Table 4.1). In all four, single mother families face above-average likelihoods of being in poverty (D. Mitchell 1993: 59, Table 3). Britain still has lower poverty rates than do the United States, Canada and Australia; poverty rates increased under the Conservatives (Millar and Whiteford 1993), but this might be reversed under Blair's New Labour Government. The United States also features relatively high rates of deep poverty among elderly women, while the other three provide benefits that keep such women marginally above the US poverty line. But only Canada directs sufficient resources to substantially reduce older women's relative poverty.

To what extent are there separate programs for labour market and family needs and risks? In all four, at least some separate programs remain, although there are others which do not differentiate between claims based on needs or risks generated in the labour market and those arising in families. Provision for the aged in Britain (National Insurance) and the United States (Social Security Old-Age Survivors' and Disability Insurance) is, to use Fraser's (1989: 150–1) terms, 'hermaphroditic ... internally dualized and gendered', in that eligibility is based on both labour market participation and associated payroll contributions and on marriage to covered wage earners. (Contributory old-age provision, such as the State Earnings-Related Pension Scheme in Britain and the Quebec/Canada Pension Plan in Canada, does offer benefits for survivors, but not to living spouses, less faithfully mirroring the logic of male breadwinner–female housewife families than the others). Such differentiation within programs is less visible and therefore, arguably, does less politically to underline gender difference than do programs which do not combine such claims bases. Need-based old-age provision, as in the main Australian old-age pension, need-based programs for the aged in Canada (Seniors Benefit) and the United States (Supplemental Security Income), and the general Income Support program in Britain, covers both retired workers and the dependants of those workers within the same framework, making no distinctions among the elderly poor on the basis of their previous positioning in the gender division of labour.

Gender differentiation of programs historically has been strongest for the United States and Australia. With the exception of the need-based old-age pension, Australia's social assistance programs target people as (poor or unemployed) workers or as caregivers and family members, with different expectations about employment attaching to the two. The US system until very recently has been strongly categorical, with categories reflecting family or work-based needs. Yet the shift in emphasis from AFDC to EITC means more people will be assisted under the rubric of the 'working poor'. With the assumption that mothers should be employed and the addition of stringent work requirements to state-run welfare programs under TANF, welfare has been restructured to be much more like unemployment assistance, with caregiving responsibilities bringing no exemption from work requirements and only minimal public support. Unemployment insurance remains a program for labour market risks. The old-age insurance system has sub-programs that correspond to retired workers' and survivors' benefits, while dependants' benefits are differentiated through the notion of auxiliary entitlement – programs are gendered, even though access to them is made gender-neutral. Thus, while programs remain differentiated, to the extent that the labour market changes, the clienteles of the programs may become less gender-differentiated.

Britain and Canada had less strongly differentiated provision. But recent changes in Britain's social assistance transfer the unemployed from the non-categorical Income Support system to Jobseeker's Allowance, leaving behind the 'unemployables' – single mothers and elderly people (who might be removed from Income Support if the Basic Pension is upgraded). There are attempts to encourage women to take up part-time work, so that they would be channelled to Family Benefit, a program aimed, like EITC in the United States, at the working poor. Britain's social insurance system has distinctly gendered claims bases. Canada's social insurance system caters principally to workers and their survivors, not containing dependent spouses' benefits. The new Seniors Benefit will assist elderly people based on need. CAP, the social assistance program for the non-aged, was non-categorical, but the new provincial schemes may go back to categorical assistance; the Child Tax Benefit, however, goes to both working and non-working poor, and does not differentiate based on marital status.

To what extent do these states' systems of social provision generate and sustain gender differences through processes of claiming state benefits and participation in different programs? In all of these systems of social provision, men make almost all of their claims on the basis of their paid work, while fewer women's claims are so based. A partial exception comes in men's use of need-based programs; nevertheless, men's reasons for needing such programs almost always stem from unemployment or retirement rather than from caregiving responsibilities. Thus, men get benefits almost exclusively from programs designed to compensate for failures in the labour market, while in contrast, most women – though the proportion is declining – have made their claims based on familial or marital roles to programs targeted at compensating for family 'failures', the break-up of marriages due to divorce or the death of their husbands or the need to raise children alone. Men – even single fathers – very rarely make use of these programs.

Men make up the majority of unemployed claimants in all four countries, women the vast majority of sole parent beneficiaries. In the three countries with work-based old-age programs, men are the majority of those making claims on their own work record, but increasing numbers of women are in this category as well. Men make almost no claims as dependants or survivors under old-age insurance in the United States and Britain. Thus, women make up almost this entire category of claimants. Women predominate among those getting survivors' benefits or both retired-worker and survivors' benefits in Canada, but because one can get both types of benefits simultaneously, men receive these as well, though at a lower rate than women. And, because of their relatively greater economic vulnerability, women predominate among those claiming income-tested old-age pensions in Australia or need-based provision in the other three countries. While there are now women wage earners (and even breadwinners), the sphere of family work continues to be a female one – even if the male breadwinner model has broken down, the female caregiver model remains hegemonic, although it may be 'other women' hired for the purpose, disproportionately immigrants and women of colour, doing the caregiving (Jenson 1997a; Glenn 1992; Windebank 1996).

But while we can discern overall gender differences in the claims made by men and women, we must also be aware of differences across the four countries, across cohorts of women, and across classes and racial/ethnic groupings. The majority of clients of welfare states today are elderly, and their labour market experiences were very different than current working-aged cohorts, who are much more likely to be employed, and, particularly in the United States and Canada, more likely to be employed consistently over their lives and in full-time work. Policy changes in the 1960s and 1970s opened to women the formally gender-neutral identity of citizen-worker – though one with strong associations with the traditionally male pattern of work. Women have entered the paid workforce in increasing numbers with each successive cohort. To the extent that their work is similar to men's, they too have made and in retirement will make claims as workers (and now under the same terms of eligibility and benefits as do male claimants). Among working-aged men and women, especially in North America, the quality of benefits may depend more on the distinction between good and bad jobs than on differences between programs targeted on caregiving versus employment. We can expect class and racial/ethnic differences among women to show up in terms of their access to labour market programs and the quality of benefits to which they have access. It is also likely to influence political mobilisation, in different gendered political identities – (citizen-) worker versus (citizen-) mother (stay-at-home or part-time worker).

What is the future for women's caregiving claims? The most salient question in the United States may be whether such claims will survive at all. An optimistic scenario would see them grafted on to work-based claims; a pessimistic one would see them disappearing and the quality of life deteriorating (Hochschild 1995). Canada faces similar dilemmas, although buffered by the stronger safety net. In contrast, in Britain, given the rather dismal state of the labour market for women and the pervasive mandating of care, it seems likely that there will be less change from the current situation, in which gender difference in claims is strong. Australia presents a less negative picture of continuing gender differentiation in claims, but greater access for women to labour market positions – though this is based on data from before the Coalition

Government took power. We might expect, then, a slower decline in women making family-based claims in Australia than in North America. What is the relationship between gender differentiation and gender inequality? American scholars have tended to see a direct link between differentiation and inequality, identifying a 'two-tier' welfare state with inadequate social assistance programs serving a predominantly female clientele and a relatively more generous contributory social insurance targeting a male clientele (see, for example, Pearce 1986; Nelson 1984, 1990; Fraser 1989). But, first, not all countries have systems bifurcated between social insurance and social assistance – Australia has only social assistance, while other welfare states have universal components. Second, while social assistance does generally offer benefits inferior to social insurance, it is not limited to women or to family 'failures' in all countries. For example, men claiming non-contributory, means-tested unemployment benefits outnumbered men claiming unemployment insurance in Britain. Third, many women – a larger number than social assistance clients – are incorporated into the top tier of the US welfare state, indirectly, on the basis of their marriage to men who have made contributions to social insurance programs; they get lower benefits than do wage earners, but they are entitled to the same standardised treatment and to nationally set, inflation-indexed benefits accorded to men under social security. Finally, emerging forms of non-contributory programs to assist the families of the working poor, such as the EITC in the United States, Britain's Family Benefit, Australia's Additional Family Payment, and Canada's Child Tax Benefit, confound the strict distinctions made between feminine, familial social assistance and masculine, work-based social insurance. Many of these programs are operated with little surveillance. Their appearance may be tokens of a breakdown of the distinctions made during the 'golden era' of the welfare state between unemployables and workers, and of the emergence of a new set of distinctions based on quality of employment. And things look somewhat different from an Australian perspective. There is differentiation in the types of claims men and women make, but in the unified system of social provision, there is little benefit inequality. Pension levels are set at the same relatively low level for elderly retired wage earners and homemakers, sole parents, and the unemployed.

Within formally gender-neutral need-based and labour market-based programs we see the reflection of the disadvantages accruing to women given their caregiving responsibilities at home and vulnerabilities in the labour market. Because men are generally better positioned in the labour market, they are more assured of access to public social insurance and private occupational pension benefits, and reap the rewards of higher benefits in income-graded systems. In this case, public provision merely ratifies men's 'privately' generated economic advantages. But in the United States and Canada, some women, too, particularly those with advantaged educational backgrounds, have access to some of the 'good' jobs (disproportionately but not entirely in the public sector); thus, women are stratified into 'good' and 'bad' jobs and social provision. As economic restructuring and welfare reforms aimed at increasing selectivity and market incentives proceed, and as marital bonds remain fragile, gender-neutral social insurance provision for 'typical' workers and social assistance for the casualties of non-standard employment may further undermine the position of anyone outside the primary labour market, a category disproportionately made up by women but not exclusive to them. Thus, the character of gendered arrangements in the labour market is critical for women's and men's prospects in income maintenance programs.

Social Rights

To what extent can both men and women make individual claims for social protection? An important aspect of social benefits as they affect gender relations is the extent to which they allow individual claims for benefits or 'familise' recipients through derived benefits or household means tests. In the US and British social insurance programs, married women are made eligible for dependent spouses' pensions on the basis of their husbands' contributions and employment history and face barriers to establishing their own individual claims if they engage in the non-standard employment that often goes with marital caregiving duties. But such derived rights are vulnerable in the face of marital dissolution, although increasing protection for divorcees may change this. In income-tested social assistance programs, the use of household means tests undermines women's abilities to claim benefits as individuals – in the unemployment assistance programs of Britain, Australia and Canada (and, until recently, in the AFDC-UP program in the United States), eligibility is conditioned jointly on the incomes of both spouses in the case of married couples, which effectively disqualifies the second earner, usually the woman, from benefits when her income alone is interrupted. Yet Australia has gone further than the others in individualising access for caregivers within marriage. Women's independent claims to benefits are also undercut by rules defining households which presume that when a woman is living or sleeping with a man (who is not her husband) the woman is being financially supported by that man.

How much protection do these systems give to workers vis-à-vis the market? These systems have long been seen as market-reinforcing for workers (see, for example, Esping-Andersen 1990: 51). Certainly, for the aged, long contribution records have been required to get full benefits. Private pension coverage is increasingly important to maintaining standards of living but access is declining; gaining access demands not only employment, but usually also a 'good' job. Contributory unemployment benefits are linked to recent, steady, full-time labour market experience and their duration has been shortened in Britain, Canada and the United States. The level of social assistance benefits for unemployment is relatively low in Australia, Britain and Canada, thus encouraging paid work. But, previously, social assistance had been of more or less unlimited duration, so that those unable to find work could depend on at least a publicly supported subsistence. Unemployment assistance is now subject to increasingly stringent efforts to move workers back into the labour force or into participation in work-related activities. The 'dole' can function as a bribe against unrest and a guarantee against starvation, but the authors of new unemployment schemes – usually renamed in 'active' mode ('Job Search Allowance', 'Employment Insurance') – appear to aspire to more than passively supporting those without jobs. Through new casework methods or shifting work incentives by tying benefits to even part-time work effort, these countries are restructuring the system of social provision for those of working age to reflect what are understood to be the imperatives of 'globalisation', with demands for labour market 'flexibility' (Eardley and Thompson 1997; Rhodes 1996). The United States has no national unemployment assistance, but locally administered general relief has functioned in a way similar to the dole for residents of some areas, particularly high-unemployment inner cities or reservations populated by African-Americans, Native Americans and other racial or ethnic minorities. Yet, given America's lower unemployment rate, there is less tolerance for non-work and, recently, more effort at forcing people into low-wage work, or simply off benefits, with little concern for how they support themselves (Danziger and Danziger 1995). Indeed, some have argued that the very high imprisonment rates of men, particularly African-Americans and Latinos, function to 'sop up' some of the US unemployed (Western and Beckett 1997) and to give public employment – as construction workers and guards in prisons – to white men.

As long as women with children were defined as unemployable, various schemes which tied workers to the labour market were targeted mainly at men. But now women, too, are being defined as employable, albeit unevenly, and to the extent that they depend on their own employment to sustain their households, they are also subject to these work-enforcing shifts. In addition, to the extent that social insurance remains superior to social assistance and as implicit and explicit disentitlement moves workers from positions in which they can claim social insurance, women workers' position in the workforce will be increasingly consequential for their well-being.

What of men's and women's capacities to form and maintain autonomous households? Men have long relied on market work to sustain households; the welfare state was a back-up, not an alternative, to employment. That remains the case. But jobs with family-supporting wages are fewer, and the safety net less comprehensive. More men, particularly but not only in the United States, are falling outside the circle of jobs and social security that allows them to sustain households. Women rely on the market to an increasing extent, but not as much as men. Income sources are more mixed among women: some rely on male partners, even more are in dual-earner households or support themselves. Some women support households through state benefits. Among older people, women are essentially guaranteed a subsistence-level benefit. Many women have individual access to benefits, either through their own work or because access to benefits for some divorcees has been protected, but the related problems of derived benefits and of aged women's poverty continue to vex policy-makers.

Most political concern of late focuses on women of working age. Social politics across the four countries has featured contestation surrounding women's roles – paid worker, part-time worker/primary caregiver or full-time mother, the extent to which women's employment, unlike men's, should be up to individuals' choices, and how states should enforce parental financial responsibilities in cases of marital breakdown.

Prior to the elimination of AFDC in the United States and CAP in Canada, and, perhaps, the implementation of the new British child support scheme, one could say that all four countries allowed more independence for mothers vis-à-vis marriage and the family than for workers vis-à-vis the market. Social assistance provided an 'exit option' (Hirschman 1970) with, we would argue, positive effects for women within gendered power relations. In Britain and Australia, a single mother can maintain a household without access to a male wage and without herself working for pay – there are as yet no work requirements. In Canada and the United States, this is no longer the case. Although women may be able to gain temporary state support, there is no entitlement to assistance, and requirements to take paid work are part of the plans of many states and provinces. In addition, in all four countries anyone with children claiming social assistance is required to co-operate in identifying and finding the absent parent. Some would argue that this alone precludes real autonomy, as women are being forced to sustain relationships with partners with whom they have broken. (Although all programs formally make some allowance for concerns about contact with violent partners and the like, there are fears that this will not be implemented properly.) Others contend that the relationships being sustained are between absent fathers and their children, whom they have a responsibility to maintain; this should not have a bearing on custodial parents' autonomy. Yet in Britain, this argument is weaker than in the other three countries, given that women must be maintained economically in part by former partners if they claim some form of social assistance – as nearly all single mothers in Britain do.

Sole parent benefits were established with the aim of allowing white single mothers to pursue the distinctive, non-commodified life pattern deemed appropriate for other white mothers; this continued to be the case even as women of colour and indigenous women laid claim to sole parent benefits. Public provision construed single mothers as unemployable, as full-time caregivers rather than as potential workers. This has eroded completely within the US system of social provision, and to a greater or lesser extent in the other three countries. (Tax systems, however, may be a different case; see McCaffery 1997.) Changing gender relations have helped to propel policy changes, and new assumptions about gender – specifically that women can be expected to be employed – will have far-reaching implications for men and women. All four countries have developed incentives for single mothers to take paid work (sometimes part-time), such as wage supplements, subsidised services, pass-throughs of portions of child support awards and the like, as well as disincentives for staying on public support. Yet there are some significant differences among the countries in regard to models of motherhood as embedded in social assistance and other parts of policy regimes, ranging from enforcing difference, dependency and inequality (Britain), supporting difference, equality and women's choices about employment (Australia – at least under the Labor Party), and enforcing sameness and employment for everyone (the United States and, to a modified degree, Canada).

Britain manifests the least change with respect to gender relations; indeed, in some ways, the traditional division of labour has been reinforced. Thus far, British sole parents have remained exempt from work requirements. Pragmatically, given the pool of unemployed male workers, moving single mothers into the labour force was not the highest priority of the Tory Government. But the policy on single mothers' work also reflects the view that mothers' caregiving responsibilities are primary, and that employment must not interfere with these duties. Millar (1996: 47) notes that part-time work has come to be seen as compatible with mothers' caregiving, although government policy has been neutrality – 'lone parents should "have a choice" whether or not to take paid work' (Millar and Whiteford 1993: 63, quoting UK Department of Social Security). Yet, in contrast to the situation in North America (where single mothers' work is increasing) and Australia (where it has been relatively stable; McHugh and Millar 1997), decreasing proportions of single mothers are working for pay – while married women's employment is rising, as it is across the four countries. And in Britain, again in contrast to North America, increasing proportions of single mothers are depending on social assistance (from less than half in the mid-1970s, to over two-thirds by the mid-1980s; Millar and Whiteford 1993). Millar (1996: 47) describes the government dilemma: 'Should single mothers be allowed to continue to make this "choice" when more and more married mothers are "choosing" work? And especially when that choice is so costly in terms of social security benefits'. But to force single mothers on benefits to work – one solution to conservative concerns about the 'culture of dependency', embraced enthusiastically by Americans – would both challenge the primacy of mothers' caregiving and open up the issue of child care availability and cost for all women (Millar 1994: 29–30).

Offsetting some of the rising cost of social expenditures for single mother families through enhanced child support enforcement allowed cutbacks without upsetting traditional gender roles: men's responsibilities to maintain their families and women's to care for children. Yet the overall set of changes made to policies affecting single mothers in Britain adds up to an effort to transfer state responsibility to women and their former partners by getting child support and maintenance from absent parents and increasing mothers' part-time work, which then entitles them to the employment-related Family Benefit. This minimises the government contribution but deprives women of an independent income sufficient for maintaining a household. Nor do women gain good employment opportunities (given the character of most part-time work in Britain). Opposition to the child support legislation has been widespread among feminists, but it was middle-class men's resistance which prompted changes (Millar 1996; Lister 1994b). The New Labour administration promises to be less indifferent to poverty and social exclusion than its Conservative predecessor. Yet, on the question of women's work, it has not broken entirely from the models of motherhood that make caregiving a priority even if it attempts to 'modernise' motherhood so that women return to employment, especially part-time, after children are in school. Feminists, now more likely to have political influence, resist work requirements, but generally support women's right to care (or not) (see, for example, Lewis 1997).

Australia is now pursuing a policy of encouraging sole parent pensioners to enter the labour force while their children are young, and requiring work after children reach the age of sixteen. In other words, full-time caregiving will only be supported through the sole parents' pension for a limited period (Cass 1994: 109). Under the previous Labor administrations, women's employment was supported in various ways, as part of an ensemble of reforms promoted by 'femocrats', feminist women in the state bureaucracy, and their allies in the Labor Party and outside the state (Eisenstein 1996). The Social Security Review, led by feminist academic Bettina Cass, paid special attention to the situation of single mothers in its quest for a more active and less exclusionary society. In contrast to the model of motherhood – full-time domesticity and economic dependency – enshrined in the earlier system of widows' and supporting parents' pensions, the review promoted the notion that women, particularly when their children were older, should be employed, but that government should help them overcome barriers to employment, including inadequate child support and needs for child care and training (Millar and Whiteford 1993; McHugh and Millar 1997).

Under the ALP, there was a gradual policy shift to supporting women's employment, with protections retained for older cohorts of women who had been full-time mothers and housewives. (In contrast, such women were expected to be able to compete in the labour market immediately in the United States.) But there was also support for women's economic independence even apart from employment, seen in the individualisation of some benefits and direct payments to carers as part of the 'Working Nation' and other reforms. The support to women's employment and their economic independence has now become a matter of partisan politics, as the Liberal–National Coalition Government promised a return of the tax allowance for housewife-maintaining families (D. Mitchell 1997).

The changes under way in Canada have until recently seemed fairly similar to those in Australia; that is, there were moves to encourage paid work among mothers receiving assistance and women's employment more generally was supported through child care initiatives, similarly championed by representatives of women's groups. Yet labour market conditions and regulations have more closely resembled the United States. Single mothers are unevenly required to be workers – some provinces have been like the United States in imposing strict work requirements on assistance beneficiaries, others have not (P. Evans 1992); but whatever the extent of formal requirements, in practice, Canadian policy has been less draconian in forcing the commodification of women's labour. However, with the end of CAP in 1995, the guarantee of social assistance to any needy Canadian was eliminated and some provinces have instituted tougher work requirements and workfare; Canada has moved closer to the US model for single mothers. Election victories by conservatives such as Premier Harris in Ontario further this trend; indeed, Harris immediately cut benefit levels and imposed stronger work requirements in welfare, but, interestingly from the point of view of ideologies about gender and caring, retained an exemption for mothers of young children (Lightman 1997). Thus, single mothers may still in practice be eligible for state benefits that allow them to maintain a household without recourse to the market – at least until their children are no longer infants – but without an entitlement, they must rely on the political will and whims of party élites and electorates.

The logic of US social policy is based most strongly of the four on gender sameness and the predominance of the market, with women, including mothers, to be treated – like men – principally as workers, and, moreover, as workers whose caregiving responsibilities may be easily taken care of. Since the 1960s, US social assistance programs have had the shortest period of support allowed for full-time mothering. But now there is no entitlement to assistance and motherhood will no longer bring an exemption from commodification. Single mothers (or other caregivers) receiving welfare are to be required to enter the paid labour force or participate in workfare (work in exchange for welfare benefits), whatever the age of their children (with a twelve-week leave after childbirth).

Welfare reform – meaning increasing restrictions and work require-ments, occasionally with enhanced child care services or training, or abolishing AFDC – has been a politically popular proposal among Republicans and almost all Democrats. Two main paths for reform were (and to some extent still are) in play, associated with the Democrats and Republicans respectively, yet both are premised on the idea that mothers, even of very young children, should work for pay. Both operate within the dominant policy discourse, which valorises paid work above caregiving and which pushes all towards a model of citizenship based on paid work.

Welfare used to be a 'wedge issue' used by Republicans against the Democrats (Weir 1998; Weaver 1998). The Republicans' favoured policies will further limit full-time caregiving – indeed, even the pos-sibility of maintaining a home – as an option for poor mothers (Jencks and Edin 1995). By mandating gender 'sameness' with a vengeance, in which only labour market success allows anyone the capacity to have a family, Republican policies attempt to use the mechanism of market discipline to curb child-bearing by single women and the poor generally. However, market mechanisms alone no longer work to prevent autonomy for better-off segments of the female population, who can support themselves without men – and do, as high rates of divorce and single motherhood indicate. Here, we see differences between '*laissez-faire* feminists' (Klatch 1990), who do not want state subsidies or regulation of personal behaviour, and social conservatives who target 'illegitimacy' as the source of all social ills (Title I of the Personal Responsibility Act is directed at reducing 'illegitimacy' without increasing abortions), and ultimately hope to prevent non-marital motherhood altogether (even for those who can afford it). But they are all unwilling to commit state resources to supporting men's wages or women's caregiving work.

In 1992, the then presidential candidate Bill Clinton promised to 'end welfare as we know it', and require welfare recipients to work after two years of benefits, although with various guarantees of child care and public employment if jobs were not to be found; this looks like a liberal (that is, residual) version of Sweden's or France's supports for single mothers, which also require paid work. But, like Cold Warrior Richard Nixon opening the door to Communist China, Democrat Clinton's embrace of a stance that had formerly been anathema in his party changed political dynamics irrevocably. Although Democrats sought to retain control of the welfare issue, the call to end welfare was seized on mainly by Republicans, who moved the debate far to the right – to outright elimination of a right to assistance. After the Republicans captured the House of Representatives in 1994, President Clinton in 1996 signed a Republican welfare bill that was much more restrictive and less generous that his own, unsuccessful, plan.

US Democrats wanted to make AFDC more like unemployment insurance – a short-term benefit to help claimants 'get on their feet' but pushing all into the labour market with the stick of short benefit duration and the carrot of job training, day care subsidies and health insurance. Some still pursue this at the state level. But the main focus of the Clinton administration has been on 'making work pay' for women as well as for men through enhancing the EITC, increasing the minimum wage, and extending the minimum wage to now-working welfare recipients.

Both visions of reform are premised on imposing the logic of the market on all citizens. Those segments of the populace that do not receive any government welfare (whatever other government largesse they may enjoy) – that is, a large majority of the non-elderly – must depend on their capacities in the labour market to gain access to valued resources, including health benefits. It is here that the residualism of US provision for those of working age has its political effects. There is widespread sentiment that mothers as well as fathers 'must' work in order to have a decent lifestyle and to support children. It is this compulsion which is to be extended to welfare recipients.

Feminism's influence on welfare reform is contested, and complex, due in part to the coincidence of the end of the entitlement to social assistance and the shift from supporting mothers as full-time caregivers to expecting their employment. Organised feminists almost all opposed the specific legislation which eliminated AFDC, although many legislators allied with women's equality forces did not oppose the bill. But there were – and continue to be – differences over whether full-time caregiving should be preserved as an option within welfare, or whether social assistance should move women towards employment with greater public support (for example, child care and health insurance). To what extent do feminists partake in the dominant assumptions about the market? Some who support a modern-day 'maternalist' approach (that is, full-time caregiving as an option) have blamed mainstream liberal feminism and its emphasis on paid employment for helping to undercut an entitlement to social assistance for single mothers (see Mink 1995). Others would separate the issues of the social right to assistance – a safety net – from expectations about employment for caregivers, but here there is at least partial agreement that it is reasonable to expect participation in the labour market, if there are proper supports (see Bergmann and Hartmann 1995).

Esping-Andersen has argued that in liberal regimes 'concerns of gender matter less than the sanctity of the market' (1990: 28). Historically, this has not been true. All four of the countries examined deliberately created gender differentiation and tolerated gender inequality within their systems of social provision. Women's access to benefits that might support an autonomous household was and is hedged in with racial, gendered and class-based restrictions, but to the extent that it has existed and has been generalised to all single mothers, it is premised on women's – or at least mothers' – exclusion from the compulsion of proletarianisation. The sanctity of motherhood has shielded women from the sanctity of the market. This continues to be the case formally in Australia and Britain and informally in Canada, although motherhood is no longer defined as a lifelong occupation. There is an ongoing redefinition of the proper gender division of labour to include women's paid labour, but caregiving is still to be supported. Only in the United States, then, does the market really matter more than 'concerns of gender', at least as those concerns have been invoked to protect mothers of young children from the compulsion to sell their labour power in order to survive.

The more coercive work requirements in the United States versus the others are likely related to the different ways in which welfare politics have been racialised (Quadagno 1994). Australian, Canadian and British sole parent pensioners are overwhelmingly white, while a majority of US claimants are African-American or Latina; white women were a significant proportion of AFDC recipients, but for various reasons had less public visibility and were less likely than racial minority mothers to be on the program for long periods (United States Department of Health and Human Services Office of Family Assistance 1991: 6; Bane 1988). US women of colour have been subject to requirements about combining motherhood and paid work that have differed historically from those applying to whites (Bell 1965; Collins 1990; Glenn 1992). The standards applicable to women of colour are being made requirements for all, a trend reinforced by the increasing proportions of all women in the labour force. African-American family forms, understood as 'matriarchal', and which do differ from idealised traditional forms, were targets of criticism in the welfare debates (Franklin 1997). US media paid disproportionate attention to the long-term 'dependency' of primarily African-American and Latina women. Yet there is a greater problem of social exclusion and economic deprivation in the United States, reflected in high rates of reliance on welfare, tied to the history of racial discrimination and racial labour markets, as well as to higher levels of economic inequality. Analogous problems exist in Australia and Canada – indigenous populations in both countries are terribly deprived and marginalised, but they form a very small proportion of the population and, moreover, are geographically concentrated away from the biggest urban centres. Meanwhile, Ann Phoenix (1996) has argued that in Britain, race has not been a notable feature of the discourse on welfare as black women were not even considered 'true' British citizens.

The differences in the ways the four states support the capacity to form and maintain an autonomous household also reflect overall differences in the gender division of labour, as discussed in Chapter 3. We see a pattern of stronger traditional arrangements in Australia and Britain than in North America, with somewhat higher rates of housewifery and higher rates of part-time versus full-time paid work for all women and more deeply institutionalised supports for breadwinners. Thus, Australia and Britain, despite recent changes, still offer single mothers the capacity to maintain an autonomous household without participation in the labour market for a certain period of their children's lives. The United States requires that all who want to maintain a household obtain the means of supporting that household through the market. While Canadian policy is moving towards greater work requirements, it has not as yet gone as far towards all-encompassing commodification as has the United States, as is evidenced in various anti-poverty programs serving both employed and unemployed people (Myles and Pierson 1997). For many women in both the United States

Table 4.2: Family Types, 1991 (Percentages)

	Couples without children	Couples with children	Single fathers	Single mothers
Australia	31.0	43.0	1.2	7.8
Canada	32.7	54.6	2.3	10.4
United Kingdom	39.2	47.2	1.9	11.7
USA	40.9	38.3	4.4	16.5
Denmark	39.5	47.2	2.1	11.2
Finland	50.0	43.0	1.0	6.0
France	36.9	52.9	1.5	8.7
Germany	38.1	50.4	1.8	9.7
Italy	23.3	66.3	3.0	7.5
Netherlands	36.1	53.7	2.4	7.7
Norway	45.1	43.8	1.9	9.2
Sweden	53.5	38.0	1.2	7.2

Notes: 'Children' refers to children from 0 to 15 years old living in the household. For Canada the data are from 1986. For France, Norway, Sweden and the United States the data refer to 1990.

Sources: Eurostat 1995; Census of Canada 1991.

and Canada, the market – particularly since it has been subjected to equal opportunity regulation – does offer wages capable of sustaining independent households. Although the US state does not support women's capacity to form and maintain autonomous households through generous social provision, the market coupled with anti-discrimination and a very residual system of social provision has both allowed and forced a great many women to be independent of men. Among these four liberal countries, despite the lack of public social support, the United States has the highest rates of single motherhood, at 28 per cent of all families with children, compared with 20 per cent in Britain, 15 per cent in Canada and 14 per cent in Australia, and divorce, with 21 divorces per 1000 married women per year, compared with between 11 and 13 per 1000 in the other three countries (see also Table 4.2). But for the poorest women, whose likely husbands are unable to support families (Wilson 1997) and who themselves tend to have poor earning capacities, the market offers little and the state is offering less and less (see, for example, Jencks and Edin 1995); market-generated stratification is creating increased differentiation among women, helping to create schisms among those who would promote women's equality politically.

CHAPTER 5

Body Rights, Social Rights and Reproductive Choice

The comparative study of welfare states has given surprisingly little attention to the role of the state in the sexual and reproductive lives of its citizens. This omission is particularly remarkable in such a long-standing, and nationally significant, area of public intervention in private life. Historically welfare states have concerned themselves with maternal and child health; with birth legitimacy and the moral character of the unwed mother; with natalism, eugenics and the peopling of the nation; and with the regulation of contraception, abortion, adoption, wet-nursing, homosexuality and incest. Maternal and child health and welfare services have their origins in the same period as the first old-age pensions and unemployment assistance, and were shaped in the same historical conditions of industrialisation and democratisation. Recent scholarship points to women's civic and religious movements as critical forces behind their development (Lewis 1980; Reiger 1985; Michel and Koven 1990).

The field is as fit as others for comparative inquiry. Like other social policy institutions, maternal and child health arrangements are historical constructions, differentially shaped by time and place, politics and culture. That the participation of women and women's groups in their development has been more active than in other social policy institutions might seem to suggest distinctive sources of variation among countries, and the possibility of types different from those based on social rights for workers, such as age pensions and unemployment insurance. However, there is also evidence that their contours may be similar. In one of the few comparative studies to date, Sonya Michel and Seth Koven (1990) identify differences in the early development of maternal and child welfare provision in 'weak' (Great Britain and the United States) and 'strong' (France and Germany) states, arguing that women had greater influence in the weak states. Lewis (1994) argues that Michel and Koven confuse the weakness of the British state with its decentralisation, so that women were active participants in its local and voluntary reaches but not in the building of its central institutions. She does not dispute its difference from the stronger and more unitary states of continental Europe. The overall picture is that while women's organisations played a critical role in getting the needs of mothers and children onto the political agenda, the scope and development of services which eventuated depended on wider characteristics of the welfare state.

Hernes (1987: 51–71) has seen 'reproduction going public' in the post-war period. Writing of Scandinavia, she refers most directly to care work and social reproduction, but her phrase also aptly describes the politicisation of needs associated with biological reproduction. Since the 1960s welfare states have faced new demands ranging from the support of contraceptive services to, currently, the use of advanced technology, such as in vitro fertilisation and surrogate parenthood. This chapter is concerned with one such service, abortion, and what it can tell us about the development of the liberal welfare states of Australia, Great Britain, Canada and the United States.

Reproduction covers a broad range of welfare state activities and functions. Abortion proves a particularly interesting case study. Its choice is at first sight paradoxical, for it is the negation of reproduction. At the same time, women's movements have supported its availability as part of the reproductive autonomy essential to women's freedom in modern society. Abortion is particularly interesting for the present study because it presents a challenge to liberal ideology with respect to woman's individual personhood.

The notion of individual rights is quintessentially liberal. The ideology of possessive individualism (Macpherson 1962) centres on the proposition that the individual is the rightful possessor of his or her bodily capacities. While such rights have been most commonly associated with the capacity to work for wages, possessive individualism has a potentially wider reference to men and women as possessors of their bodily capacities in sexuality and human reproduction (Pateman 1989). The assertion that a woman has the right to control her own body is a clear statement of her proprietorship in her person, and the right to choose an expression of her free will. These claims assume an essential individualism in which the woman properly acts in the pursuit of her own needs and wishes. Her rightful action is limited only by the freedom of others to do likewise. The question of reproductive rights raises the question of women's equality in liberal society in particularly acute form, for it pits her claim to equality as a possessive individual against her connectedness to others.

Contemporary women's movements claim reproductive rights of this liberal kind. They have argued that such rights are essential pre-conditions for women's full participation in paid employment and public life, and that the lack of them is a source of unchosen depend-ence on husbands. The demand for a right to abortion is particularly problematic, for the discourse of rights in turn raises issues about how a woman's rights are limited by the potential rights of others. Political conflict over the right to abortion has been waged in precisely these terms.

Liberal welfare states have produced similar debates over the politic-ally contentious area of women's rights to reproductive choice. Peter Taylor-Gooby (1991) notes two important features of the liberal welfare state type. Its limitations, deriving from its formation without the achievement of a class alliance, tend to perpetuate a continuing class struggle, but one waged among individuals through the market. He suggests that citizenship demands are instead channelled through the law, as claims to legal rights and legal equality, and also as the entitle-ments of individuals. This has been true of liberal movements for reproductive rights. Using the language of citizenship, they have sought civil rights to autonomy in the exercise of reproductive functions, and social rights to the support of the welfare state in access to the medical services necessary for the expression of these rights. Opposition too has been framed by liberal discourse. The claim to a civil right to abortion has been met by counter claims about the competing rights of the foetus, of a male sexual partner, and of the parents of a pregnant minor. Claims to social rights in support of abortion services have further evoked responses about the moral rights of medical personnel and of taxpayers.

There is significant common ground for comparing the development of abortion services in these four countries. They share a majority cultural heritage, and the legal heritage of British common law. The political forces active in abortion politics, including medical professions and women's and anti-abortion movements, are aware of and in touch with one another. Given these similarities, one might expect similar development of abortion rights and services in these countries. At the same time, though, there are also notable differences between them. One of these is religious culture, Canada having large Catholic constituencies and the United States active traditions of religious fundamentalism. There are also important legal differences, in that the two North American countries have written constitutions affirming the

rights of citizenship and traditions of judicial activism in the interpretation of such rights.

Abortion rights are matters of law and culture. Abortion services,
where legal, are subject to medical authority, with access gained through
the health care system. Significantly for the present discussion, the
British welfare state is often distinguished from the others by a commitment to social democratic universalism in key sectors (Taylor-Gooby
1991). In fact the health systems of three of these countries, Australia,
Britain and Canada, contain important elements of universalism, while
the American health care system does not. These differences bear upon
the way these governments have responded to the abortion issue.

All four countries have seen significant change to abortion law since
the late 1960s. Legal changes have gone furthest in North America,
where abortion in the first trimester of pregnancy has come to have the
status of a right. In all countries, too, the reform, repeal and decriminalisation of abortion has aroused intense engagement of groups both
supporting and opposing women's access to abortion. In some countries
this politicisation of the abortion question has been turned against the
social rights of the welfare state, and the four countries vary substantially
in the support available to a woman seeking legal abortion.

Body Rights, Social Rights

Following Marshall (1950), reproductive rights may be understood as a
form of citizenship in which civil, political and social rights are entailed.
These forms of right are interdependent and held in an unstable
equilibrium in the institutions of a democratic-welfare-capitalist society
(Taylor-Gooby 1991). There is no necessary complementarity between
the three dimensions of citizenship, and indeed in the case of abortion
there is acute tension between them.

The establishment of a civil right to abortion makes the service a
legitimate commodity for trade, subject to the consent of medical
authority. In turn, civil rights create the basis upon which claims may be
made for the state to replace the market with a minimum standard of
access to services, a social right to secure an abortion. The importance
of civil rights is here twofold, for civil rights also define group interests
and solidarities in the expression of political rights. In the case of
abortion, the political mobilisation around the recognition of reproductive rights has drawn less upon class than upon medical and other
professional interests, religion, morality, and the changing position of
women in paid employment and in the family. Coming after the formation of the modern welfare state, both civil and social rights to abortion
have been the subject of intense political contestation.

In British common law abortion is a criminal act, with exceptions permitted in specified circumstances. In many countries the direction of legal change has been for these circumstances to be broadened, from risk to the life of the mother to risk to her physical and mental health. The effect of these changes is to make abortion legal in certain defined circumstances, framing it as a legitimate form of medical treatment. Here the notion of right attaches to abortion only in the sense of a more general right to health care needs as judged by medical authority, and we refer to this as 'medical entitlement' to abortion. In some countries, however, abortion has been given the status of personal right, attached not to medical need but to the legal personhood of the woman. Her claim to abortion thus rests on her rights as an individual secure from the interference of the state. We refer to this as a 'body right' to abortion.

As in previous chapters, we see social rights to assistance in sexual and reproductive life as operating at the nexus of state, market and family, and these services as differentially structured as public entitlements or provided under market or market-like arrangements. Social rights to abortion services bear most directly on women's decisions about when and under what conditions they will undertake parenthood and caregiving responsibilities, and the role of economic and market factors in constraining such decisions. Such rights also have consequences in terms of personal autonomy and class and gender stratification. Control over her reproductive capacities supports a woman's ability to maintain employment and to function outside the economic dependence of marriage or to limit her dependence within it. Thus a social right to abortion bears upon women's position in the sexual division of labour both in the home and in the public economy. The availability of abortion, free or at low cost, is part of the wider decommodification of health care services, and in this general sense makes the citizen more independent of the market economy than would otherwise be the case. However, these connections are less direct than in the case of social rights to welfare state support for employment and as income maintenance, and their effects are relatively weak. Moreover, the need for abortion occurs only at a point in time, and is experienced as highly personal.

When abortion is legal, a social right to the termination of pregnancy at little or no cost is unlikely to have significant independent effects on social stratification, but the lack of such a right may be expected to compound more general market disadvantage. Social rights are, however, likely to have considerable significance for women's autonomy within marriage and for young women's independence of parental authority. Social rights are thus of great significance for the individuation of women within the gender order of the family. Hence, the primary importance of a social right to abortion lies in its underpinning of a woman's personhood and autonomy, which are the foundation for her participation in social and economic life.

Body Rights in the Liberal States

Abortion prior to quickening was legal under the British common law in the nineteenth century, but was brought under regulation by the twentieth (Ginsburg 1989: 43–57; Petersen 1996: 80–1). The British Offences Against the Person Act of 1861 removed any distinction of foetal age, but in 1929 the Infant Life (Preservation) Act opened the way for abortion to preserve the life of the mother. This ground was broadened in the 1938 decision of *R v Bourne*, in which preservation of the life of the mother was extended to include circumstances in which she would be made a 'physical or mental wreck' if made to carry the child (Mason 1990: 101–2). The move to further widen the grounds for abortion began in Britain in the 1950s, and was under way in all four countries by the late 1960s. The first wave of liberalisation extended the medical grounds under which abortion was permitted to include the physical and mental health of the woman, and in some cases also foetal abnormality.

A number of common factors underlay the move to reform abortion laws. Among these were consumption economies which by the 1960s were drawing married women into paid employment. In their different ways both commercial advertising and radical cultural movements emphasised pleasure and autonomy in personal life. Behavioural changes included more widespread non-marital sex and a reshaping of the life cycle. Improved birth control technology, especially the pill, played an important part in these developments, and at the same time generated higher expectations about the control of fertility. Medical professions found the abortion issue increasingly problematic, while illegal abortion was known to be widespread. Women's movements raised the consciousness of women about their right to equality with men, and argued that sexual freedom and the control of fertility were critical to women's individual autonomy. Finally, political climates were favourable to the liberalisation of law in areas of personal and sexual life. Laws were passed in several countries decriminalising suicide and homosexuality and abolishing capital punishment. The need for abortion law reform was brought to popular attention by the case of Sherri Finkbine, an American woman who sought an abortion after having taken Thalidomide. A rubella epidemic in the same period also served to awaken women's consciousness about abortion.

Liberalisation and Medical Entitlement

The first wave of change in abortion law began in Britain and established a degree of medical entitlement in all four countries by the early 1970s. The British campaign was spearheaded by the Abortion Law Reform Association, a left-leaning single-issue group led largely by élite women. As grounds for law reform, it cited public opinion in favour of change, medical confusion about existing law, and the widespread illegal sale of abortifacients. Major medical groups opposed radical change in the law but conceded the need for a degree of revision, concurring with the Church of England that abortion should remain a medical decision.

The Abortion Act 1967 permitted abortion when, in the opinion of two doctors, it was necessary to protect the physical or mental health of the woman, with the health ground very broadly defined. The degree of risk to the woman's health was defined as circumstances in which the risk to her life or health was greater by continuing the pregnancy than by terminating it. The effect of this provision was to make abortion available in the normal circumstances of early pregnancy (Francome 1984: ch. 4). The Infant Life (Preservation) Act had set twenty-eight weeks as the point at which a foetus was assumed to be 'capable of being born alive'. In 1974 the time limit was reduced to twenty-four weeks. In 1990 abortion was brought under the supervision of the Human Fertilisation and Embryology Authority, under the Human Fertilisation and Embryology Act. This Act defines specific grounds on which abortion may be permitted. These are that the continuation of pregnancy would involve risk of injury to the physical or mental health of the pregnant woman or any existing children of her family; that an abortion is necessary to prevent grave permanent injury to her physical or mental health; that continuation of pregnancy would involve risk to her life; or that there is a substantial risk that if the child were born it would suffer from serious physical or mental abnormalities. The first of these grounds applies only in the first twenty-four weeks of gestation and permits the consideration of social factors in the assessment of health. The Act makes provision for the use of the abortifacient RU-486, and this drug is now marketed in England (Petersen 1993: 109–28; Petersen 1996: 84–9).

The British Act was quickly followed by reforms in both Australia and Canada. In Australia abortion is governed by the laws of the separate states. During the 1960s abortion law reform groups were established in all states, campaigning in association with civil liberties and progressive church organisations. Abortion law reform predated the involvement of a rising women's movement (Coleman 1988: 76).

In 1969 South Australia passed an act closely modelled on the British Act. The law went beyond the guidelines of the Australian Medical Association at the time (Siedlecky and Wyndham 1990: 79). In Victoria and New South Wales liberalisation came via judicial decision, in Victoria after a bitter campaign to expose police corruption and in New South Wales in a prosecution aimed at pre-empting the exposure of corruption (Coleman 1988: 78–80; Petersen 1996: 88–90). The Menhennit ruling in Victoria (in *R v Davidson* 1969) and the Levine judgment (in *R v Wald* 1971) in New South Wales were based on the *Bourne* case, and allowed broad interpretation of health grounds. These rulings quickly gave wider access than under the South Australian legislation, effectively establishing abortion on request, mainly through free-standing clinics in those states. The legality of abortion has been less clear in other states, but practice has generally followed the models established in South Australia, Victoria and New South Wales. In early 1998 moves to reform abortion law in Western Australia were provoked by the arrest of two well-regarded doctors on the basis of a literal interpretation of the law. Medical and feminist groups joined in the reform campaign, with doctors withdrawing abortion services when the Parliament was deadlocked over the terms of legislation. Legislation was passed, making abortion legal in the first twenty weeks of gestation, with the informed consent of the woman. She must be offered counselling. Late abortions are subject to stringent limits.

A more limited liberalisation of abortion law was passed in Canada in 1969. The measure came as part of a wider reform package of the newly elected Trudeau Liberal Government, which also included measures legalising contraception, divorce and homosexuality. Initial impetus came from élite legal and medical organisations seeking to clarify the law in the light of contemporary practice. The Canadian legislation provided that an abortion would not be criminal if performed in an approved or accredited hospital and approved by a hospital 'therapeutic abortion committee' on the ground that continuation of the pregnancy would or would be likely to endanger the life or health of the woman. Hospital committee approval required the agreement of three doctors not including the doctor who was to perform the abortion.

In the United States, as in Australia, the medical regulation of abortion falls under the jurisdiction of the states. Attempts to clarify and liberalise state laws began in the early 1960s. In a detailed case study of abortion law reform in California, Luker (1984: ch. 4; see also Sollinger 1993) argues that the impulse to reform came largely from small groups of élite professionals in law and medicine. California statutes dating from 1849 made the procuring of a miscarriage a criminal offence except where necessary to preserve the woman's life. Medical opinion was increasingly divided between 'strict' and 'broad constructionists' of the law. The 1967 California reform law permitted abortion in an accredited hospital, subject to determination by the hospital's therapeutic abortion board that the pregnancy would 'gravely impair' the physical or mental health of the woman. By 1973 abortion reform statutes had been passed in one-third of all states.

Thus by the early 1970s all four countries had instituted legal provisions distinguishing therapeutic from criminal abortions. The effect of these reforms was to define therapeutic abortion as a legitimate form of medical treatment, subject to regulation by medical authorities and under medical (usually also hospital) control. These reforms, many of which did little more than bring the law in line with common practice, were outcomes of élite movements and typically included at least a degree of support from within the medical profession. In most cases reform preceded any significant participation by the women's movement or other popular political organisations.

As a form of medical care, access to legal abortion depended on the attitudes of individual doctors. In all countries medical decisions varied widely by region, and by the class and race of the woman. In much of the United States and Canada access also depended on the operation of hospital abortion committees and varied significantly from one hospital to another. In Canada, groups opposed to abortion captured control of hospital boards, and many Canadian hospitals declined even to establish committees. Abortion became most freely available in Britain and Australia, where medical grounds were quickly extended to include 'social' reasons and, where medical authority allowed, amounted to abortion upon the request of the woman. The California law had a similar effect: by 1970 virtually all women applying for abortions were being granted them (Luker 1984: 94).

Beyond Liberalisation: Body Rights

In the United States and Canada the move to liberalise medical regulation of abortion gave impetus to new movements among women for the repeal of abortion law and its decriminalisation. These movements claimed abortion as a woman's right, part of a wider set of rights to the control of her body and its reproductive functions. By 1988 abortion in the first trimester of pregnancy had attained a status of right to some degree in both countries.

In the United States an activist women's movement began to challenge the strategy of reform even before the passage of the California law (Luker 1984: ch. 5; Petchesky 1986: 125–32). National support came from the National Organization of Women and the National Association for Repeal of Abortion Law. By 1973 four states had passed repeal legislation, including a 1970 New York bill giving abortion on request in the first twenty-four weeks of pregnancy. The bill imposed no residency requirement (Francome 1984: 104–5).

The movement towards repeal culminated in the decisions of the United States Supreme Court in the paired cases of *Roe v Wade* and *Doe v Bolton*, commonly referred to together as *Roe v Wade*. The ground for the decision had been prepared by several cases immediately preceding it. In the 1965 case *Griswold v Connecticut*, concerning the use of contraceptive measures, the Court had recognised the existence of a constitutional right of privacy within marriage. This decision was extended to single persons in 1972, when the Court ruled that the marital couple were not an entity but two individuals each of whom had rights to privacy. In *Roe v Wade* the Court held that the right to privacy in marital and sexual life was broad enough to encompass a woman's right to decide whether to terminate her pregnancy. This right was by no means absolute, and the Court maintained that the decision did not entail an unlimited right to do with one's body as one pleases or to abortion on demand. The right to privacy also attached to the doctor–patient relationship. The Court held that the abortion decision in all its aspects is inherently and primarily a medical decision, and affirmed the right of the physician to administer medical treatment according to the doctor's professional judgement.

The interests of the state were found to be divided between that of preserving and protecting the health of the pregnant woman and that of protecting the potentiality of human life. The decision held that these interests were separate and distinct, each becoming 'compelling' at a different stage of pregnancy. The Court resolved these competing interests through a developmental, trimester framework. State regulation of abortion was unconstitutional during the first trimester. During the second, the state might intervene to protect the woman's health. In the third, associated with foetal viability, the state's interest in potential life could justify prohibition of abortion except when necessary to preserve the life or health of the mother. The decision in the accompanying case, *Doe v Bolton*, invalidated statutory requirements that abortions be performed only in accredited hospitals, but limited the performance of abortion to licensed physicians (Francome 1984: 122–7; Petchesky 1986: 289–95; Rodman, Sarvis and Bonar 1987: 102–3; E. Rubin 1987: ch. 3; Petersen 1993: 149–55). The Supreme Court decision invalidated virtually all state laws governing abortion, including legislation for both reform and repeal. With access no longer fettered by hospital restrictions, the way was cleared for the establishment of free-standing abortion clinics.

The rights conferred under the *Roe v Wade* decision are ambiguous. While the decision appears to entitle the pregnant woman to an abortion in the first trimester of pregnancy, such right is clearly mediated by the medical authority of the attending physician. The right is thus ambiguously a right of the woman to seek an abortion or a right of the doctor to practise medicine in accordance with his or her professional judgement. This right is further limited by the developing rights of the foetus, which become significant in the last trimester.

In Canada the liberalising reforms of 1969 also stimulated moves towards repeal and decriminalisation. The 1971 Report of the Royal Commission for the Status of Women had recommended abortion on request in the first twelve weeks of pregnancy, but the force of its position was weakened by substantial dissent from within (Jenson 1997b: 296–7). Further change came through an alliance between women's groups and liberal doctors. The central figure in Canadian abortion politics has been Dr Henry Morgentaler, a Montreal doctor. When the 1969 reform law proved ineffective in making abortion available to Canadian women, Morgentaler provided abortions from a Montreal clinic without the required accreditation and committee certification. He was arrested for the first time in 1970 and repeatedly for more than a decade thereafter, serving a prison sentence in 1975. By the 1980s, abortion had become a widely accepted aspect of medical practice in Quebec (Jenson 1997b: 302).

The history of Morgentaler's jury acquittals and judicial convictions on appeal over nearly two decades is intertwined with Canadian constitutional development and the aspirations of the women's movement to secure constitutional support for women's right to equality. In 1975 the Supreme Court of Canada declined to recognise abortion as protected under the 1959 Bill of Rights. It faced the issue again in 1986 when Morgentaler and two others appealed convictions to the Supreme Court on the grounds that the 1969 abortion law was inconsistent with the Canadian Charter of Rights and Freedoms. In 1988, in *Morgentaler v Canada*, the Court ruled the law unconstitutional because it violated a woman's right to 'life, liberty and the security of the person'. Three majority judgments agreed that in delaying abortion or making it practically unavailable the 1969 law was detrimental to the health of the woman, and that this was a violation of her security of person. In considering the competing interest of the state in the protection of the foetus, the judgments found that the delays and procedures employed were disproportionately harmful and hence not reasonable limits to the rights of the woman (Day and Persky 1988: 180–95; Mandel 1989: 273–307; Campbell and Pal 1989: 197–200; Tatalovich 1997: 73–9).

The effect of the decision was to decriminalise abortion at the national level. An attempt to enact new legislation governing abortion was defeated on a tied vote of the Senate in 1991. The bill proposed that abortion remain within the criminal law but be permitted when performed by a medical practitioner on broad health grounds. It had been opposed by both pro-life groups, who thought it too permissive, and pro-choice groups, who objected to the recriminalisation of abortion. The opposition by doctors was decisive. Fearing criminal liability under the new law, they withdrew from abortion work in large numbers (Brodie 1992; Tatalovich 1997: 83–95). In the stalemate that has followed *Morgentaler*, Canada continues to have no federal law governing abortion. The legal vacuum has been filled by provincial governments using their powers to regulate and fund health care (discussed further below).

Several writers (Jenson 1992: 26; Gavigan 1992: 118; Tatalovich 1997: 78) distinguish the status of abortion in Canada from the rightful status given it by *Roe v Wade* in the United States. They point out that the *Morgentaler* decision struck down the existing regulatory regime as violating the woman's security of person, but did not preclude its replacement by further legislation. In the legal vacuum that remains, abortion has been legitimised as a medical procedure, and women's right is mediated by medical authority. This distinction is a fine one. It is true that the Canadian Supreme Court has not affirmed access to abortion as a right of the woman in the same terms as given in *Roe v Wade*. The *Morgentaler* decision nevertheless clearly attached effective and timely access to abortion to women's right to security of person, and *Roe v Wade* as much as *Morgentaler* defined access to abortion as inherently and primarily a medical decision. On these arguments, it is clear that the right of Canadian women to abortion is closer to the body right of women in the United States than to the medical entitlement of Britain and Australia.

The Reaction to Liberalised Abortion

In all four countries, though to varying extent, the liberalisation of abortion law has served to crystallise opposition movements seeking to reverse the gains. The US Supreme Court decision in *Roe v Wade* brought a much stronger response than earlier reform legislation, and is widely credited with responsibility for the formation of the Right to Life movement.

In Britain, the Society for the Protection of the Unborn Child and the more extreme Catholic LIFE pursued parliamentary and activist campaigns to tighten the abortion law (Francome 1984: 158–82). Private

Member's bills to restrict grounds and reduce time limits have so far failed, but the maximum time period has been reduced from twenty-four to twenty weeks. In Australia initial opposition came from Catholic and Lutheran groups (Francome 1984: 149). The first Right to Life group was organised in 1970, and soon became active on a national level. This and other anti-abortion groups have continued to campaign for stricter laws governing abortion and for restrictions of other kinds, the campaign becoming extremely vocal in the 1980s. These groups are clearly associated with the American Right to Life organisation (Coleman 1988: 89; Siedlecky and Wyndham 1990: 97). A number of Private Member's bills have been introduced to state and federal legislatures without success. Since its election in 1996, the conservative Liberal–National Party Government has often depended on the vote of an independent senator, Brian Harradine, for the majority necessary to pass legislation through the Upper House. Deeply opposed to abortion, he has been influential in government decisions to ban the abortion pill RU-486 and to exclude family planning assistance from Australia's foreign aid programs. While the federal health minister, a doctor, has unequivocally ruled out change in federal policy on abortion, both Catholic organisations and feminist groups have recently begun to mobilise (H. Pringle 1997: 108; Wainer 1997), prompted by the case of *CES v Superclinics (Australia) Pty Ltd* (1995), in which a woman sued doctors for failing to diagnose her unwanted pregnancy and hence denying her the opportunity to seek an abortion. In the first hearing of the case the judge found for her but ruled that she was not entitled to damages because abortion was an illegal act.

In Canada anti-abortion feeling mounted in response to the repeated challenges of Morgentaler, who was seen as flouting the law as well as taking human life. Pro-life groups have been active in political lobbying and in the streets and clinic doorways. Opposition to the decision in *Morgentaler* has been spearheaded by a series of constitutional challenges. In *Tremblay v Daigle* 1989 a putative father sought an injunction to stop his former partner having an abortion. The case was lost, the judges ruling that the legislature had not intended to confer the status of legal person upon the foetus. Catholic crusader Joe Borowski has mounted a series of cases maintaining that the foetus is a person and thus has rights protected by law. These cases have been unsuccessful. The Saskatchewan Supreme Court ruled in 1984, and the Saskatchewan Court of Appeal upheld in 1987, that there is no existing basis in law justifying the conclusion that foetuses are legal persons (Mason 1990: 130; Brodie 1992: 95; Tatalovich 1997: 79–80; see also Shaffer 1994). In 1989, the Supreme Court of Canada declared the matter raised by Borowski moot following the *Morgentaler* decision.

American opposition to abortion, having begun among Catholic professionals, quickly came to include newly mobilised mass participation
by women with children, members of fundamentalist churches and
moral conservatives (Luker 1984: ch. 6). The movement mobilised
rapidly and began to apply many of the activist protest strategies of the
civil rights and women's movements. Politicised at the highest levels,
opposition to abortion has affected elections to the presidency and been
a prominent issue in presidential appointments to the Supreme Court.
Harassment and terrorism directed against the staff of abortion clinics
culminated in four deaths in 1994 (Gober 1997: 1010). Violence of this
kind also began to occur in Canada in the 1990s. In both countries
attempts to control pro-life groups' aggressive picketing and harassment
of clinics have led to further rounds of court action defining rights and
limits of free speech (Tatalovich 1997: 71–3, 221).

State governments responded to the decision in *Roe v Wade* with
legislation limiting and regulating abortion, some directly contradicting
the Supreme Court decision. Court challenges have resulted in a series
of decisions largely confirming *Roe v Wade*, but there has been a
tendency to fetter the abortion decision with limitations. The July 1992
decision in *Planned Parenthood of Southeastern Pennsylvania v Casey* interpreted *Roe v Wade* more narrowly than before and lowered the judicial
status the Court had previously given abortion as a right. It also
abandoned the trimester construction. A bare majority upheld the
central tenet of *Roe v Wade* that a woman has a right to choose abortion
up to the point of foetal viability. In that decision the Court ruled that
states may impose a number of conditions on abortion, including a
waiting period of twenty-four hours, notification of the parent of a
minor, and conditions establishing informed consent. The decision
ruled invalid the requirement that a woman notify her partner of her
intention to abort unless the legislation provided significant grounds for
the requirement to be waived (Petersen 1993: 156; Tatalovich 1997: 70).

In summary, legislative and judicial developments in these countries
over the last two decades have resulted in two bases for women to have
access to legal abortions: as a 'medical entitlement' and as a 'body right'.
In a comparative analysis of Australia, Britain, Denmark, New Zealand
and the United States, Kerry Petersen (1993: 100) distinguishes three
models for the legal regulation of abortion. Taken together, her first two
models correspond closely to the category of medical entitlement used
in the present analysis. In the abortion reform model, to which Britain,
New Zealand and, in Australia, the Northern Territory and South
Australia correspond, the original criminal statutes have been altered by
legislation providing for lawful abortion where the medical practitioner
believes appropriate grounds exist. In the judicial model, found in the

Australian states of Queensland, New South Wales and Victoria, lawful grounds within criminal statutes have been defined by judicial decision. Though the reform and judicial models are similar in practice, the judicial model gives abortion a less secure status because it leaves doctors vulnerable to prosecution. Petersen's elective model, to which Denmark and the United States correspond, removes abortion from the criminal law and confers a degree of right upon the woman.

In Britain and Australia abortion has become largely accepted as a legitimate medical treatment, part of the woman's entitlement to medical care. Access is mediated by medical authority, requiring in some jurisdictions the concurring opinion of two or more doctors. Medically justified grounds include not only physical but also mental health, the latter often acknowledging social factors affecting the well-being of the woman, her other children and the future circumstances of a foetus were it to be born. These grounds amount in many circumstances to abortion upon request, though it may matter a great deal to what medical authority the request is addressed. In the two countries of North America abortion has been given judicial endorsement as forming part of the rights of citizenship in liberal society, an expression of the woman's constitutional rights to individual freedom and personhood. The abortion decision is equally mediated by medical authority, the US right being ambiguously the right to privacy of the woman and the right to privacy of the medical consultation.

Abortion has been much more highly politicised in the countries of body right than of medical entitlement, where it has been sheltered by the claim of medical authorities to professional autonomy. The liberal politics of body right have exposed abortion to counter-mobilisation by coalitions of conservative forces responding to deeply rooted social change, most visibly in women's roles and family life. Much of the opposition has come from women defending the value of traditional family life. The abortion issue is believed, for example, to be responsible for the failure of the Equal Rights Amendment to the American Constitution (Luker 1984: 205; Petchesky 1986: 271; Ginsburg 1989).

Liberalism and the Rights of Others

The liberal ground of body right structures politics in the individualist terms of liberal ideology, and that ground has proved more vulnerable to a politics asserting the rights of others than has medical entitlement. There is a clear pattern in which those countries giving body rights to women also give more recognition to competing rights of others. The rights of medical personnel are similar in all countries and are not discussed here. There is little difference in the rights accorded to the husband or other male partner of the woman. More substantial differences are to be found in the implicit acknowledgement of foetal rights and the relative rights of a pregnant minor and her parents.

The rights of a husband or other male sexual partner to a role in the abortion decision have been asserted in a number of countries. To date these claims have not been accepted in any country, though Canada came close to doing so. They were denied in English cases in 1979 and 1987 (Mason 1990: 115–16), and most recently in the July 1992 decision of the United States Supreme Court. Greatest recognition has been given in Canada, where under the 1969 law two-thirds of hospital abortion committees required the consent of the husband and some also required the consent of the male responsible for the pregnancy of a single woman. In 1981 the Ontario Supreme Court ruled that foetuses and natural fathers had rights, drawing upon the 'birth for benefit' provision of Scottish law giving rights of inheritance to a foetus subsequently born alive (Mason 1990: 130). This decision was subsequently overturned, and the consent requirements of hospital abortion committees invalidated in the judgment of the Supreme Court of Canada in 1988 in *Morgentaler*. Two cases have been brought since then, in both of which putative fathers have sought injunctions to prevent abortions. In each case the injunction was granted but subsequently reversed on appeal (Brodie 1992: 91–6; Gavigan 1992: 133–40).

In none of these countries has the foetus been given legal recognition as a person, though such cases have been brought before the courts repeatedly in all four. There is, however, an implicit right of the foetus expressed in the limitation of the abortion of a potentially viable foetus to circumstances in which the woman's life or physical health is jeopardised. Thus British law limits abortion on lesser grounds to the first twenty-four weeks of pregnancy. In the United States, tacit recognition of the potential rights of the foetus was formalised in the trimester framework of *Roe v Wade*. Similarly, in Canada, majority opinion in *Morgentaler* held that the law had a valid purpose in the protection of foetal life. In the United States the right to life of the viable foetus has been strengthened by a 1989 Supreme Court Decision in *Webster v Reproductive Health Services* permitting states to require a test for viability of any foetus believed to be of twenty or more weeks gestation. The opposition of 'foetal rights' to the rights of the woman has been claimed to justify extensive intervention in the lives of pregnant or potentially pregnant women. Cynthia Daniels (1993) reviews arguments on behalf of foetal rights in cases involving the forced medical treatment of a pregnant woman, criminal prosecution of a drug-addicted pregnant woman, and the attempt to exclude women from certain types of jobs because of their fertile status.

The vulnerability of body rights to the competing claims of others is clearest in the conflict between the rights of a pregnant minor and those of her parents. In Britain and Australia the right of a minor to abortion is treated in the more general context of consent to medical treatment and is defined as a matter of medical discretion. The *Gillick* case (*Gillick v West Norfolk and Wisbech Area Health Authority and the Department of Health and Social Security* 1986) in Britain provides the precedent in both countries. This case concerned the right of public authorities to give contraceptive advice to a minor without the consent of the parent, and resulted in a House of Lords ruling that the doctor might do so where the minor was able to understand the nature and consequences of the procedure and after having attempted to persuade her to involve her parents (Mason 1990: 50–2). In contrast, the issue continues to be heavily politicised in the United States. *Roe v Wade* having left the issue undecided, a 1976 Supreme Court decision invalidated blanket pro-visions requiring parental consent to the abortion of a 'mature minor'. Subsequent judgments have elaborated the principle that states may require that parents be notified or consulted providing the minor has the freedom to seek approval by a court before such notification. The court may determine either that she is sufficiently mature and well-informed to make her own decision or that an abortion would be in her best interests. The Supreme Court decision of July 1992 permitted states to require parental notification, but continues to require an alternative route through the courts.

Whatever rights are ostensibly theirs, women in all four countries must exercise such rights in and through the medical profession. The terms of the decision are thus finally not those of the woman herself but of medical ethics and the autonomy of medical practice. As Kerry Petersen (1996: 99) observes, women's secondary position denies them recognition as responsible and moral decision-makers. While broader questions of gender and power in medical practice are beyond the scope of this book, it is important to note how centrally these issues condition women's actual experience of seeking and having an abortion. Also not explored here are circumstances in which women's rights to the control of their fertility are limited not by the denial of abortion but by its imposition. Policies of this kind have commonly operated with respect to certain groups of women deemed to be unfit mothers, including the very young and women with physical and in-tellectual disabilities. It is also important to note the discriminatory use of health and welfare services, including abortion, contraception and sterilisation, with and without the consent of the woman, to control fertility among some racial and immigrant groups (Daniels 1993; Roberts 1997).

Social Rights to Abortion

Whether legalised as medical entitlement or body right, access to medically legitimate abortion has caused markets in illegal services largely to disappear in all four countries (Francome 1988: 463; Siedlecky 1988: 25; Tietze, Forrest and Henshaw 1988: 482; Sachdev 1988a: 72). At the same time, the numbers of abortions being performed have increased significantly since the 1960s. It has been estimated that in the early years after legalisation in the United States some two-thirds of legal abortions replaced formerly illegal procedures (Jaffe, Lindheim and Lee 1981: 13–14). After steep rises in the first decade after legalisation, rates in Britain and Australia appear to have been stable since the early 1980s. Abortion rates in the United States have declined slowly over that period (Gober 1997).

Abortion rates differ strikingly in the countries under consideration. Abortion is almost twice as frequent in the United States as in the other three countries. In the mid-1980s there were 28 abortions per 1000 women aged 15 to 44 years. Within that country, rates are almost twice as high among black and minority women as among white women. This compares with 16.6 abortions per 1000 women aged 15 to 44 in Australia, 14.2 in England and Wales, and 10.2 in Canada in the late 1980s (Henshaw 1990: 85). The figure for Canada does not include abortions performed outside hospitals, that is, in clinics or doctors' surgeries. Paul Sachdev (1988a) estimates that these increase the rate to 11.2. Reflecting the situation before the 1988 decision in *Morgentaler*, even this corrected figure does not necessarily represent the present situation in Canada. While birth rates also vary among these countries, the magnitude of differences is much smaller. In 1995 crude birth rates per 1000 population were thirteen in the United Kingdom, fourteen in Canada and Australia, and fifteen in the United States (World Health Organization 1995).

Medically regulated in all four countries, the provision of abortion services has tended to be shaped by the health care system into which it has been absorbed. Thus the effective availability of abortion services depends on the way in which health care is organised and the role of the welfare state in supporting the facilities and expertise required. The important dimensions for the social distribution of access to abortion are the scope and form of public provision and the division of health care into public and market sectors, the working of the system in giving access to abortion within the permitted time period, and the role of medical regulation in the operation of hospitals and free-standing abortion clinics. Together these determine the availability of a social right to a minimum standard of access to abortion services.

Taylor-Gooby (1991: 96) notes that elements of social democratic universalism make Britain anomalous in the group of liberal welfare states. In actuality the health care systems of virtually all liberal welfare states contain such social democratic elements, with universalist principles underlying those of three of the four considered here. Only in the United States is the social right to medical care based on classically liberal, class-divided arrangements.

Universalism in health care provision takes two forms, the direct provision of health services by public authorities, as in the British National Health Service, and indirect support through universal compulsory insurance, as in Canada and Australia. Both forms make health care available to all citizens at little or no direct cost, but they differ in their relation to markets for medical services. While direct provision replaces the private market with public services, the insurance model delivers public support through the private market.

The first wave of medical legitimation of abortion largely limited the procedure to hospitals and the hospital framework of medical authority. Campaigns to widen access to abortion have in a number of countries included challenges to this limitation, including the establishment of free-standing clinics for first trimester abortions. Set up by private philanthropic and commercial bodies, these clinics provide low-cost services and are organised to facilitate processes of medical authorisation.

In Britain the extension of therapeutic abortion under the 1967 Abortion Act was directly assimilated into the hospital services of the pre-existing National Health Service (NHS). Effective access to NHS abortion services depends both on the working of the NHS system in general, including its patterns of appointments and waiting lists, and on resistances by medical authority reflecting covert opposition to abortion. A woman seeking an abortion under the NHS must attend the general practitioner with whom she is registered and request referral to a specialist gynaecologist. If her termination is approved it will be performed in hospital without cost to her. The most significant factor affecting the availability of an NHS abortion is the attitude of senior gynaecologists, and there is marked variability from region to region on this account. There are also repeated and lengthy delays which, when compounded by the uncertainty of medical approval, make many women seek abortions outside the NHS. Because of these factors less than half of all terminations are provided through the public health system. Abortion is thus an exception to the general pattern of NHS services in England and Wales, in which well over 90 per cent of care is provided by the NHS. This proportion was stable over a decade from the early 1970s to the early 1980s (Paintin 1985: 7–9).

Commercial and non-profit services provide the remainder of terminations in about equal proportions, mainly from fee-charging abortion clinics. These clinics advertise, accept self-referred patients, and provide services within two to five days at relatively low cost. A first trimester abortion in a private clinic currently costs £320 or more (Marie Stopes International 1997). Some clinics reduce fees for women unable to pay the full charge.

In Australia abortion was quickly accommodated within the established system of health care funding, but that system itself has been the subject of political contention. Universal compulsory health insurance was reinstated in 1983, and provides general practitioner and public hospital treatment at little or no cost to the patient. The health system permits the patient free choice of doctor outside hospital. As numbers of abortions have risen many hospitals have imposed quotas on the numbers performed (Siedlecky 1988: 26). This limit has had most severe consequences in South Australia, where the first free-standing clinic was established only in 1992. Most abortions are provided in clinics, where a first trimester abortion currently costs about $A170 to the patient after collection of the insurance rebate. About 10 per cent of eligible clients do not claim the rebate, usually to ensure privacy, and these women face total charges of about $A300 (NHMRC 1996: 3–5). Opposition to abortion in Australia has more frequently been directed to legal restriction than to the denial of public funding. Moves to remove abortion from the schedule of insurance benefits were defeated in 1979 and 1989 (Siedlecky and Wyndham 1990). In practice abortions remain difficult to secure in some states, particularly Queensland and Tasmania (Ryan and Ripper 1993; NHMRC 1996).

The US health system is a patchwork of arrangements applying to different social groups. The largest part of the population is covered by private insurance, usually provided as a fringe benefit of employment. By 1983 some 63 per cent of the population had private insurance (Gilbert and Gilbert 1989: 124–5). Most private insurers cover abortion, but it is common for this to be a part of maternity coverage, which is often an expensive optional supplement and is not always offered to unmarried employees and dependants (Jaffe, Lindheim and Lee 1981: 52). A means-tested public insurance program, Medicaid, covers a further 10 per cent of the population who have very low incomes. Medicaid is a joint federal–state program in which states must meet federal requirements to qualify for federal funds. Entitlements vary significantly from state to state. Some 15 per cent of Americans have only partial or no insurance cover from either public or private sources. Some of these are low-income workers who do not qualify for Medicaid, while others live in areas where Medicaid benefits are unavailable (Gilbert and Gilbert 1989: 126).

In the period following *Roe v Wade* the provision of social rights to abortion has been rapidly and heavily politicised. The decision evoked campaigns to put limits on the public funding of abortion services. A 1977 Supreme Court decision in *Beal v Doe* ruled that a state might restrict funding under the Medicaid program to medically necessary abortions. In the same year Congress passed the *Hyde Amendment* precluding the use of Medicaid funds for any abortion except where the life of the mother would be endangered, and the Supreme Court subsequently upheld the restriction. Both Houses of Congress voted to retain this limitation in 1993.

In *Roe v Wade* the Supreme Court had not found grounds for a right to abortion in the equal protection provisions of the American Constitution. In a 1977 case, *Roe v Maher*, the Court focused again on the constitutional question of the right to abortion. It held that because a woman could turn to a private source of support without state interference, a state's policy to deny Medicaid support for elective abortions did not infringe her fundamental right to privacy (Rodman, Sarns and Bonar 1987: 115–16). In the language of rights, the Court divorced a civil right to abortion from a social right, holding that the Constitution did not confer a social right to a minimum standard of access.

In the first years after *Roe v Wade* some 25 per cent of all legal abortions had been funded through Medicaid. By 1978 the number funded through Medicaid had been reduced to 1 per cent of the previous figure (Rodman, Sarns and Bonar 1987: 115–16). Some states have continued to provide abortion funding, and these states account for by far the largest number of Medicaid-eligible women (Tietze, Forrest and Henshaw 1988: 476). It was estimated that of the women denied Medicaid-funded abortions in 1978, some 84 000 obtained them in the private sector, a maximum of 3000 obtained illegal abortions, and some 14 000 gave birth (Cates 1981).

The Reagan and Bush periods saw the White House instigate barriers to abortion in the bureaucratic machinery of the state. These measures extended constraints on abortion beyond Medicaid, applying to any form of federal financial support. Department of Health and Human Services regulations prohibited doctors and counsellors in federally funded clinics from discussing abortion with women. Food and Drug Administration regulations precluded the mention of abortion in information accompanying oral contraceptives. One of the first actions of the incoming Clinton administration was to remove some of these restrictions. It lifted the prohibition on abortion counselling in federally funded family planning clinics, rescinded the ban on foetal tissue research, and allowed women in the armed forces to obtain abortions at military hospitals, providing they were paid for privately (Tatalovich 1997: 176).

The most significant erosion of support came with the decision of the US Supreme Court in *Webster v Reproductive Health Services* in 1989. The case upheld a Missouri statute prohibiting the use of public employees or facilities for performing abortions not necessary to save the mother's life. The statute also prohibits the use of public funds, employees or facilities for the purpose of encouraging or counselling for an abortion unless necessary to save the mother's life. The definition of public funds or facilities is extremely broad, covering all public employees and private facilities receiving indirect public support. Raymond Tatalovich (1997: 70) regards this case as marking the turning point to narrow the woman's right to abortion conferred by *Roe v Wade*.

In the United States some 80 per cent of abortions are now provided in free-standing private clinics or doctors' surgeries, with large providers accounting for most services (Tietze, Forrest and Henshaw 1988). In 1997 the cost of a first trimester abortion ranged from $US200 to $US400 (National Abortion Federation 1997). Major medical funds cover abortion providing the woman or her husband has sufficiently comprehensive insurance. There are few services outside metropolitan areas, some 94 per cent of non-metropolitan counties having no abortion provider. State limitations on access to second trimester abortions and access by minors are causing increasing numbers of women to travel interstate. The politicisation of abortion has led many rural doctors to stop providing the service (Ginsburg 1989: 55; Gober 1997: 1004–6).

Canadian health care is funded through universal compulsory insurance, nationally based but administered by provincial governments. Established before the 1969 reform legislation, the health system absorbed the funding of abortion services where these had been approved by the relevant hospital therapeutic abortion committee, and, in Quebec, funded clinic abortions even before the *Morgentaler* decision (Jenson 1997b: 302). The system provides free in-patient and out-patient care, with funded physician services subject to a degree of cost sharing in some provinces. Most doctors bill the medical fund directly.

The 1988 decision overturning the 1969 legislation evoked strong reactions from provincial governments. While Ontario and Quebec moved to pay for all abortions, whether performed in hospitals or clinics, all other provinces announced measures to limit abortions to hospitals or to withdraw public funding (Mandel 1989: 292; Day and Persky 1988: 20–1). The strongest reaction came from British Columbia, where the provincial government instituted regulations withholding funding from abortions except where the woman's life was in danger. The measure was quickly overturned by the Supreme Court of British Columbia, but on grounds which did not prevent provincial governments from denying health insurance coverage of abortion (Tatalovich

1997: 218–19). As recently as 1995, the Alberta Government proposed to restrict funding to 'medically necessary' abortions, but was deterred by organised medicine (Tatalovich 1997: 219). Before the *Morgentaler* decision free-standing abortion clinics were legal only in Quebec, but Morgentaler and his associates had also established clinics in Toronto and Winnipeg which were legalised in the decision. Morgentaler has continued to challenge provincial restrictions of abortion funding to hospital providers (Tatalovich 1997: 219–21).

By 1990 there had developed extreme variations in entitlement and access to abortion from province to province (Brodie 1992: 89). Provincial responses to *Morgentaler* have tended to follow the contours of Canada's political economy, urban industrial provinces including Catholic Quebec maintaining support for abortion while primary producer areas have withdrawn support. These variations are compounded by significant variations in the inter-provincial distribution of medical resources, and in regulations governing the charging of fees under the Canada Health Act (Mandel 1989: 295; Tatalovich 1997: 221–2). By 1995 patient costs for clinic abortions varied significantly from province to province. In Ontario and British Columbia patients paid no fees; in Quebec, Newfoundland, Nova Scotia and Alberta they paid partial costs; while in Manitoba and New Brunswick clinic patients had to bear the cost of both physicians' fees and clinic user charges. The fees in these last circumstances could be as high as $C400 for a first trimester abortion. In 1995 the federal health minister began moves to force provincial governments to treat abortion in the same terms as other medical services (Tatalovich 1997: 222).

Abortion, Decommodification and Social Stratification

Abortion is now readily available in all four countries, as a medical entitlement in Britain and Australia and as a body right in the United States and Canada. The pattern of civil and social rights presents the conventional account of the welfare state with a paradox, for it associates the strongest civil rights with the weakest development of social rights. The source of this paradox lies in the identification of abortion with liberal ideology in the North American cases.

In comparison with the other liberal welfare states, the United States accords women both the greatest rights and the least. However much eroded since the Supreme Court decision of 1973, *Roe v Wade* gave women, in consultation with medical practitioners, the right to choose whether or not to proceed with a pregnancy. The effect of judicial decriminalisation in Canada has been similar. While women in these countries must negotiate their decision through medical channels, they begin the discussion with a presumption that the right of choice is their own. In this sense, the body right of North American women is stronger than the medical entitlement of their sisters in Britain and Australia. In these countries of medical entitlement women must argue their needs in the indirect language of health, without the presumption of right. At the same time, however, body right to abortion has been more vulnerable to political erosion than has medical entitlement, and is probably also more unstable. The claim to body right casts abortion in the language of possessive individualism, and in doing so evokes the broader terms of that ideology. Key among these terms are individualism and the market, while not included is social equality.

These links are clearly visible in the development of abortion policy in the United States. The concession of women's body right in *Roe v Wade* was quickly followed by political mobilisation against it in the streets, in the Congress and in the courts. These forces have aimed at overturning the right to abortion, and the judicial reversal of *Roe v Wade* remains their primary goal. But the forces opposing abortion have meanwhile sought to reduce the numbers of terminations taking place, and in the process have politicised the machinery of the welfare state. The breadth of this politicisation is extensive, reaching beyond hospital and medical authorities to embrace virtually every government instrumentality, including those governing drug approval and foreign aid. Moreover, the liberal terrain of body right has proved more vulnerable than that of medical entitlement to the limitation of woman's right by the potential rights of certain others, primarily the foetus and the parents of the pregnant minor. The competing rights of both receive more recognition in American law and practice than under the medical regimes of Britain and Australia.

The denial of a social right to a minimum standard of equality in access to abortion also follows the lines of classic liberalism. Identifying freedom with the market rather than the state, the ideology of possessive individualism divorces the issue of right in law from that of effective right in actuality. Implicit in this divorce is protection of the competing right of a further unnamed other, the taxpayer, whose moral commitments may preclude sharing in the support of abortion through the collective auspices of the welfare state. While anti-abortion forces have attempted similar initiatives in the countries of medical entitlement, they have been largely ineffective in the face of the claims of medical authorities to professional autonomy.

Legal abortion is not now an expensive service. Nor is market price necessarily a deterrent, as the history of illegal abortion has long made clear. The high rates of abortion in the United States suggest that for most metropolitan women market provision is not a significant barrier.

At the same time, American provision through the market reproduces social stratification in abortion services. Access to insurance funding reflects the occupational stratification of employment benefits. Poor women denied Medicaid support have to fund private services from scarce resources, and not all are able to do so. States in which Medicaid finance for abortion was not available had much lower abortion rates than those in which it was provided (Haas-Wilson 1993: 506). Currently only fifteen states fund abortions for indigent women, or have a court which has ruled that the state constitution prohibits restricting state funding for this purpose (Gober 1997: 1009). The far-reaching restriction of federally funded services under *Webster v Reproductive Health Services* may have similar effects on some middle-class women. For women outside metropolitan centres the cost of abortion is increased by the cost of locating a service, of travel and accommodation, and of lost wages during a waiting period. In combination with legal restrictions, market provision also puts abortion out of reach for many teenage women unsupported by their parents. Given their high abortion rates, these effects are felt especially strongly by black and minority women.

In Canada the establishment of body right is beginning to evoke an anti-abortion backlash against social rights to abortion services. A pattern of unequal access to abortion appears to be emerging in which the political economy of inter-provincial differences is reproduced in access to abortion. This pattern is compounded by the limitation of free-standing clinics to metropolitan centres in the industrial provinces.

In Britain and Australia medical entitlement presumes social right, but differences between direct provision through the NHS and indirect support through universal insurance result in different outcomes for the women seeking abortion. In Britain delays, regional variations and the limitation of NHS support to hospital services has resulted in the emergence of a large private market for commercial and non-profit providers. Market abortions are more expensive in Britain than in any of the other three countries, leaving scope for stratification by race and income to be reproduced in access to private abortion services. Working through the market, Australian insurance funding covers clinic as well as hospital services. The Australian health care system provides the greatest equality of access of all four countries, but differences remain in the access of women in different states and regional areas. Women from rural and remote areas face the greatest barriers.

Abortion in Liberal Welfare States

In the case of the liberal welfare state, the development of abortion services has taken two divergent paths. In Britain and Australia, the countries of medical entitlement, élite movements for abortion law reform have resulted in its limited legalisation as a form of medical care. In the result, the civil right to decide whether a woman will abort her pregnancy lies not with the woman but with the doctor(s) and the medical system. Women's access and her social right to a minimum standard of abortion services depends on the character of the health care system and its integration with the private market in medical services. The health care systems of both these countries have significant elements of social democratic universalism, and in principle these systems confer an equality of social right. In actuality, however, direct provision through the British NHS has provided less-effective access than the insurance-supported market system of Australia.

Women's movements have claimed that the right to abortion is about woman's individual personhood in liberal society and her right to personal autonomy in decisions concerning her body and fertility. Such a claim has been recognised in its fullest form in the liberal welfare states of North America, where such a body right has been recognised on the central terrain of possessive individualism. In the result, the right to abortion has been given expression in liberal terms, as a freedom to be exercised primarily through the medical market. On the same ground, a social right to an equal minimum standard of access has been denied. Abortion is largely a market service in the United States, the market providing services at competitive prices but through a limited number of large providers concentrated overwhelmingly in metropolitan centres.

Taylor-Gooby (1991) suggests that in the liberal welfare state gender conflicts tend to be waged through the legal rather than the welfare system, and that these conflicts become subsumed into the class conflicts of the market. This aptly describes the United States, where the liberal state is not contradicted by social democratic universalism in the health care system. But neither is such universalism in and of itself sufficient to guarantee a social right to abortion. A dual system of free public and expensive private services has emerged in Britain, and social rights are being withdrawn in some Canadian provinces. As access to low-cost abortion in the early stages of pregnancy depends most directly on the use of the services of free-standing abortion clinics, it is women who must travel who are most disadvantaged in all countries.

Whether as medical entitlement or body right, the outcome of the establishment of a civil right to abortion is much the same, for legal abortion is available in much the same degree in all countries. Medical entitlement has, however, proved more stable than body right in the face of mobilisation against women's access to abortion. The extreme controversy unleashed in the United States has been such as to render the body right conferred by *Roe v Wade* an 'empty shell' for many women: public funding is denied, fewer medical students are trained in the procedures, and terrorism deters practitioners from the field (Petersen 1996: 98). Body right is vulnerable to the internal contradictions of liberalism in a way that medical entitlement is not, for it pits woman's claim to autonomy as an individual against the potentially equal rights of a range of others. It is significant in this regard, however, that in no country has the right of a husband or other male sexual partner been recognised. More overtly politicised than medical entitlement, body right is also vulnerable to the competing rights of the generalised other in the taxpayer, pitting the civil right of all women against the social rights of the most disadvantaged. Where the liberal body right to abortion has been established, the social right to effective access has been weakened.

This conflict only restates the central contradiction of the liberal welfare state, between the freedom of the possessive individual in the market and the need of the person unable to command market resources. Abortion, however, states this contradiction in the distinctive terms of woman's claim to full and equal status as a possessive individual. In other instances civil rights have facilitated the support of social rights, mobilising political forces against possessive individualism in the development of the welfare state. In this instance the claim to a right to abortion on the high liberal ground of body right has constituted opposing forces in the same liberal terms, not supporting but undermining the welfare state.

Abortion does not fit at all neatly into the frameworks of established welfare state types. Civil rights to abortion services in the first trimester of pregnancy have become established across a much wider range of countries than the 'liberal' group discussed here (Glendon 1987). Moreover, such social rights as underpin effective access to abortion services depend quite directly on the character of the health care system in each country, and neither do these sit comfortably with the welfare state typologies generated in the study of economic policy and income support arrangements. What, then, can the comparison of civil and social rights to abortion services in these four countries have to say about the meaning of the liberal variety of the welfare state?

The liberal type identified by scholars such as Esping-Andersen (1990) is predicated upon a commitment to the ideology of possessive individualism and the market as the preferred means of meeting social needs. The present comparison of abortion rights and services considers the possibility that this ideology may be carried beyond fields of need in which the politics of class and income are salient, shaping access to abortion services in its own image.

These are not the only countries in which a woman may choose abortion as a matter of individual decision. In a review of abortion law in twenty countries of North America and Western Europe, Glendon

(1987) lists five others which permit elective abortion in early pregnancy. These are Austria, Denmark, Greece, Norway and Sweden. What distinguishes these from the United States and Canada is the support of more genuine abortion choice through the provision of significantly more comprehensive support in pregnancy and child care in the types of welfare state found in continental Europe and Scandinavia.

The ideology of possessive individualism does not infuse medical entitlement to abortion in Britain or Australia to the same degree. There are, nevertheless, differences between these countries and others whose welfare states take different forms. Glendon notes differences between the Anglo-American common law and the civil law traditions among countries permitting 'abortion for cause' on the 'soft' grounds of exceptional hardship for the pregnant woman. These are England, Finland, France, what was then West Germany, Iceland, Italy, Luxembourg and the Netherlands. She argues that France and Germany have evolved forms of regulation which place the needs and interests of the pregnant woman in a context rooted in communitarian rather than individualistic values (Glendon 1987: 15–22, 33–9). In comparison with *Roe v Wade*, 'The West German decision emphasises the connections among the woman, developing life, and the larger community' (Glendon 1987: 35).

Nor are the universalist elements of health care systems of otherwise liberal welfare states necessarily inconsistent with the market principle. The United States is exceptional in its lack of public provision, and that country has developed the largest private market. The health insurance systems established in two of the other three countries work to underpin rather than to replace private markets for medical services. In Australia and, though unevenly, also in Canada most abortions are provided through clinics operating on a fee-for-service basis. In Britain abortion is exceptional among medical services in being provided as often through private auspices as through the National Health Service.

If the distinguishing features of the liberal welfare state are taken to be an ideology of possessive individualism and a structural preference for market principles, then abortion services appear to have the same broad character in at least some degree. Civil and social rights to abortion in these countries have been generated in a distinctive politics giving direct representation to gender, religion and professional interest. The form these rights have taken, however, also appears to have been shaped by the ideologies and institutional forms of the broader social policy context.

Civil and social rights to abortion refer to only part of the broader spectrum of reproductive rights. Our focus on abortion reflects our concern with liberal ideology, and particularly its concern with individual personhood and security from infringement of the rights of the individual by the state. Hidden from view in this formulation is the wider question of civil and social rights to the resources and circumstances required to produce and bring up children in health and economic security. This requires a broader conception of liberty as including positive freedoms, and positive rights to their enjoyment. While a conception of this kind is available within new or social liberalism, this view is more often identified with social democratic conceptions of the state. The contemporary women's movement has been subject to forceful criticisms for reducing the issue of reproductive rights to abortion. The most telling such criticism is that it has given priority to the concerns of largely white, middle-class women while disregarding the limitations which poverty, racism and social policy place on the procreative choices of poor, black and minority women. Dorothy Roberts (1997: ch. 7; see also Ross 1993) argues for an interpretation of reproductive freedom that recognises the right to abortion as one aspect of a broader right to autonomy in reproductive decisions, and which would include advocacy against forced contraception and sterilisation as well as support for social rights to maintain a family. Jane Jenson (1997b) notes similar divisions within the Canadian movement. She argues that the movement for reproductive rights should reframe its political discourse beyond the individualistic right to choose, so that it encompasses the right to bear children and raise them in a dignified and equitable way. She would link abortion rights to child care and economic policy, to immigration and training policy, and to all aspects of social interdependency (Jenson 1997b: 293–302).

The liberal terms of privacy and possessive individualism are not the only language within which body rights can be conceived. Rosalind Petchesky (1995), reviewing examples from non-capitalist societies, radical democrats and slaves, shows that constructions of self-propriety may be based on concepts as varied as sovereignty over the body, right to its use, caretaking of one's body, and the creation of the self through the body. Jean Cohen (1996) argues that the right to bodily privacy is critical for the formation of personal identity, and hence identifies body rights with a more expansive notion of freedom than the liberal freedom from intrusion by others. What distinguishes the liberal form of body rights to abortion in the United States and Canada, and of medical entitlements in Britain and Australia, is the relative absence of these other meanings in state constructions of reproductive freedom. In these countries the language of reproduction constructs the body in more singular terms, as the exclusive property of the individual.

CHAPTER 6

Liberalism, Gendered Policy Logics and Mobilisation

In this chapter we shift from analysis of single policy areas to over-arching policy logic. The distinctive character of the gendered policy logic in each of the four countries is outlined around three sets of dimensions which reflect the gender reasoning underlying policy. We explain the particular patterns identified through a review of how gender equality issues have been represented in the political system since 1970. This entails considering the influence on policy development relating to gender equality of political party configuration, labour mobilisation and the strength and strategy of the women's movement. But these influences are not operating in a vacuum. In the United States, Canada, Great Britain and Australia they are operating within the context of a liberal political tradition and policy legacy which likely influences the character of political discourse in distinctive ways; for example, we would not expect left politics in these countries to find identical expression to that of social democracy in the Nordic countries. On the other hand, we would expect that differences in dominant party orientation, the level and character of labour mobilisation and the strength of the women's movement would be associated with cross-national variation in the expression and influence of the liberal political tradition on contemporary policy.

While social policy frameworks have identifiable structures we recognise that these are rarely static and that at some periods they are in considerable flux or even crisis. The 1980s and early 1990s witnessed considerable questioning of the post-World War II settlement. Such a compromise between capital and labour, under which trade union movements accepted some limitation on their behaviour, in exchange for rising wages and the social and economic policy developments which have come to be identified as the Keynesian welfare state, characterised all four countries although its scope, characteristics and the intensity of commitment to it varied (see, for example, Jenson 1989). The questioning of these arrangements occurred in all four countries and was reflected in a pervasive, if not always consistent, restructuring of the welfare state. This was to a significant extent a restructuring of responsibility for provision of services between state, market and family; in several respects it was a restructuring around gender. This is particularly evident in the usually unspoken assumptions about the distribution of responsibility for care work, both paid and unpaid, which underlie the increased public policy focus on community care of dependent people. It is also evident in the changing criteria for access to benefits and services and in the increased social regulatory role of the state in several countries. Contributing to the need for change in service provision and organisation was the long-term change in gender ideology, evident to varying degrees in all western countries, from a preference for the breadwinner/dependent family to accommodation of the dual-earner household in varying forms, despite the continuing household gender division of labour, especially in caregiving. Coinciding with these changes, the increased globalisation, or at least internationalisation, of production, trade, foreign direct investment and financial flows and the associated economic restructuring were having an effect on the availability and quality of employment. Consequently, as the reliance on the labour market for survival was being increased, both because of a change in individual preferences and pressure associated with changed benefit access criteria, the possibilities for achieving an adequate standard of living through reliance on the labour market were being lessened. The phenomena of the restructuring of the welfare state and the broader economic restructuring are an integral part of the context within which gender policy logics and the representation of gender equality issues in the political system are being played out in all OECD countries, including the four considered here.

Policy Regimes and Policy Logics

We now turn to identification of the distinctive character of the gendered policy logic in Australia, Britain, Canada and the United States. Each of these welfare states is stratified by gender, as it is by class, and there is considerable evidence of a class logic pervading all policy areas. Is there an analogous gender logic? Is there an overarching gender logic reflected in the policy frameworks relating to income maintenance, labour market participation, services facilitating such participation, and reproductive rights and services? Is there a coherence in the principles underlying policy across these three policy areas in each country? Three sets of dimensions reflect the gender reasoning underlying policy.

First, the welfare state as a mechanism of stratification brings into focus issues of class and gender stratification and in some countries stratification by race. It also brings into focus the related issue of gender sameness or gender difference. It is recognised in analyses of various theoretical hues that while welfare state programs mitigate patterns of stratification they may also be mechanisms of stratification. Historically, most welfare state analyses concentrated on the issue of class stratification. In critiquing this approach, early feminist analyses concentrated on gender stratification. Increasingly it is recognised that both types of stratification and their interaction must be considered if a comprehensive analysis of welfare state stratification is to be achieved. For example, neither gender sameness nor gender difference automatically entails equality. The key issue is the social context within which the policy orientation is located. A labour market gender sameness policy orientation which does not recognise difference in condition associated with family and class location is a recipe for inequality. On the other hand a commitment to sameness which entails a removal of barriers to equal participation, whether these be associated with family and/or class location, can contribute to labour market gender equality, although who benefits will depend on the orientation of the legislation. For example, equal opportunity legislation is more likely to benefit those who are in the upper reaches of the labour market whereas equal pay legislation, depending on its format, has the potential to spread benefit throughout the labour market. A policy that recognises difference may also have a contradictory outcome. For example, a gender difference approach may reinforce women's difficulties in escaping 'different roles' (as was illustrated in Chapter 3).

Second, the distinction between the achievement of equality in civil rights and its achievement in human or social rights is important for understanding the differences in policy logics across countries and apparent contradictions within particular countries. Emphasis on one or the other is a significant thread running through debates in several policy areas. In the case of civil rights, equality entails treating everyone the same, since 'Every individual has the same presumptive right as every other individual to individual autonomy subject only to those limitations the state can justify as reasonable'. In contrast, equality in human rights entails treating people as equals, which implies recognising their differences, since here we are talking of 'individuals in their capacity as members of groups which are disadvantaged for arbitrary reasons' (Abella 1991: 22). The recognition of difference in condition as a basis for policy is far more contentious than the recognition of equal treatment. An important issue is whether or not the ability to exercise civil citizenship rights can be divorced from the ability to exercise certain social rights.

While the achievement of civil, political and social rights is crucial to full citizenship, we also stress the significance of rights in affording women a minimum income, or the right to earn one. While women's standards of living are generally lower than men's, this right is important in giving women an exit option from personal economic dependence.

Third, the division of responsibility between state, market and family and the related issue of public versus private provision of services are pervasive themes in welfare state analysis but interpretations vary considerably. For example, while the division of responsibility for services and benefits between state, market and family has received considerable attention in recent welfare state analysis most of this has concentrated on the relationship between state and market with relative inattention to the family aspect. From a gender point of view this aspect is crucial because the relationship between the family and the labour market and that between the family and the state encompass the relationship between paid and unpaid work, including the social division of caring work. With regard to the public–private issue there is a marked tendency to treat the private as a homogeneous domain, that is, as non-public or non-state. However, it is crucial from both class and gender points of view to recognise the difference between market and family provision. The relations between state, market and family are reflected not only in the allocation of responsibility for provision of services but also in the regulatory role of the state, an aspect that is of considerable consequence for gender relations and an aspect that has been the focus of considerable controversy and restructuring over the past decade in some countries.

The United States provides the most coherent exemplar of the primacy of the market, which is associated with a relatively coherent gender sameness approach to policy. Aspects of this policy orientation, evident in their most extreme forms in the United States, are relevant to a lesser extent in the other countries. Canada comes closest to the United States in terms of policy logic. Great Britain also presents a relatively consistent policy logic across the three areas of income, labour market and reproductive rights but is in many respects at the opposite ends of several continua to the United States. Australia, while presenting similarities with elements of all the others, is in several respects distinctive.

The United States

The analysis of income maintenance, labour market participation, related social provisions and legislation, and reproductive rights and services in the United States indicates a commitment to gender sameness that entails the treatment of women, like men, mainly as workers, based on a traditional male worker model. The primacy of the labour market for survival is assumed. This reflects a separation, and assumed independence, of state–market and state–family relations without an acknowledgement of market–family interaction; in particular, without acknowledgement that status in the family may constrain possibilities in the market and vice versa. In so far as household status, for example motherhood, is recognised in social policy it is assumed to be a temporary barrier to labour market participation and responsibility to overcome this barrier rests with the individual. It is noteworthy that this is the framework within which abortion is understood. When the state does undertake solutions to market failure they tend to be market solutions, for example, tax credits to individuals to aid with the purchase of child care on the market and/or the encouragement of firms to provide workplace child and elder care. Even where there is a recognition that workers have family responsibilities, as reflected in the Family and Medical Leave Act (1993), the take up of leave provision is dependent on individual and/or family resources and is not supported by public provision of income support.

The US policy configuration reflects a strong commitment to the development of civil citizenship rights and a weak commitment to social rights. This is reflected most obviously in relation to the strong civil right to abortion accompanied by the absence of a social right to health care to facilitate the exercise of the civil right irrespective of socio-economic status (discussed more fully in Chapter 5). It is also evident in the relatively strong emphasis on anti-discrimination and equal opportunity legislation but the relative absence of social provision to facilitate the exercise of the equal access rights (discussed in Chapter 3).

Is there congruence in policy orientation across the three areas in the United States? The gender sameness orientation of income maintenance policy and the reliance on labour market participation for survival reinforce the primacy of the market. The strong civil citizenship rights orientation, as exemplified by a civil right to abortion in the absence of the social right to services to facilitate the exercise of this right, also points to reliance on the market. However, the relative lack of support services for labour market participation for those with caring responsibilities, and without the resources to purchase those available through the market, may in fact reinforce gender difference. A further contradiction of US policy is that the objective of lessening the role of the state through increased targeting of benefits and services, as is being attempted in much of the welfare state restructuring, necessitates a greater regulatory role for the state. The politically contested nature of the state, market, family division of responsibility was clearly evident in the US Republican Party 'Contract with America' document, much of which concerned a commitment to lessen the regulatory role of the state vis-à-vis the market but to strengthen its regulatory role vis-à-vis the families of welfare recipients (Gillespie and Schellhas 1994). A good example of this is the replacement of Aid to Families with Dependent Children (AFDC) by Temporary Assistance to Needy Families (TANF), which increased both labour market requirements and the social regulatory role of the states (rather than the federal government). The market orientation emphasis is also reflected in the Earned Income Tax Credit (EITC), which has been increasing in significance over the past decade (Myles and Pierson 1997). It is noteworthy that this approach to income maintenance through the tax system lessens the direct regulatory role of the state (discussed in Chapter 4).

There is clear evidence of a gender logic, namely, gender sameness operating in the US policy system. Key constraints on the realisation of the equality potential of such a strategy are the reliance on the market, even to the extent of using market solutions to market failure, but in the absence of acknowledgement of state, market, family linkages. This exemplifies the failure to acknowledge in public policy the complex and inextricable connection of the public and private spheres and in particular the connections between state action and the two dimensions of the private sphere – the family and the market – and the interaction of these two dimensions. The adherence in US policy to the assumption that the public and private spheres are independent of one another means that a key source of gender inequality is occluded. It also means that the economic barriers to the exercise of civil citizenship rights are obscured and as a consequence the salience of these barriers is reinforced: when social citizenship rights are minimal then class differences assume primary importance in the distribution of resources and life chances. This is equally true for women and men and it is in this context that gender relations are played out. Well-developed market services provide a range of quality and options, linked to price, which enhances the choices of the economically well-endowed but severely constrains the choices of those who are not.

Canada

Canada is often identified by people outside North America as having a welfare state similar to that of the United States but Canadians typically point to the differences. In addition to the universal public health care system, they identify Canada as reflecting greater compassion and comprehensiveness in its social provision. There is clear evidence of two institutional forms – if not two 'worlds of welfare' (Tuohy 1993) – existing within the Canadian welfare state in the mid-1990s: a social democratic institutional form, exemplified by the universal health care system, is located within a more encompassing liberal institutional form.

Concentrating on the explicit gender policy logic of the Canadian welfare state, a further layer of dualism can be identified. The gender logic pervading the policy orientation of the Canadian welfare state is a gender sameness tempered, on the one hand, by an equal opportunity orientation and, on the other, by a commitment to social protection, each of which is circumscribed, to varying degrees, by a commitment to the primacy of the market. While this is in some respects similar to the United States, it is also different in that traditionally there has been, and to some extent still is, a stronger reliance on the state as a mechanism for the solution of market failure problems in Canada. While this is a weak role relative to that in several European countries it does reflect some recognition of the links between status in the family and status on the labour market and the mutual constraints imposed by these. Social provision in Canada includes not only maternity leave but parental leave and, more significantly, benefits in both cases.

The recognition of the family–market status linkages is also reflected in the policy discourse on child care in Canada. There have been periods when child care has had a high political profile in Canada and when the extensive analysis and lobbying by interest groups appeared to be bearing fruit; for example, in 1987 a National Child Care Strategy was announced by the federal government only to be abandoned in 1992. Yet, the nature of the provision proposed involved a significant element of market subsidisation and this was the part of the plan that was implemented. This is consistent with the mixed family, market, public and/or non-profit solutions which form part of child care discussions in Canada. Despite this, it is significant that public child care is still on the political agenda and is recognised as an economic issue if only at the level of political rhetoric.

The Canadian policy configuration reflects a historically strong commitment to the development of social rights from the 1950s up to the early 1970s, and since the 1970s a relatively strong commitment to the development of civil citizenship rights. The latter commitment was strengthened along US lines by the ratification of the Charter of Rights and Freedoms which formed Part I of the Constitution Act 1982. The Charter constitutionally affirmed the right to equality in employment and explicitly permitted legislation such as employment equity. Like the United States, Canada has a relatively strong emphasis on anti-discrimination and equal opportunity legislation and, as in the United States, it is relatively effective at the élite level, as reflected by comparatively low levels of gender-based occupational segregation. Legislation to apply this to the majority of the labour force in Ontario by its social democratic New Democratic Party Government in 1995 was reversed by the successor Progressive Conservative Government before it could be implemented. Abortion in Canada is affirmed as a civil right but not a social right. Despite being legal, it is still a highly charged issue and protests against its availability are persistent, reflecting the fact that it does not have the same status as other civil rights. While Canada's universal health care system could facilitate access to abortion services, abortion is not a health service like any other. Consequently, the majority of those seeking abortions are dependent on market solutions.

Is there a congruence across the three policy areas? A gender same-ness orientation of policy in relation to labour market participation is supported by anti-discrimination and equal opportunity provisions. Reliance on market participation and market provision of services is circumscribed by the acceptance of a legitimate role for the state in the event of market failure. The Canadian pattern encompasses social provision which recognises gender difference. It combines gender same-ness with a commitment to lessening the impact of barriers to equal participation – this is reflected in pay and employment equity pro-visions, although the weak complaint-based approach to equal pay has not significantly altered gender-stratified patterns of pay. The recog-nition of the impact of familial status on labour market participation is also reflected in maternity and parental leave and more significantly in the associated benefits. Although the services for labour market participants with caring responsibilities are low by Scandinavian or French standards, the range of support services for labour market participants is consistent with the policy orientation towards gender sameness in the labour market.

Great Britain

Historically, the British social policy framework is widely identified as the male breadwinner–female housewife model (Jenson 1986; Lewis 1992; Pedersen 1993). This model is built on the assumptions of women's primary place in the home and the fear that strong state income support would lessen the responsibility of males for their dependants. These assumptions are reflected in the 'firm dividing line between public and private' that characterises strong male breadwinner states (Lewis 1992: 159). The fracturing of the traditional assumptions are obvious from the increase in female labour force participation over the past few decades but the influence of the traditional model is still pervasive, as is indicated by the exceptionally high level of part-time work by women, much of it relatively few hours. Adherence to the traditional model has not precluded a push for greater reliance on private sources of support for sole parents but, consistent with the strong male breadwinner model, the character of this push is quite different from that adopted in the United States. The emphasis in Britain is on collecting child support from fathers rather than compelling mothers to enter the labour market on a full-time basis, as in the United States. The recent push to get more sole parents into the labour force assumes part-time participation with the continuation of some state support, which is still linked to the collection of child support from fathers. These policy choices reflect the primacy of the family for support via the male breadwinner's participation in the labour market as opposed to direct market compulsion for all. The lesser labour market compulsion on mothers is also reflected in the relatively higher levels of income support for sole parents. It is noteworthy that the Labour Party Government elected in May 1997 has put an increased emphasis on labour market participation. This is reflected in welfare-to-work measures including such measures for sole parents. Consistent with the gender difference policy orientation which has historically characterised the British social policy framework there is an implied acknowledgement that status in the family may constrain status on the market. What distinguishes Britain is the fact that the solution is seen to rest in the family unit, although market solutions are available to those who can afford them (Bradshaw et al. 1993). Public assistance will be forthcoming if the family unit is a sole parent full-time carer unit. Otherwise the solution must be found on a purely private basis.

Policies to promote gender equality in employment in Britain have gone through a trajectory broadly similar to those in other countries: equal pay for equal work (late 1960s to early 1970s), equal pay for work of equal value (mid to late 1970s to early 1980s); anti-discrimination laws (late 1970s to mid-1980s), employment equity/affirmative action (mid-1980s on). However, Britain has never taken up labour market gender equality policies in a major way. What action it has taken has been to a significant extent mandated by the European Union and has been challenged by the British Government on several occasions even when the challenge was contrary to the position of the Equal Opportunities Commission. Britain still has relatively high female–male wage differentials. Although better than the United States and Canada in this regard it is worse than both in its relatively high levels of gender-based occupational segregation. The relative inaction in this area is consistent with the gender difference orientation which characterises income maintenance policies and the reluctance to put in place public policy measures which acknowledge the linkages between status in the household and status on the labour market.

The British policy configuration reflects a relatively stronger commitment to the development of social rights than to the development of civil rights in the gender equality area. Reflecting this, the civil rights status of abortion is relatively weak in the sense that abortion is permitted 'for cause' and as a medical service, rather than as a body right, while social access is relatively wide due to the National Health Service. However, abortion is exceptional among medical services in that its provision is divided almost equally between private clinics and the National Health Service. This is due to the delays in the public system and also uncertainty about medical approval – both of which illustrate the weakness of its civil right status. The relatively well-developed social citizenship rights reflect the legacy of social democratic universalism, which permeated the post-World War II settlement. This legacy is most clearly reflected in the National Health Service, although it has been under some threat since the early 1980s. The social democratic universalism element was always clearly circumscribed within a liberal framework in all other areas of social provision and has been further circumscribed throughout the 1980s and 1990s, as the pressure of retrenchment of the welfare state has gained in strength. As in the United States and Canada, a lessening of the role of the state is an integral part of the debate on the restructuring of the welfare state.

What then is the distinctive character of the gendered policy logic of the British welfare state as reflected in the three areas? The key theme that emerges in relation to social rights is the influence of the male breadwinner–female housewife logic which implies strong gender differentiation. While this has been modified to a certain extent, its influence is still evident across income maintenance and labour market policy areas. It is evident in the very limited support for public child care and the gender difference approach that characterises some social rights. It is also evident in the less than enthusiastic commitment to employment equality strategies and in the assumptions underlying the policy emphasis on community care for dependent people which has been a central plank of welfare state restructuring (O'Connor 1996: 13–29). While there is compensation for difference in condition for sole parents as well as maternity leave and benefit, the general pattern is one of gender difference without a consistent commitment to equality.

Australia

Despite similarities stemming from the common liberal political tradition, the Australian welfare state stands out in many respects as distinct relative to the United States, Canada and Great Britain. This is most clearly evident in labour market-related issues, at least up to the early 1990s, and in its income maintenance system of which the Industrial Relations Awards System and the universal means-testing approach to social provision are the distinguishing mechanisms. The distinctiveness characterisation fits with Australia's identification as a 'wage-earner's welfare state' (Castles 1994) comprising a 'women's and a men's welfare state' (Bryson 1995). The wage earner's welfare state designation refers to the 'use of wage regulation as the primary instrument of social protection and the distinctive pattern of social policy outcomes resulting from it' (Castles 1996b: 91).

Australia was historically committed to a strong male breadwinner–female housewife model and this was reflected in the labour market system until 1972, when the first equal pay decision was made, and until recently in the income maintenance system. It has now moved away from its earlier treatment of women as the dependants of men to a system of formal gender neutrality within which women are treated as independent citizens but caregiving is still a basis for claims (Shaver 1995). Despite this formal neutrality, as reflected in the individual basis of claims and the fact that the caregivers' pension is the same as other allowances and open to both women and men, women still tend to make claims on the basis of their family status and men on the basis of their work status (Bryson 1995). Of course, this is not unique to Australia.

Female labour force participation has increased considerably in Australia over the past few decades but it is still lower than in the other three countries and there is still a relatively high level of part-time work by women. This indicates considerable fracturing, but not the demise, of the traditional male breadwinner–female housewife model. The persistence of traditional gender-based patterns has been the impetus for relatively strong labour market anti-discrimination and affirmative action provisions – this reflects a strong recognition of gender stratification and inequality since the early 1970s. These actions have been very successful at the mass level, as reflected in relatively low female–male pay differentials, but not at the élite level, as is indicated by the relatively high gender-based occupational segregation. It is noteworthy that the former is the result of the award system and the strong minimum wage commitment, each of which exemplifies the collectivist approach that has traditionally characterised Australia. While the award system is now formally gender-neutral, it also has considerably less impact due to the shift to enterprise bargaining.

In terms of the state, market, family responsibility dimension we find the role of the state is stronger in Australia than in the United States, Canada and Britain. In the context of these countries, social rights are well-developed. Australia is distinctive not because of means-testing but because that means-testing effectively excludes those with higher incomes and/or means. Several policies reflect a recognition of the linkages between market and family status. This is most evident in the strong commitment to public child care provision since the 1980s and the prominence accorded to ILO Convention 156 on Workers with Family Responsibilities (ILO 1993).

The gender logic underlying policies in relation to income maintenance, labour market participation and reproductive rights in Australia in the 1990s fits the gender-neutrality rubric. This is modified by a recognition of gender difference as reflected in family status. The implications of a gender-neutrality focus for gender and class stratification, in particular whether or not it will lessen these patterns of stratification, depend on the commitment to and effectiveness of the policies to compensate for gender difference. A weak commitment and/or low level of effectiveness implies the continuance of existing stratification patterns. In this regard, the Australian debate on the restructuring of the welfare state is of considerable importance. This debate has focused to a large extent on lessening the role of the state vis-à-vis the market with little reference to the implications for family. This reflects little acknowledgement of the mutual interaction of status in the family and status in the labour market. The debate is characterised by the same contradictions identified in other countries.

The Primacy of the Market with Varying Intensity

Rather than consistently distinct policy logics in these four countries we find variations on a series of continua, the most important of which are the stratification dimensions and the related gender sameness, gender difference orientation of policy, the public–private or division of responsibility between state, market and family, and the civil rights, social rights emphasis of equality achievements. The dynamics of all three are conditioned by the extent to which class stratification is recognised as a factor influencing life chances and the ability to exercise citizenship rights. While absolute consistency across policy areas in gender logic and in the division of responsibility for services between state, market and family is not evident in any of the four countries, the United States has the most coherent policy framework as reflected in its adherence to gender sameness and the primacy of the market. Parallel to this, it also has the strongest civil rights orientation. Canada is most similar to the United States in its policy framework and orientation but within the context of a welfare state encompassing two institutional forms – social democratic and liberal – and a legacy of universalism in several aspects of policy. Its commitment to gender sameness and the primacy of the market is tempered, reflecting some acknowledgement of the linkages between family and market status. Great Britain is at the opposite end of the gender sameness, gender difference continuum to the United States. Its gender difference orientation is situated within the context of a relatively strong tradition of social rights, a weaker civil rights tradition and a stronger role for the state than there is in the United States. Like Canada its welfare state incorporates a social democratic institutional form in its National Health Service. Within the gender difference orientation there is compensation for difference in family and market status but there is not a consistent commitment to equality. Australia's gender-neutrality logic can be situated on the continuum between gender sameness and difference. The context is an institutional legacy of centralised wage negotiation and, historically, a relatively strong role for the state. Consistent with this, the neutrality orientation is coupled with a recognition of the linkages between family and market status which is most clearly reflected in the area of child care. It is also reflected in its health care system which, like those of Canada and Great Britain, is universal in its orientation.

There is a policy legacy of universalism, or at least a discourse of universalism in public policy, which has mitigated the class influences on life chances in Australia, Canada and Great Britain, although the universalism influence is lessening in all of them. This lessening of universalism is exacerbated by the changing context within which trade is taking place, one in which the influence of globalised production is increasingly felt through a process of economic restructuring, which is in turn felt through labour market restructuring and the restructuring of the social policy regimes.

The pressure for the restructuring of the welfare state has come from · diverse sources. Much of the media coverage has concentrated on the fiscal deficit and the purported contribution of health and social services and especially income maintenance expenditure to this. While the fiscally driven critique of the welfare state in all four countries has had adherents across the political party spectrum the intensity and scope of the critique has varied considerably even among contributors professing the same political party allegiance. The most trenchant critique has come from advocates of the new-right arguments for lessening the redistributive role of the state, increasing the role of the market and lessening regulatory controls, who also often advocate a strengthening of the social regulatory role of the state. While in its extreme form this critique has tended to be confined to conservative party and organisation spokespersons, elements of this argument have been evident in the statements of the right wing of parties avowedly in the left and centre of the left–right political party spectrum. While these critiques have varied in timing and intensity across countries, their influence is clearly evident across all four countries and has influenced the context of mobilisation around gender equality.

Mobilisation and Policy Logics

Historically, none of these countries reflected a commitment to gender sameness, gender neutrality or gender equality. Yet, since the 1960s, to some extent, there has been a shift in thinking away from gender difference in all four. How do we explain the trajectories evident in the gender logics underlying policy in these countries in the contemporary period? There are really two related questions that need to be answered. First, how have gender equality issues been understood and represented in the political system in the different countries? Second, given the particular ideologies, or visions of gender relations, what determines success in effecting change in government policy?

There is overwhelming evidence of liberal influences on the origins and development of these welfare states. Consistent with this, all have been characterised by a recognition of gender difference and/or a public–private division which in practice was a gender division (Orloff 1991; Jenson 1986; Lewis 1992; Shaver 1987; Andrew 1984). However, each has also been characterised by its own variant of this policy logic and in the contemporary period, movement from, or at least modification of, this policy logic. Neither the historical nor contemporary policy differences across countries identified throughout this book are purely the result of different levels of commitment to the liberal tradition. Patterns of class and gender mobilisation have influenced the equality policy preferences espoused and the political strategies pursued. The framework through which we seek to explain the similarity and/or variation of the gender policy logics is built around these elements, taking into account national and historically specific institutional structures. It is informed by Marian Sawer's (1991) analysis of the relative success of the Australian women's movement in effecting changes in government policy over the 1970s and 1980s. The four factors she identified as specific to the Australian situation are consistent with four of the five factors which compose the more encompassing framework we propose. Before outlining this framework it is necessary to discuss our use of the concept of 'gender equality movement'.

The term 'gender equality movement' is used here to refer to the movements for women's equality in the sense of gender equality, widely identified as the feminist movement. There is no single movement in any country. When we use the term 'feminist movement' we recognise that the term 'feminism' has a broad range of connotations. Similarly, the women's movement in all four countries encompasses a range of movements with shared but also diverse emphases. We use the term 'feminism' to refer to analysts and/or activists who recognise gender as a fundamental structuring mechanism in contemporary societies. There is no single feminist analysis of the welfare state and significant differences in emphases and in policy prescriptions are evident in published analyses. Liberal, socialist and radical perspectives, the first two of these paralleling long-standing analytical and political approaches in western countries, identify the major traditions in feminism from the 1960s to the present. We acknowledge that these designations are not universally accepted and are less used now than in the 1960s, but aspects of the tendencies reflected under these designations consistently appear in new forms. Our concern here is not with establishing definitive designations. Rather it is with identifying key strands of the women's movement that have had resonance within the four countries since the 1960s. While all feminist analyses give primacy to gender and the achievement of gender equality they differ significantly in their explanations of the source of gender inequality and in the proposed solutions, and there are differences in emphases within schools (J. Dale and Foster 1986; Williams 1989).

The primary focus of liberal feminism is on inequalities associated with sex discrimination and associated attitudes. This leads to an emphasis on anti-discrimination and equal opportunity policies directed to increasing the representation of women in politics and in public and private institutions, especially at senior levels. This is by far the most influential of feminist approaches at a policy level in most countries. Its achievements are reflected in equal opportunity and equal rights institutions and policies. It is important to acknowledge that many equal opportunity organisations move beyond a focus on equal rights and identify deeper sources of gender inequality (this point is made in relation to the Equal Opportunities Commission in Britain by J. Dale and Foster 1986). It is also important to recognise that the solutions proposed by liberal feminists are generally supported by other variants of feminism; their reservations relate to the adequacy of these solutions in combating what are identified as the most important sources of gender inequality.

Radical feminists are at the other extreme from liberal feminists in some respects. They adopt a highly critical approach to many mainstream institutions including welfare state institutions. Consequently, they are less likely to involve themselves in reforming these institutions than are liberal feminists. The major significance of radical feminism for welfare state analysis relates to the implications of its campaigns on violence against women, its involvement in the provision of services for women, including refuges for battered women and rape crisis centres, its involvement in abortion rights campaigns and its campaigns to broaden the perception of legitimate political space and activity.

The socialist or materialist feminist position recognises the importance of class and gender and their interaction in the analysis of the structuring of inequality – this is reflected in links to the labour movement and social democratic and labour parties. Socialist feminists stress the material basis of gender inequality and the importance of recognising the interaction of gender, class and race in analysing inequality. The socialist feminist position is of enormous importance for welfare state analysis because of its focus on understanding the gender division of labour and the mechanisms perpetuating it. Again there are degrees of emphasis on the economic determination of gender inequality and the influence of male dominance and degrees of optimism about the possibilities for the amelioration of gender inequality under capitalism.

These three strands of feminism share a vision of gender equality which involves equality of participation and the minimising of gender differences. In the late 1970s this view was challenged by 'difference' or 'cultural' feminism, which focused attention on the analysis of androcentric cultural standards. Nancy Fraser captured the key difference between these approaches as follows: 'The proponents of equality saw gender difference as the handmaiden of male domination . . . Difference feminists, in contrast, saw gender difference as the cornerstone of women's identity' (Fraser 1997: 177). Whereas the equality groups emphasised the politics of redistribution, the cultural feminists stressed the politics of recognition and focused on cultural demands. Neither of these approaches adequately reflected differences among women based on race, ethnicity, sexual orientation and the like. This became a much stronger focus of analysis and mobilisation throughout the 1980s and while this is reflected explicitly in the proliferation of diverse strands within the feminist movement within all countries it is also reflected in a broadening of the focus of all of the original strands to encompass to varying degrees elements of the two political approaches, which Fraser calls redistribution and recognition. We find all of these strands of feminism, and others, in all four countries, though there is variation in strength and visibility of the various strands, not only cross-nationally but over time in individual countries. Despite cross-national variation in level of mobilisation, strategy and tactics, the Black Women's Movement has been the most influential among the other strands (Collins 1990; Barnett 1995; Vickers, Rankin and Appelle 1993; Lovenduski and Randall 1993; Lucashenko 1994; Huggins 1994).

Cross-national differences among feminist analysts, most notably the difference between Scandinavian analysts and those in Britain and the United States, on whether or not the state is inherently oppressive of women or is a potential resource have often been pointed out (see, for example, Hernes 1987). Differences among feminist analyses in Australia, Canada, Great Britain and the United States are clearly evident but are interpreted more appropriately as positions along a continuum than as extreme positions. Indeed, the differences are often a reflection of responses to different political party configurations and political opportunity structures. It is noteworthy that the reproductive rights movement, which became central to the gender equality movement in all four countries, was independent of the women's movement in its early stages and drew more significantly on the general ethos of reform supported by élite women in medicine, law and liberal church circles.

The framework through which we analyse the representation of gender equality issues involves five elements.

1 *Social movement mobilisation and orientation* – Social movement orientation refers to the political strategy pursued by gender equality movements, in particular, with regard to the state. Is the state perceived as inherently oppressive of women or is it a potential resource? If the state is a resource, is participation in state institutions in the development and implementation of policy the most effective approach or is change more effectively achieved through external pressure?

2 *Mobilisation of anti-feminist movements* – While such movements are often characterised as against equality in their orientation they invariably stress equality in their programs. The emphasis is on equality but within the context of difference and traditional gender roles, including a traditional gender division of labour.

3 *Political party configuration* – This term is used to refer to the relative strength of left, centre and right parties. We are interested in this configuration because of its likely influence on the representation of gender equality issues, both directly in terms of party positions and more importantly in terms of its influence on the context within which social movements and groups represent these issues. There is considerable evidence that parties on the left of the left–right political spectrum – social democratic and labour parties – are more favourably disposed to gender equality issues than parties to the right of the political spectrum, with centre parties occupying an intermediate position. This is borne out in analyses of these and several other countries (Lovenduski 1986; Randall 1987; Lovenduski and Randall 1993; Kaplan 1992; Katzenstein and Mueller 1987). Yet, there

is cross-national variation in the commitment to gender equality of parties of the same political hue and variation over time in the commitment of individual parties. It is also important to recognise that the same label does not imply the same orientation. Australia and Canada have Liberal Parties but the Australian Liberal Party is more appropriately categorised as a moderate-right conservative party – a fact which is reflected by its consistent coalescing with the National Party, which is on the far right of the political spectrum by cross-national standards (Castles and Mair 1984). A caveat must also be entered in relation to parties of the left across these countries. The British Labour Party, the Australian Labor Party (ALP) and the Canadian New Democratic Party (NDP) are affiliated to the Socialist International and each is characterised in cross-national classifications as a 'moderate-left' party, although on the centre side of this designation relative to other moderate-left parties. While the British Labour Party and the ALP have their origins in the labour movement, the roots of the Canadian NDP are far more diverse (Brodie and Jenson 1988). In relation to the US Republican and Democratic parties there is general agreement on their right and centre designations in terms of US politics (Castles and Mair 1984). Yet, it must be recognised that these parties are coalitions of relatively diverse interests and this diversity is often reflected in intra-party divisions on gender equality issues. While acknowledging this complexity we argue that the political party configuration is crucial to the character of the political opportunity structure within which gender equality advocates operate.

4 *The political opportunity structure* – We are using this concept, as developed by Sydney Tarrow, to refer to access to state institutions, the stability of political alignments and the relationship to allies and support groups (Tarrow 1983: 28–34). We are particularly concerned with the political opportunity structure confronting the gender equality and anti-feminist movements.

5 *The institutional context and legacy* – Examples of this are the unitary or federal structure of government, the centralisation of government, the potential for bureaucratic policy machinery and the industrial relations framework.

The United States: The Women's Movement as 'A Sophisticated Interest Group'

The women's movement in the United States is one of the highest profile movements in the world, yet the gender equality policy outcomes have been less encompassing than in several countries with weaker movements. On the other hand, civil citizenship rights in the United

States are as strong as, or stronger than, elsewhere in the OECD and the decrease in gender-based occupational segregation over the past three decades has been among the best in the OECD. This does not preclude the persistence of occupational segregation and the existence of a glass ceiling which limits the percentage of women in the most senior positions. These apparent contradictions give rise to a question about the compatibility of mass and élite strategies. Before considering this we outline how gender equality issues have been represented in the political system over the past three decades and the characterisation of the contemporary US women's movement as 'a sophisticated interest group' (Costain and Costain 1987: 210).

The United States, like Canada, has had significant commission reports that have served to inform not only policy-makers but also the public about gender issues. The most noteworthy are *American Women*, the 1963 report of the President's Commission on the Status of Women, which was established by President Kennedy in 1961, and *A Matter of Simple Justice*, presented in 1970 by the President's Task Force, established by President Nixon. The President's Commission led to the establishment of the Interdepartmental Committee on the Status of Women and the Citizens' Advisory Council on the Status of Women. It also recommended state commissions on the status of women and these were established in all but one state. In addition to their impact on policy priorities these commissions served to publicise issues relating to gender inequality. This happened within the context of considerable mobilisation by women, increased labour force participation and an increase in tertiary level educational participation. Both the Citizens' Advisory Council and the state commissions were assisted to a considerable extent by the Women's Bureau, which is the oldest bureaucratic women's equality policy unit in the United States, having been established in 1920 with a mandate to monitor the working conditions of wage-earning women. The National Organization of Women (NOW) was formed in 1966, at least in part out of frustration at failure to implement gender equality policy, in particular, the failure of the Equal Employment Opportunity Commission (EEOC) to enforce the 1964 Civil Rights Act gender provisions. NOW concentrated much of its energies on fighting sexual discrimination in employment through legal action.

The US gender equality movement has never been monolithic and the dominant orientation has varied over time (Costain and Costain 1987; Davis 1991) although liberal feminism has always been the core of US women's mobilisation. Since the mid-1980s there has been more diversity in the movement and in its organisational locus. This is reflected in enduring and widespread grass-roots activities (for example, rape crisis centres and women's bookstores) along with more properly political structures such as the 'permanent flexible alliances' of women's groups who work on a common agenda (Harder 1990), for example, the National Women's Conference Committee which works on state law reform and which grew out of the former state commissions on the status of women. The Council of Presidents, which is composed of representatives of over eighty national women's organisations, works at the federal level, adopting each year a set of legislative priorities called the Women's Agenda (McGlen and O'Connor 1995: 300–1). In addition, there has been a proliferation of women's caucuses in professions and the growth of specific issue organisations around abortion rights, peace and nuclear disarmament (McGlen and O'Connor 1995: 300–1). The diversity is also reflected in an identifiable feminism on the right of the political spectrum, distinctly different from any of the traditional feminist orientations in professing a libertarian and pro-market orientation (Klatch 1990).

As in several other countries there has been a persistent tension between those who wished to pursue formal legal equality versus those who favoured protective legislation which recognised difference in condition (Freeman 1987). This difference is captured in the opposing positions on the Equal Rights Amendment (ERA), which was accepted by Congress in 1972 but which did not gain the support of sufficient states to ensure ratification by 1982, and thus failed to be incorporated in the Constitution. The ERA has a long and contentious history. It was first submitted to Congress in 1923 and immediately caused a split between those feminists who argued for the fundamental importance of gender equality (many of them Republicans) and 'social feminists' who asserted the importance of protective legislation for women (many of them Democrats). The ERA remained on the political agenda but did not become the focus of sustained concerted action again until the 1960s. NOW endorsed the ERA in 1967 and some of its members resigned on the grounds that it would negate protective legislation. Consistent with this position, the AFL-CIO (American Federation of Labor and Congress of Industrial Organizations) testified against it at the Senate hearings. In 1970 the Citizens' Advisory Council on the Status of Women argued on the basis of legal advice that it would result in the extension of women-only benefits to men rather than their abolition. This was associated with success in the campaign for acceptance by the Senate in 1972 (McGlen and O'Connor 1995: 45–6). The division among gender equity proponents on the ERA illustrates the complexity of the issues related to equality versus difference. Support for the ERA is consistent with the US focus on civil citizenship over social citizenship rights. Our analysis indicates that, despite the failure to ratify the ERA, the thinking on which it is based – gender sameness – is now the taken-for-granted framework for public policy in the United States.

After the defeat of the ERA in 1982, the focus of the women's equality movement became more diverse. The 1980s also saw increasing mobilisation around political representation. From 1971, with the formation of the National Women's Political Caucus (NWPC), there was an explicit commitment by at least a section of the women's movement to influence political parties from within by getting more women elected to political office (Freeman 1975: 161). The founding of the non-party NWPC and Emily's List, a support group to elect pro-choice Democratic women is an outcome of this commitment. Yet, there is widespread consensus among analysts that the women's movement directed relatively little pressure for policy change through political parties prior to the 1980s (Costain and Costain 1987). The objective of getting more women elected to political office was not crowned by early success but the proportions of women officeholders at state and national levels increased from 4.3 per cent in 1981–83 to 10.3 per cent in 1993–95 (Centre for the American Woman and Politics 1993).

Anne Costain and Douglas Costain (1987) identify three periods in terms of the dominant approach to attaining political influence by the contemporary US women's movement, as represented by NOW and the Women's Equity Action League (WEAL), which was formed as a breakaway from NOW in 1968. During the formative period of 1966–72 the movement concentrated on protest and working through political élites. In the routinising period, 1972–77, a range of tactics was used, including constitutional amendment, legislative lobbying and political protest. During the institutionalising period from 1978 onwards, legislative lobbying has been the preferred tactic together with an emphasis on electoral politics, especially since 1980. Writing in the mid-1980s, Costain and Costain concluded that political parties had been largely tangential to the successes and failures of the women's movement. They argue that the characteristics of the American political system, especially its highly decentralised decision-making structure, the highly decentralised organisation of political parties and the diversity of their policy preferences, frustrate social movement efforts to change policy (Costain and Costain 1987: 208–9) and that the successes achieved by the women's movement have come largely through 'sophisticated interest group' behaviour, the legitimacy of which is based on the demonstration of strong grass-roots support for the positions advocated. As a tactic this affords access to policy-makers in Washington. Parallel to this many of the most significant equality achievements by the US women's movement have been achieved through the courts; for example, abortion rights, anti-discrimination and equal opportunities decisions.

While not doubting the importance of legal action and lobbying it is important to recognise that the political party in power has influenced considerably the scope and possibilities for gender equality activity not only through the composition of the Supreme Court and other senior appointments but also by its support, or lack thereof, for the limited bureaucratic policy agencies that exist in the United States, such as the Women's Bureau (Stetson 1995) and the EEOC. The Reagan–Bush period was one of constraint on all of these grounds for the women's equality movement, whereas it was relatively favourable to the counter-equality movement, coinciding with the identification of the Republican Party with anti-feminism. These developments reinforced the shift of the women's movement towards lobbying the Congress, which was controlled by the Democrats. The emergence of the gender gap in party identification and voting in favour of the Democratic Party was associated with considerable activity by gender-equality activists within that party. This is reflected in recent electoral outcomes.

Where does the United States fit in terms of the five-point framework outlined above? Unlike the other three countries it has both a strong gender equality movement and a strong anti-feminist movement. The latter was particularly active during the ERA ratification process through the Stop ERA and the Eagle Forum organisations and continues to be active not only around abortion issues but also around the role of the state vis-à-vis the family – for example, Concerned Action for America actively campaigned against the Family and Medical Leave Act until it was passed in 1993. Throughout the Reagan–Bush period the counter-equality movement enjoyed a favourable political opportunity structure relative to the gender equality movement. In contrast, the Clinton administration has provided a relatively positive opportunity structure for the women's equality movement, at least in terms of equal opportunity and access to positions of influence. The most obvious manifestation of this is women in cabinet positions and in senior administrative positions. In view of the length of presidential office-holding by the Republican Party over the past twenty-five years, it must be asked whether or not the absence of reliance on the government as a mechanism for achieving gender equality, identified by Marian Sawer in her comparison with Australia (Sawer 1991) is an inherent characteristic of the US women's movement or a realistic response to the political opportunity structure.

The dominant orientation of the US women's equality movement has been consistently liberal feminist, as has its strategy, and while this has had little success in achieving mass economic gains it has been relatively successful in the equal opportunity and anti-discrimination domain, which has been of particular benefit to better-educated women, and in the strengthening of civil citizenship rights. These gains would appear to be relatively secure since they are consistent with the overall policy framework and tradition – although they are not unchallenged as is evidenced by abortion. In terms of its lack of success in relation to mass equality issues, such as pay equity, it is noteworthy that the context, in terms of the highly decentralised industrial relations framework, provided institutional barriers and the weak and declining labour union movement meant that allies were sparse. In contrast, the civil rights orientation finds a fertile context not only in the policy tradition but also in the existence of numerous supportive rights organisations.

Canada: Bureaucratic Policy Machinery, Social Movements and Political Parties

In reviewing the range of equality strategies pursued in Canada over the past twenty-five years and the process of representation of gender equality issues one cannot escape the significance of two royal commissions – the Royal Commission on the Status of Women in Canada (1970) and the Royal Commission on Equality in Employment (Canada 1984) – and the bureaucratic policy machinery to which they gave rise.

The Royal Commission on the Status of Women was established in 1967 by the Liberal Government. Several factors were associated with this decision, including pressure to ratify, and to live up to the conditions of, ILO and UN conventions relating to gender equality and the influence of initiatives being taken in other countries, especially the United States where President Kennedy had established the President's Commission on the Status of Women (Findlay 1988: 5). The Royal Commission's Report in 1970 included 167 recommendations. Several concerned policy machinery and these were the first to be implemented. Delay in implementing the other recommendations led to the founding of the National Action Committee on the Status of Women (NAC), an umbrella organisation for national and regional women's groups, with the objective of monitoring the implementation of the Royal Commission recommendations (Vickers, Rankin and Appelle 1993: 4). These included equal pay for work of equal value, equal opportunities and anti-discrimination legislation, maternity leave and benefits, child care and several objectives relating to gender equality in federal public services employment. Two of the chief concerns of the NAC since its inception have been child care and pay equity.

The Royal Commission recommendations on policy machinery were consistent with the recommendations of the UN Commission on the

Status of Women, which had advocated national advisory commissions on the status of women as early as 1963 (Heitlinger 1993: 78). In 1971 the Office of Equal Opportunity in the Public Service Commission was established, as was a Minister Responsible for the Status of Women, and an Office of the Coordinator, Status of Women, within the Privy Council Office. Associated with the latter, an Interdepartmental Committee was established to develop a strategy for implementing the recommendations. It recommended the creation of several new status of women agencies. One of these was the Women's Program in the Department of the Secretary of State, established in 1972. Its mandate was to administer grants to equal rights groups. From its inception it had an explicitly progressive orientation (Findlay 1988) and it was part of the Citizen Participation Program. The Citizenship Branch of the Department of the Secretary of State had a low profile until 1968 when it became actively involved in sponsoring and funding advocacy organisations. This change was associated with a change in the political configuration, represented by the election of the Trudeau Liberal Government which emphasised national unity and identity in its challenge to Quebec nationalism and was initially committed to citizen participation. This commitment was brief but, despite political hostility to such participation from 1972 onwards, the patterns established endured at least until the late 1980s. The state, pursuing a national unity strategy, had created constituencies, including the women's movement, that demanded the continuation of funding and supported or opposed government policy and action depending on their own political perceptions of particular issues (Pal 1993). The financial benefits of this strategy for the women's movement were greatest in the early 1980s and were considerably lessened in the late 1980s with the second electoral victory of the Conservative Party in 1988. Several of that party's policies had been opposed by organisations receiving funding, for example the NAC.

The uniqueness of the Canadian state strategy throughout the 1970s and 1980s lies in the funding of advocacy groups and the emphasis on citizenship development and national unity. Leslie Pal (1993) argues that this funding was most important for the Women's Program, where the impetus for funding was linked to the recommendations of the Royal Commission on the Status of Women and obligations associated with the United Nations-sponsored International Women's Year in 1975. This funding was crucially important for the NAC and several of its constituent organisations during the 1970s and early 1980s.

In 1983 the Government established the Royal Commission on Equality in Employment with a mandate 'to explore the most efficient, effective, and equitable means of promoting equality in employment for four groups: women, native people, disabled persons, and visible minorities' (Canada 1984: v). This Commission was in part a response to the findings by several parliamentary task forces that the four designated groups were under-represented in public sector employment and when employed were concentrated at the lower levels of the occupational spectrum. It was also a response to the mobilisation of the four designated groups. This mobilisation was facilitated at least in part by funding from the Citizenship Programme run by the Department of the Secretary of State. Several other factors gave a high profile to the issue of equality in employment throughout the 1970s and early 1980s. International Women's Year, the designation by the UN of 1976–85 as the Decade for Women and the 1975 and 1980 world conferences on women (held in Mexico City and Copenhagen) all helped to highlight gender inequalities, including labour market inequalities. Canada had made a commitment to achieving the goals of equal opportunities and economic independence for women in *Towards Equality for Women* (Status of Women Canada 1979). This was Canada's response to the UN World Plan of Action for the Implementation of the Objectives of International Women's Year adopted at the Mexico City Conference for Women in July 1975. A further impetus to measures to achieve equality in employment was Canada's ratification in 1981 of the UN Convention on the Elimination of All Forms of Discrimination Against Women, which endorses affirmative action.

The Royal Commission reported in 1984 and while its focus was employment equity the principles it established have also influenced pay equity legislation. It pointed out that existing Canadian legislation had little impact on the gender earnings gap. The failure was related to the inadequacy of most existing legislation, with its focus on equal pay for equal work, but also to the failure to enforce legislation rigorously, including the Canadian and Quebec Human Rights Acts, which embodied the equal pay for work of equal value concept. The Commission also made several recommendations relating to child care provision and funding arguing that its absence not only inhibits access but impairs the quality of participation. The major direct outcomes of the report were the 1986 federal Employment Equity Act and the Contract Compliance Programme but it also influenced provincial legislation (O'Connor 1998a).

In 1982, the Canadian Charter of Rights and Freedoms constitutionally affirmed the right to equality in employment without precluding 'any law, program or activity that has as its objective the amelioration of conditions of disadvantaged individuals or groups' (Section 15 (2)). This clause was a direct response to mobilisation by the women's equality movement and is seen as a high point in its political effectiveness. It also demonstrates the limited effectiveness of the Canadian

Advisory Council on the Status of Women (Geller-Schwartz 1995: 52–3) (see Chapter 5). The Charter of Rights and Freedoms introduced a new element into the political and legal context of the gender equality campaign in Canada. It was also the impetus for the founding of LEAF (Women's Legal Education and Action Fund) in 1984 when the equality clause came into force. This fund was to be used to finance court action on equal rights cases – preferably winnable cases arising under the Canadian and Quebec Charters. The Canadian Government also instituted a fund – the Court Challenges Programme – to support Charter cases. Its announced abolition by the Conservative Government in 1993 was strongly opposed by equality advocates and it was reinstated by the successor Liberal Government. LEAF has had considerable success in the cases taken, sometimes reacting to cases challenging on Charter grounds gains that women had already made, and in education and lobbying.

Where does Canada stand in terms of the framework outlined above? Canada has had a relatively strong women's equality movement since the 1970s. It has changed considerably in character over the two decades as have the range of demands made and the political strategy pursued. It has changed from a movement with a strong liberal feminist orientation to one strongly influenced by a materialist analysis. It has also become more diverse in membership with a strong emphasis on the inclusion of visible minority and disabled women. The political opportunity structure has also changed. The Liberal Party was in power throughout the 1970s and up to 1983. During this period, especially in the earlier years, there were relatively close contacts between the women's movement and the Liberal Party. This created a relatively favourable political opportunity structure within which equality demands could be pursued. During this period the NAC was strongly committed to a liberal feminist agenda, recognising the state as an important instrument of change; for example, it used a high profile tactic of an annual lobby of cabinet ministers. The period of Progressive Conservative Party Government from 1983 to 1993 was one of a deteriorating context for the women's equality movement – reflected in lesser funding and less access to government ministers, including refusal by ministers to participate in the annual lobby day – and an improving scenario for the anti-feminist movement, represented by REAL (Realistic Equal Active for Life) Women. This was assisted by the electoral emergence in the late 1980s of a right-wing populist party – the Reform Party – which was overtly anti-feminist. The 1980s also witnessed considerable changes in the NAC. Progressively throughout the 1980s it put a greater emphasis on economic inequality and the need for structural change – demands which are more challenging to the status quo than the equal opportunity focus of the 1970s. Much of its public mobilisation now involves the formation of coalitions with unions, church and community groups around broad gender and economic equity issues. Many of these have little connection with the activities of the gender equality bureaucratic policy machinery, which has been the hallmark of Canada's official gender equality strategy over the past twenty-five years but which has been very limited in its ability to systematically review government policy (Burt 1990; Status of Women Canada 1993; personal communication from Status of Women Canada, 1995; O'Connor 1998a).

Great Britain: Diverse Movement in a Changing Context

Britain differs from the United States, Canada and Australia in having a unitary structure of governance and even among countries with such a structure its political and administrative system is recognised as highly centralised and difficult to penetrate. This is one of the reasons cited for the lack of influence of the feminist movement. On the basis of comparative research in the early 1980s Joyce Gelb concluded that the structure and values of British politics tended to isolate feminists from the political mainstream and from potential allies (Gelb 1987; see also Lovenduski 1995). One must also recognise that the strategic choices made by the movement also influenced the outcome.

Historically the women's movement in Britain is strongly identified with the Women's Liberation Movement (WLM). The WLM, which was a grass-roots movement of autonomous women's groups, held high profile conferences from 1970 to 1978. The original demands of the movement were equal pay, equal education and employment opportunities, free contraception and abortion and 24-hour child care. Three others had been added by 1978: financial and legal independence; freedom from sexual coercion; and action against violence against women. The last conference was characterised by a split between the radical and socialist wings of the movement. Despite the significant theoretical and strategic differences, considerable coalition activity continued after this (Lovenduski 1986: 72–83). While the WLM was not disposed towards involvement in state institutions there were gender equality advocates, including women in the Labour Party, at this period who worked for such involvement. This resulted in the 1975 Sex Discrimination Act, which had all-party support, and the associated Equal Opportunities Commission (EOC) which was opened at the end of that year. During the 1980s the 300 Group, again non-party, had the objective of getting 300 women elected to Parliament.

During the 1980s the grass-roots groupings became even more complex with the rise to prominence of the black feminist movement and women peace activist organisations. The black feminist movement was, and continues to be, extremely influential in questioning the inclusiveness and orientation of the movement. This greater diversity at the grass-roots level was paralleled by greater integration of other elements of the movement into key political and economic institutions. Joni Lovenduski and Vicky Randall (1993: 7) argue that during the 1980s the liberal feminist goals of integrating women into positions in which they would be able to pursue equality objectives became more influential – many women's equality advocates pursue this strategy while not identifying themselves as liberal feminist.

The EOC was established to oversee the implementation of the Sex Discrimination Act and it is also the agency in charge of developing equality legislation. This Act came into force in the context of several pieces of equalising legislation during the 1970s. EOC commissioners were chosen to represent employers, unions and government departments with no explicit concern to include women's equality movement representatives. This was associated with considerable tensions between the agency and the gender equality movement in the early period. Relations improved greatly in the 1980s due to changes in orientation and strategy on both sides. These included a greater recognition of the importance of women's issues in the trade union movement – recognition not only associated with the unions' loss of power but also with acknowledgement that restructuring had a strong gender element. Despite the retrenchment ethos of the Thatcher Government the EOC was relatively successful not only at maintaining its budget but also at developing its work. EU directives, which had to be implemented, strengthened its hand.

Relative to the other three countries there is a stronger adherence in the public policy framework to the traditional male breadwinner–female housewife model in Britain. Yet the traditional logic has greater impact in some areas than in others. As with the ERA in the United States the issue of protective legislation has divided British feminists. Until the 1960s protective legislation was broadly considered appropriate and desirable. Since the 1970s the predominant model is one of equality, implying the abolition of protective legislation (Lewis and Davies 1991). Jane Lewis and Celia Davies see the arguments about equality in the 1980s as somewhat hollow in their failure to recognise that women enter the labour market on different terms than men, and to consider the impact of status in the family on status in the labour market. It is noteworthy that these contradictions not only characterise the political party system but are also evident within the gender equality movement.

The issue of child care services reflects the strong influence of the traditional model. Randall (1995) argues that the particular combination of issue type and policy-making tradition conspired to make it a marginal issue. She contends that both the redistribution entailed and the fact that it brought to light issues about the 'ideology of motherhood' made it unappealing to the Conservative governments in power from 1979 to 1997. This combined with the 'national policy style', which 'has entailed a reluctance to intervene either in the labour market or in the "private" family sphere', resulted in its marginalisation (Randall 1995: 327). In a related article Randall (1996) points to the limited feminist mobilisation around the issue especially up to 1980. She attributes this to the diverse strands within the movement, ambiguity in thinking about motherhood, paid employment and the proper role of the state and the way in which 'immediate concerns' such as child care were perceived by the WLM in terms of the movement's overall transformative objectives. Whereas campaigns for abortion rights and against rape and violence could be seen as symbolising or prefiguring a society where women would have reproductive freedom, the demand for publicly provided child care did not 'occupy the same logical space' (Randall 1996: 503). By the time feminists, often in coalition with Labour Party and trade union colleagues, began to make a concerted effort on child care the Conservative Government was in power. It was intent on cutting back rather than expanding the role of the state in the state, market, family nexus.

Summing up in terms of our framework we find a relatively divided women's equality movement in Britain which did not enjoy a favourable political opportunity structure for the eighteen years to 1997, during which the Conservative Party was in power. Lovenduski and Randall (1993) point to the British feminist 'mistrust' of involvement in state institutions and the likely associated loss of opportunities but also point out that some of the attitudes were a realistic response to a relatively impenetrable administrative and political environment. They argue that relative to other liberal democracies the British political system is 'unusually centralized and difficult to break into' (1993: 363; see also Pierson 1994). This was particularly evident during the Thatcher period. Yet, while it closed off opportunities it also changed the political opportunity structure in a positive way from the point of view of the women's movement: it made the trade union movement and the Labour Party more receptive to integrating the demands of the women's movement. It will be interesting to see whether or not this bears fruit during the tenure of the Labour Party Government elected in 1997.

No strong anti-feminist movement has emerged in Britain. This may be associated with the fact that the political environment was relatively hostile to the gender equality movement, and abortion as a long-established medical entitlement was not a political issue in the same way as in the United States and Canada. In addition, the women's movement was not and was never seen to be in the ascendancy in terms of policy influence – the European Union was perceived to be the gender equality force to be challenged by counter-equality forces in Britain.

Australia: An Alliance Between the Labor Party Government, the Women's Movement and the Labour Movement

The contemporary women's equality movement in Australia as elsewhere has diverse strands and its origin cannot be neatly dated. For the present analysis we concentrate on developments since the early 1970s. This is an important break-point. The late 1960s saw 'the arrival from the United States of a more assertive form of feminism – women's liberation', which in the context of a better-educated female population, many of whom had been politicised by the anti-war movement, had a strong mobilising influence and contributed to a change in the way in which traditional equality demands were articulated (Sawer 1995: 23). The contemporary movement has three main elements: grass-roots organisations, women in the labour movement and the Women's Electoral Lobby (WEL). The latter organisation, which was founded in 1972, is non-party and focused on bringing women's equality issues – child care, equal pay, equal opportunity and reproductive rights – on to the political agenda. It gained immediate prominence because of its very effective election strategy in the same year. This election brought the Labor Party back into power after twenty-three years of Liberal–National Party Coalition government. Since the new government was strongly committed to women's equality issues, some of the demands made by WEL enjoyed almost immediate success, in particular its demands for greater representation of women in the government and bureaucracy (Sawer 1995). While WEL has received considerable attention because of its high profile success, it is important to acknowledge that much of the success of the Australian women's equality movement, especially in terms of achievements such as pay equity, which benefited the mass of women, is a story of the concerted action of diverse strands. It involved not only elected women and feminists in the bureaucracy – the 'femocrats' – but also the successful organisation of women in the trade union movement and the pressure on, and criticism of, the feminists in the bureaucracy by grass-roots movements.

Australia is not unique among these four countries in having a relatively strong labour party and union movement. However, there are some key elements, especially institutional structures which, combined with the political party configuration over the 1970s and 1980s, made the Australian situation favourable to the achievement of mass equality gains. The Australian Labor Party has been Australia's single largest party for almost all of the period since 1910 when it formed the world's first majority Labor government (Rawson 1991) but the Whitlam Government in 1972–75 was the first labour government in almost a quarter-century. That Government's concern with gender equality issues was consistent with the acknowledgement by social democratic and labour parties cross-nationally at this period of the importance of gender equality in the context of their broader commitment to equality. The US civil rights movement helped to raise the profile of equality issues throughout the western world at this time. The concern with gender equality issues by the Whitlam Government was also a reflection of electoral concerns – the ALP had traditionally fared relatively poorly among women voters. These concerns were heightened by the activities of WEL.

Considerable gains were made during the Whitlam Government's tenure both in relation to social programs in general and specifically to the institutionalisation of a concern with women's issues in government and in the federal bureaucracy; this was reflected in the establishment of policy machinery and the recruitment to the bureaucracy of several feminist activists both of which actions were maintained, although with varying levels of support, throughout the Liberal–National Coalition governments which followed (Watson 1990; Sawer 1991). Much of this was replicated at the state level with the result that Australia has an extensive array of gender-related bureaucratic policy machinery. Some of these measures were strengthened in the period from 1983 to 1996, during which time the ALP again held office at the federal level. The Women's Budget Program introduced in 1984–85, and from 1987 entitled the Women's Budget Statement, is particularly noteworthy. This required Commonwealth departments and agencies 'to provide a detailed account of the impact of their activities on women for a document circulated by the Prime Minister on budget night' (Sawer 1990: 228). This enhanced the effectiveness of the requirement introduced in 1983 that all cabinet submissions must include a statement of their impact on women (Sawer 1990: 228). The Women's Budget Statement had a significant educative role in sensitising bureaucrats and the public on the gender impact of apparently gender-neutral programs. Rather than asserting neutrality, departments were obliged to provide a gender disaggregated analysis of programs, for example labour market programs and taxation measures (Sawer 1990: 229–31). This program was abolished by the Liberal–National Coalition in 1996.

The Accord between the ALP and the Australian Council of Trade Unions (ACTU) was negotiated before the ALP was elected in 1983. This was facilitated by the strong role of the ACTU vis-à-vis individual trade unions and its ability to command their support for the negotiated Accord. It included a commitment by the Labor Government to provide tax and welfare measures and create favourable conditions for economic restructuring in return for wage and strike restraint. It included a commitment to protect the incomes of social security recipients and low wage earners from the effects of structural change. Despite early criticism that the Accord had institutionalised gender pay inequality, the period of the Accord until 1993 saw significant decreases in the gender wage gap. It was also associated with other gender equality gains. For example, the proposal to introduce maternity benefit was negotiated in 1994 as part of the Accord and is seen as an element of Australia's commitment to and compliance with ILO Convention 156 on the Rights of Workers with Family Responsibilities, ratified by Australia in 1990 (and not yet ratified by any of the other three countries). In addition to its promotion by the trade union movement, paid maternity leave was advocated by WEL and the National Council for the International Year of the Family, which was in place throughout 1995.

In analysing the relative success of the Australian women's movement in effecting change in government policies over the 1970s and 1980s, Marian Sawer (1991: 260) argues that four factors make the Australian situation unique: the Australian political tradition whereby radical social movements automatically looked to government to satisfy their demands; the window of opportunity provided by the election of reformist governments at national and state levels at a time when the political energy of the contemporary Australian women's movement was at its height; the lack of effective opposition, as anti-feminist organisations did not win the credibility with mainstream political organisations that they achieved most notably in the United States; and the existence of a centralised wage-fixing system.

What makes the Australian situation unusual throughout most of the 1970 to 1990 period is the simultaneous occurrence of these four factors. This created a relatively favourable political opportunity structure for the Australian women's equality movement, although it is important to recognise that this was more consistently true in some areas than in others. While the gender equity bureaucratic policy machinery remained intact during the government tenure of the ALP, the centralised bargaining system which was the source of the mass gender equality gains was effectively ended in October 1991. Enterprise bargaining was introduced at the end of 1991 despite an earlier statement by the Industrial Relations Commission that it 'places at a relative disadvantage those sections of the labour force where women predominate' (IRC 1991: 56; quoted in Lee 1994: 190). In recognition of this, the award system was retained to provide a safety net to protect those unable to make workable agreements with employers and to ensure compliance with ILO conventions concerning minimum pay, equal pay for work of equal value and redundancy (Lee 1994: 190). Despite these commitments by the Labor Government considerable concern was expressed by gender equality advocates. Much of this centred on the government commitment to increase labour market flexibility and the fear that this would take primacy over equality issues. Economic policy emphasised fiscal restraint and increased labour market flexibility as key imperatives of national policy to the exclusion of other considerations (Pusey 1991). This was the rationale for enterprise bargaining.

While the ALP had already seriously compromised the successful model through the introduction of enterprise bargaining, some of the other gains of the 1970s and 1980s came under challenge almost immediately on the election of the Liberal–National Coalition in 1996: for example, the Women's Budget Statement was abolished, the Office for the Status of Women budget was cut significantly and the scope of its mandate lessened. At least one analyst has detected a shift back to elements of a male breadwinner model in the early action of the Coalition (D. Mitchell 1997). Deborah Mitchell cites the government's introduction of a Family Tax Rebate paid to the primary breadwinner in its first Budget and commitments to abolish parts of the child care support structure – the operational subsidies to support family day care services, occasional care and community-based long day care centres will end after 1997 – and to cut back on others, for example, the Child Care Rebate which was introduced on a non-income-tested basis in July 1994 to help with the cost of work-, study- or training-related child care costs was changed to an income-tested payment in the 1997–98 Budget.

These changes suggest that the gains associated with the relative success of the Australian women's movement identified by Marian Sawer are under some serious challenge. They also suggest that when gender equality gains conflict with government economic objectives, gender equality takes second place. This occurs despite the existence of a range of gender equality bureaucratic policy units and the increased representation of gender equality advocates in the bureaucracy and Parliament. While the changes during the 1970s and 1980s in gender-related issues suggest the possibility of a 'woman-friendly' policy scenario in Australia, a longer term view suggests that the institutionalisation of these successes cannot be taken for granted. This longer term view suggests that the orientation of the women's movement of looking to government to satisfy its demands yields significant gains only in the context of a favourable political and economic opportunity structure.

Policy Logics in a Shifting Context

We find in all four countries a move from a relatively favourable opportunity structure for program expansion in the 1970s to a distinctly constraining one during the 1980s and early 1990s – the timing varied in different countries but the change took place in all. This cannot be associated exclusively with the changes in political configuration that occurred in particular countries. Conservative governments were elected in Great Britain (1979), the United States (1980) and Canada (1983); in addition, union density declined in all four countries. The concern with crises and contradictions of the welfare state from 1973 to the mid-1980s gave way to concerns about restructuring and globalisation. This concern grew throughout the second half of the decade not only among academics but also among politicians and the media. These concepts are open to a range of interpretations and are the focus of extensive academic analyses. It is not our objective to enter into these debates. Rather we wish to draw out some of the implications of the context characterised by a preoccupation with these terms for gender equality politics and the development of gender policy logics. As Paul Hirst and Grahame Thompson (1996) point out there is a need to distinguish between a fully globalised economy, in which the nation states are effectively powerless, and an open internationalised economy, in which nation states participate but are structurally constrained by the progressive internationalisation of money and capital markets (Andrews 1994). However, this is not the only sense in which globalisation affects the context of social policy formation. Globalisation as an ideology is promoted by particular interests (Moran and Wood 1996). This is reflected in the relationship between global pressures and domestic forces to prioritise the reduction of balance of payments deficits and anti-inflation policies over full-employment policies in several countries (Rhodes 1996: 309).

Restructuring is evident in a whole series of developments, none of which is unique to this period, but all of which are more acutely evident from the mid-1970s and throughout the 1980s: for example, rapid technological change; the growth of non-standard employment; high unemployment, especially long-term unemployment; high government deficits; falling rates of productivity growth; stagnating real incomes; and the restructuring of social programs (MacDonald 1995; Myles 1996; O'Connor 1998b). By the mid-1980s all four countries had begun to respond to these issues and this was reflected in policy output, including the restructuring of social programs. Fiscally restrictive policies were often justified by reference to globalisation, in particular the threat posed to employment by the increasing competitiveness of the globalised economy and globalised financial markets. The former was linked to the importance of attracting foreign direct investment as well as competing in international markets. There was political and business pressure to 'harmonise' programs with other countries and to increase labour market flexibility, for example in Canada vis-à-vis the United States (O'Connor 1993b). The emphasis on globalised financial markets was associated in some countries, such as Canada and Australia, with considerable emphasis on credit rating by agencies such as Moody's Investors Service and Standard and Poors Rating Group. The influence of these ratings on the cost of repaying foreign debt and on currency stability was marshalled to support arguments for the absence of choice open to domestic policy-makers.

The configuration of influences identified above and, especially, the preoccupation with fiscal rectitude has fostered an environment which is not favourable to responding to new needs through the expansion of programs. Yet, the economic and, in particular, the labour market restructuring which characterised the 1980s and 1990s gave rise to new needs that changed the traditional state, market, family balance. Female labour force participation continued to increase and this was reflected in the increase in dual-earner and single earner-carer households. But the labour market in which many of these women are participating is very different in character from that which faced the traditional male industrial worker.

All four countries have gone through a process of restructuring over the 1980s although there are considerable national variations in timing and scope (Mishra 1990). While the changing context did not result in wholesale dismantling of the post-war social policy frameworks there have been fundamental changes in some programs in several countries (Pierson 1994, 1996; Esping-Andersen 1996b; O'Connor 1998b). Not only has there been a considerable amount of 'explicit disentitlement' because of more stringent criteria for benefit and service access and duration but there has also been 'implicit disentitlement' associated with the growth of non-standard employment (Standing 1995). This growth has had major consequences for the distribution of employment quality and earnings and has militated particularly against new entrants to the labour market. Much of the analysis of restructuring has focused on the restructuring of the welfare state narrowly defined, that is, on social programs, but this is only one element of a broader phenomenon which includes restructuring of the labour market. Both elements are related and have an important gender dimension. Our concern here is with the labour market element, in particular the increasing emphasis on flexibility and the growth of non-standard forms of employment and the implications of these developments for gender equality strategies. There is now considerable evidence that in some economies, especially those of the United States, Canada and Britain, employment growth is increasingly characterised by non-standard employment, that is, part-time, temporary, contract and home-work (Economic Council of Canada 1990; Tilly 1991) and industrial policy is characterised by an emphasis on competition through static or downwardly flexible labour markets (Myles 1991a: 2). Some analysts argue that Australia is on a similar trajectory (Ewer et al. 1991). Static flexibility refers to the ability of employers to lay off workers, to lower wages and contract out work in response to changes in the marketplace. This is based on a low-skilled, low-wage workforce. It allows a rapid short-term response to changes in demand but is static in the sense that innovation is spasmodic and the adoption of new technologies slow (S. Cohen and Zysman 1987: 130–4). The emphasis on static flexibility has major implications for women since they are more likely to be in non-standard jobs or re-entering the labour market after a period without labour market experience, and consequently have to compete at the lower end of the occupational structure.

Occupation and labour market location not only have implications for labour market experience and remuneration, but also influence, both directly and indirectly, citizens' ability to exercise social rights. Even in the social democratic countries where gender equality is an explicit objective of policy, several studies have demonstrated that take up of gender-neutral services, such as parental leave available on the same conditions to men and women, varies with the man's, and especially the woman's, position in the labour market (Widerberg 1991; Kaul 1991; Haas 1992). These studies point to an important issue relating to the exercise of citizenship rights: in addition to the fact that gender-neutral citizenship rights must be exercised within a gender-structured labour market where the traditional ideal worker is full-time and assumed to be without domestic or caring responsibilities, even when citizenship rights are based on an equality principle they must be exercised within a labour market which is structured on a principle of occupational inequality and which, increasingly, is being restructured into a labour market divided into good and bad jobs. This points to the importance of focusing on the differences among both women and men in terms of labour market experience.

Despite these changes in the composition of the labour force a compensating change in the social policy framework was constrained by the new political and economic context. The challenge to the Keynesian paradigm from conservative and new-right analysts, the apparent failure of the welfare states to solve certain problems, the changing global context and the associated claim of the ineffectiveness of national solutions were all associated with a loss of confidence in collective solutions. Paul Pierson (1996) argues that the phenomenon of 'blame avoidance' characterises the politics of contemporary welfare states at least when retrenchment is considered. But what about expansion? What we are concerned with is neither traditional program expansion nor retrenchment, but the expansion and refocusing of social policy frameworks in an era of retrenchment. Many of the policies involved a restructuring of the state, market, family relationship but this was precisely the area which deficit politics was targeting for cuts. There was an explicit attempt to lessen the economic role of the state, including some aspects of its economic regulatory role, while increasing its social regulatory role. The policies being advocated by gender equality proponents had a dual focus which made their adoption particularly problematic in the context of deficit politics and this was exacerbated in some countries by political conservatism. These policies had not only a redistributive element, but also a redefinition element. This redefinition has a number of dimensions: first of these is the redefinition of the scope of public policy, which involves the recognition that the care of dependent people, which was formerly considered a private/family responsibility, is a public issue. Associated with this is the redefinition of 'worker' from the male breadwinner without caring responsibilities to earner with caring responsibilities. In terms of our focus, it involves a redefinition of the state, market, family division of responsibility. This process is ongoing and contested to varying degrees across countries and over time.

The combination of deficit politics and the deteriorating labour market situation at a period when women were entering the labour force in increasing numbers contributed to a very negative environment for gender equality. This is not to suggest that the situation was uniformly bad – socio-economic and educational differences were key influences on outcomes for individual women.

CHAPTER 7

States, Markets, Families

The defining characteristic of the liberal social policy regime is state intervention which is clearly subordinate to the market and the family. But, to a significant extent, liberal policy works through the market, as in the case of tax credits for the purchase of services such as child care, and regulation of the market, for example through anti-discrimination legislation or the setting of minimum standards for market-based services such as child care. It has a relatively strong emphasis on income and/or means-tested programs and while there may be a commitment to universalism, it is universalism with an equal opportunity focus. The implications of these arrangements for families and households and for gender relations have received little attention in comparative welfare state analysis. There are significant cross-national differences in the balance between market and family in providing benefits and services for individuals and households, and, specifically, there are significant differences in terms of gender and class consequences depending on which of the two forms of private responsibility, market or family, is supported by public policy.

Does a liberal political tradition have a congruous set of consequences for gender relations across the three policy areas of income maintenance, labour market participation and reproductive rights in Australia, Canada, the United States and Britain? The concept of policy regime refers to institutionalised patterns of welfare state provision establishing systematic relations between the state, the market and the family. Our analysis of policies relating to labour markets, income maintenance and regulation of reproduction in Australia, Canada, Britain and the United States identified significant similarities in policy orientation but also some noteworthy differences across the four countries.

Despite convergence in male and female labour force participation levels over the past couple of decades, gender-based stratification is still strongly evident in the characteristics of participation in all four countries (demonstrated in Chapter 3). This is evident not only in participation by family type and continuity of employment over the life cycle but also in part-time work, which is predominantly female, and in occupational location and pay. While each of these countries is embarked on a trajectory leading to earner-carer labour market participants, as reflected in dual and sole parent earning households, as the norm they are differently located along this trajectory. The United States and Canada most closely approximate the earner-carer model, as reflected in their relatively high full-time female labour force participation rates. The common thread across the four countries is that their social policy frameworks have not kept pace with the labour force participation developments. None of these countries has a comprehensive strategy to address gender-based labour market stratification although there is a range of relevant policies in all four which relate to the facilitation of labour market participation for people with caring responsibilities and to a lessening of inequality in pay and participation.

Given the primacy of the market and the family over the state it is not surprising that none of these countries has opted for what the OECD has termed 'maximum public responsibility' for child care. Before the Coalition victory, Australia stood out as progressive in this area not only because of its National Child Care Strategy and relatively high level of provision, even if this was increasingly provided on a commercial basis. The available public child care services are strongly targeted to 'at risk' children in both Britain and the United States. In all four countries there are tax concessions for work-based child care. Market-based provision is regulated but quality is a problem especially at the low end of the market in each of these countries. The system is multi-tiered on class lines in all four, although to a lesser extent in Australia than in the other three. Child care is one of the most explicit manifestations of the working out of class differences among labour force participants and reinforces the good jobs–bad jobs divisions in all four countries. Maternity leave, or care leave in the United States, has a stronger social rights dimension but this is constrained by stringent eligibility criteria and/or coverage. The rights dimension is further constrained by the absence of benefit in the United States, stringent eligibility criteria in Britain and its limitation to certain categories of workers in Australia.

There are noteworthy differences across the four countries in the labour market equality strategies pursued. While the policy objectives may be similar, the mechanisms for implementation and the outcomes are different. Despite the strong liberal influence on policy in Australia, as reflected in the pervasiveness of means-testing in social provision, the labour market equality strategies adopted there up to the early 1990s reflect a strong collectivist approach relative to the other three countries. This is most evident in relation to pay up to the early 1990s but is also evident in relation to expanding opportunities, especially child care, training and the consensual approach adopted by the Affirmative Action Agency. The differences in outcome associated with the different strategies are most sharply reflected in the ranking of countries in female–male pay differentials and gender-based occupational segregation. Female–male pay differentials are lower in Australia than in the other three countries while gender-based occupational segregation is most pronounced in Australia. At the other end of the continuum to Australia, Canada, followed by the United States, has the largest female–male pay differential and the United States, followed closely by Canada, has the smallest level of gender-based occupational segregation. This may reflect the effectiveness of a collectivist strategy in relation to mass rights, such as pay equity, and élite strategy effectiveness in the case of individual civil rights to equal participation and treatment. This interpretation is consistent with the finding of an inverse relationship between pay equity and occupational segregation not only in these countries but also across the OECD (Rosenfeld and Kalleberg 1990). It is noteworthy that the Australian equality advantage in gender-based pay differentials has not improved since the early 1990s. For full-time workers the situation is improving in all other countries, although not consistently as is evidenced by the worsening of the ratio in Canada in 1994.

In Chapter 4 we concluded that despite a very high degree of formal gender neutrality in income maintenance provisions there is some gender differentiation and gender inequality in all four countries, some of which occurs within programs. Gender differentiation refers to the highlighting of gender difference and the underlining of gender identities through distinctions based on the gender division of labour. Creating gender inequality involves treating different gender roles differently or treating men and women differently. In this regard Australia is least unequal since support provisions attached to employment and caring, albeit low-level and subject to means-testing, form part of a single system of benefits. All of the other countries contribute to gender inequality through several types of differential treatment. For example, benefits to those who have been principally caregivers, or who have had intermittent work histories, are less generous than those for the formerly regularly employed in the United States, Britain and Canada. But women have better access to standard employment in North America and, consequently, the prospect of better social benefits.

Labour force participation requirements are most stringent in the United States and are increasing in Canada – especially in some provinces – but without a guarantee of high quality public child care in either country.

We are again talking of a continuum in terms of the reinforcement of gender differentiation. British and US social insurance systems institutionalise distinctions between wage earners and unpaid caregivers and among caregivers based on their relationship to wage earners: widows and wives of covered wage earners, although depending on derived rather than individually based benefits, are treated better than unmarried and many divorced mothers primarily because they are incorporated into a system based on rights rather than discretion. In the case of the United States this also reflects and reinforces racial inequality – single mothers on benefits are disproportionately minority group members. Despite the persistence of gender differentiation in the US social security system, differentiation is being decreased through the emphasis on labour force participation. This is true in all countries but most explicitly in the United States, where Aid to Families with Dependent Children has been replaced by Temporary Assistance to Needy Families, which requires work from all beneficiaries, including mothers of very young children. More significantly, the increasing importance of the Earned Income Tax Credit reflects the strong commitment to labour force participation and gender sameness. The Canadian system, although similar in structure to those of the United States and Britain, has a lesser gender differentiation impact than either of these. The Australian system underlines gender difference, but with less unequal benefits than the other countries. It still divides programs into those for family needs/caregiving and labour market needs for the working aged. In considering differentiation there is a cohort effect associated with labour market participation. With the increase in female labour force participation in all four countries less gender differentiation in making claims can be expected when the present labour market cohorts retire. Given the characteristics of female labour force participation in the United States and Canada this change will come sooner in those countries.

In the contemporary period the United States is clearly at one end of a continuum where the 'sanctity of the market' has primacy over motherhood as a full-time activity. This is reflected in the requirement that those who want to maintain a household do so through labour market participation except for an increasingly short period around the birth of a child, although, as in the other three countries, a job is not guaranteed. Canada comes closest to the United States in terms of labour market participation requirements; the strength of these requirements has been increasing in several Canadian provinces throughout the 1990s. At the other end of this continuum – the primacy of motherhood end – we place Britain and Australia. The British situation is unique in its encouragement of sole parents to work part-time and insistence that they be partly supported by former partners. In contrast, Australia does support caregiving mothers as independent claimants. The motherhood end of the continuum refers to the state's provision of benefits to support the capacity of single mothers to maintain an autonomous household for a certain period of their children's lives without having recourse to the labour market. It is important to recognise that this capacity does not imply economic adequacy. Even in Britain over a fifth of sole parents were below the poverty line in the early 1990s, but the vast majority of single mothers without earnings were below the poverty line in the United States, Canada and Australia. However, as a consequence of the emphasis on labour market participation in both the United States and Canada, far fewer sole parents or married mothers are without earnings in those countries than in Britain and Australia.

Reproductive rights in these four countries afford an interesting insight into the relationship between civil and social rights. The general pattern identified in Chapter 5 is of the primacy of the civil right to abortion in the United States and Canada whereas abortion is seen primarily within the context of medical entitlements in Britain and Australia. But abortion is not seen as a medical service like any other – the existence of the condition does not ensure the treatment requested. Rather, the woman has to phrase her request in health terms. The North American pattern is consistent with the liberal welfare state commitment to the ideology of possessive individualism and the primacy of the market, although the civil right to abortion is challenged in both countries and in Canada the possibility of legislation regulating its availability has not been ruled out. There is a significant difference between Canada and the United States because of the universal medical coverage in Canada. Yet, this does not guarantee access in all areas and most abortions are provided through clinics operating on a fee-for-service basis. There is a strong market element in the procurement of abortion services in all of these countries: this is most obvious in the United States, but is also evident in Canada and Australia where the universal insurance systems underpin the market provision of services, and in Britain where, although it is covered by the National Health Service, abortion is as often secured through private clinics. In discussion of social rights in relation to reproduction, the social right to health care tends to be more salient than the social right to support one's family. Of the four countries, the United States has the least commitment to such a social right. The result is a strong link between the ability to sustain a family and labour market status.

We find significant variations in the way these welfare states affect gender and class relations. There are clear cross-national differences in policy orientation, although the fault line varies depending on the dimension considered, but there are sufficient commonalities to support the conclusion of conformity to a liberal social policy continuum when gender is incorporated into the analysis. All four countries show evidence of the influence on policy choices of a relatively limited role for the state vis-à-vis the market and family and a commitment to individual rights. The degree to which these principles may be tempered varies across countries and over time through variation in political orientations in individual countries. While we identify a strong adherence to the primacy of private provision over public provision in all four countries there is a clear division among them in terms of which form of private responsibility is supported by public policy. Canada comes closest to the United States at the market end of the continuum but, as in other policy areas, there are some 'small differences that matter' (Card and Freeman 1994).

Linking labour market and income maintenance policies we find the United States and Canada with high full-time female labour force participation and a model of motherhood based on paid work most of the time – the key difference between the two being the availability of paid maternity leave in Canada, which lessens the dependence on the labour market for survival. The market orientation in the United States and Canada is evident not only in relation to services, such as child care, which support labour market participation, but also in relation to abortion, which is affirmed as a civil right but not a social right. Again we have a less clear-cut pattern in Canada than in the United States. Canada has a universal health care system but since abortion is not a health service like any other, the majority of those seeking abortions are dependent on market solutions.

On the other side of the market–family divide we find Britain and Australia. Britain has the strongest reliance on the family for service provision with the assumption that families will be supported by a labour market participant. In the absence of a male breadwinner, public policy is financially supportive of sole parents but within the context of maintaining private responsibility through the collection of child support from absent fathers. This reflects the primacy of the family but in the context of supporting labour market participant as opposed to direct market dependence for caregivers as in the United States. Australia's position at the opposite end of the continuum to the United States is reflected to varying degrees in the social provisions to facilitate labour force participation in combination with child-bearing and rearing. It encourages independence through support for employment, as reflected in public child care services at least for some workers, but still supports full-time caregiving for pre-school and school-age children. Just as Canada tempers the market orientation of its public policy framework with publicly supported benefits and services which recognise family–market linkages, Australia tempers the family orientation of its public policy framework through its recognition of the linkages between market and family status – reflected in its support of child care both in association with labour market participation and as a full-time activity.

A second fault line in terms of public policy emphasis that parallels the line between market and family is the civil rights–social rights division. The United States and Canada have a relatively stronger emphasis on individual civil rights than on social rights while in Australia and Britain the granting of social rights as a means to exercising civil rights is more salient.

Throughout this analysis we have identified a broad movement from public policy frameworks built on the assumption of gender difference to frameworks built to varying degrees on the assumption of gender sameness. In pointing to this movement we are not implying that a commitment to gender sameness necessarily implies a commitment to gender equality. Moving from a policy orientation built on the assumption of gender difference to one built on the assumption of gender sameness should, in theory, lessen gender stratification but because of a failure to take seriously class stratification and the relationship between state, market and family the result is a reinforcing of difference among women. This is clearly exemplified in relation to labour market participation. Whereas in the past dual earning was associated with the equalisation of incomes across the socio-economic spectrum, it is now a contributing factor to increasing polarisation of the income distribution. This is not to down-play the significant improvement in household income associated with dual earning at all levels of the income distribution spectrum. It is a recognition of the polarisation of the occupational structure associated with economic and labour market restructuring. Paralleling this is the increasing polarisation of dual-earner households into high income units generally enjoying standard employment contracts and low income units in non-standard employment or households where both partners are unemployed. The former group are in a position to purchase support services such as high quality child care on the market or use paid domestic help solutions while the latter group are often dependent on low end of the market, low quality solutions.

The policy solution that moves us closer to gender and class equality is not to retreat to gender difference, understood as permanent differences between the sexes. Rather, we need to recognise the linkages between citizens' diverse positions in the labour market and their varying caring responsibilities in ways which allow men and women, parents and those without children, and people with different sorts of ties to friends, relatives and neighbours to participate as equals in both spheres. This will require some greater measure of politically mandated social support than a strict neo-liberal policy permits. If this is not present, we face a continuation, and perhaps a worsening, of the present situation in which those advantaged in labour market terms are the only ones allowed satisfactory solutions to their caregiving needs. In its long history, liberal thinking has included strands, such as new or social liberalism, which recognised the needs for social support to individuals' initiatives. Though this kind of thinking was confined to the contingencies of the capitalist labour market, there is no reason why it cannot be called upon today, in new ways, to justify social provision that supports the contingencies of caregiving.

In Chapter 6 we outlined how gender equality issues had been represented in the political system since the 1960s and asked what determined success in effecting change in government policy. Political party configuration and social movement mobilisation, in particular the level of mobilisation of the gender equality and anti-feminist movements, have influenced not only the equality objectives pursued but also how they have been pursued. This has been conditioned and constrained by the political opportunity structure and the institutional context and policy legacy. The political opportunity structure and the character of the gender equality movements proved crucial in facilitating and/or constraining the options open to gender equality advocates in particular countries at particular times. There have been changes in all countries over the period since 1970. The Australian situation gives a particularly good illustration of the impact of the range of influences identified in Chapter 6. It also illustrates the fragility of gains that do not become established as citizenship rights. From what appeared to be a very favourable political opportunity structure for gender equality advocates in the 1970s and 1980s (Sawer 1991) the situation has changed in the 1990s to one of not only the retrenchment of programs but also the dismantling of the bureaucratic policy machinery that underpinned many of the gains. This is taking place within the context of a shift from centralised to enterprise bargaining. The mass pay gains were achieved through the centralised bargaining system.

While the political opportunity structure has become unfavourable in Australia, it may have become more favourable in some respects in the

1990s in the United States with the Clinton administration and in Britain with New Labour. However, both administrations are committed to a fundamental restructuring of the social security framework in a way that is likely to constrain the ability of many people to form autonomous households, particularly among the working class and especially the long-term unemployed. Furthermore, these political changes have occurred within the context of a labour market environment that is likely to exacerbate the good jobs–bad jobs divisions among workers, both female and male.

In considering influences on policy logic, political party mobilisation is only one influence. Social movement mobilisation may be of considerable importance but must be analysed within a multi-dimensional approach which recognises the crucial importance of the political opportunity structure and the constraints and/or opportunities imposed by institutional structures and policy response patterns. We suggest that 'the natural policy response', to use Pierson's phrase, varies across countries and this influences not only government but also gender equality advocates. Whereas in Canada the establishment of a royal commission is the mechanism likely to be demanded by advocacy groups to highlight the importance of a particular issue, it is also the natural policy response of governments to the emergence of contentious issues. In the United States there have been federal and state commissions but the overwhelming sense is of the pursuit of change through a rights focus using legal advocacy. It is noteworthy that the use of the legal advocacy approach has increased in the Canadian context since the adoption of the Charter of Rights and Freedoms in 1982. There is considerably less reliance on legal advocacy in both Australia and Britain. In Australia the centralised industrial relations structure that was dominant until the early 1990s and the history of reliance by radical social movements on government to satisfy demands have conditioned the strategies of gender equality advocates and the response of governments. The highly centralised and difficult to penetrate political and administrative structure in Britain has also historically conditioned the strategies of gender equality advocates but constrained the options open to them.

We argued in Chapter 1 for an approach to welfare state analysis which acknowledges the complexity of social relations and institutional structures. To achieve this we drew on both mainstream and feminist analysis with the objective of developing an integrated analytical approach and undertook a multi-dimensional analysis of four most similar welfare states. Our analysis of the interaction of class, gender and race and the relevance of this interaction for understanding the outcomes of public policy illustrates very clearly that an exclusive focus on any one of these is inadequate to understand welfare states as mechanisms of stratification. The salience of each varies depending on the dimension of public policy that is the focus of attention and may also vary over time. There has been a tendency in comparative welfare state analysis to confine gender to the family. Our conclusion is that gender is a relevant dimension of analysis not only of the family but also of the state and market when considered individually, and is crucial to understanding the state, market, family balance in public policy. But it is only one dimension and must be considered in interaction with class and, in some instances, with race and age.

Welfare state variation is not just a question of variation in the level and character of state activity in constraining dependence on the market. The family is an integral part of the public policy framework and may be a focus of public policy in terms of service provision. These states which are often identified as displaying the primacy of the market over the state differ significantly in their approach to the two forms of private responsibility, market and family. Neither market, nor family nor state alone can provide an adequate understanding of the policy dynamic. There is now considerable agreement among comparative analysts that expenditure is an inadequate measure of welfare state variation and that quantitative and qualitative approaches are necessary to capture the complexity of institutional structures and variation. The variation across dimensions identified by our analysis illustrates that the complexity of policy logics cannot be adequately garnered from any one policy area and indeed may vary significantly over time even in particular policy areas.

The liberal welfare state is often treated as a residual category in comparative analysis. However, it is clear that the liberal designation has substantive meaning with respect to the structuring of both gender and class in the welfare states of these four countries. We reiterate that it has not been the purpose of our study to define the dimensions of the liberal 'type', or to identify the welfare states of these or other countries as members of such a grouping. Rather, we have explored the importance, or otherwise, of liberalism in its several forms, in the way social policy in these countries articulates provision through state, market and family. Many of the key processes that we have identified as changing the balance between state, market and family in the United States, Canada, Australia and Great Britain are operative to varying degrees in all welfare states in the contemporary period. Nevertheless, this ideology plays a distinctive and pervasive role, variable in nature and degree, in the policy regimes of the four countries. This is most immediately evident in the privileging of the market over provision through the state in all four countries, most particularly in respect of the centrality of labour markets. In this regard it is important to bear in mind the obvious fact that none of these countries guarantees anyone a job even when work or work effort is mandated for access to certain benefits and/or services.

Restructuring and the shift towards dual-earner families are strengthening this market dimension, and the forms of economic and class inequalities associated with it. It is noteworthy that even in the case of abortion, where the health systems of three of the four countries have social democratic elements, the market is a significant and even a majority provider. As much other research has shown, the US social policy regime is the most liberal in this respect, and Australia perhaps least so. The policy regimes of these countries also show distinctive patterns of boundedness in relations between state and family, setting stubborn limits to state intervention in areas such as equity policies and child care. The shift in liberal ideology from gender difference to gender sameness is variously represented in the policy regimes of the four countries, with Britain holding more determinedly to the breadwinner–carer family model than the other three countries and the United States moving away from it most quickly. Entailing strong preferences for 'private' over 'public' ways of meeting social need, these patterns of boundedness vary among the four countries. The United States and to some extent also Canada again show a clear and distinct pattern of encouraging families to have recourse to the market for support services, while Britain shows a clear pattern of encouraging the privatisation of need within the family, including continued dependence on former spouses.

In some respects the liberal dimension of all welfare states is being strengthened because of the increasing influence of globalisation, both as fact – increasing internationalisation of financial, investment and product markets – and as ideology. The increasing strength of the liberal world in our four countries is most sharply illustrated by the low and decreasing access to services on the basis of citizenship, the increased restrictions on insurance-based benefits such as unemployment insurance and pensions, the increased reliance, and restrictions, on income-tested programs and the increasing emphasis on the market as a mechanism for the provision of services and on relationship to the labour market in determining eligibility for benefits and services. It is also illustrated by the reluctance of the state to set limits on market activity through its regulatory role. But this is accompanied in some instances by an increase in the social regulatory role of the state. All of these changes are gender neutral but gender neutrality in the context of inequality in condition has the potential to reinforce existing stratification. As is true elsewhere, when the range and/or quality of social rights are restricted class differences are reinforced.

The liberal character of the relations between state, market and family in these policy regimes is also reflected in the women's movements in these four countries, and the strategies they have applied in mobilising women's resources, making political alliances, and in addressing the opportunity structures available to them. The appeal of these movements for women's right to full individual personhood and equality of opportunity has reflected the dominance of liberal feminism, as has their reliance on legal and bureaucratic pathways to power. The equity strategies of these movements have been written in the liberal language of gender sameness, individual rights to equal pay and equal opportunity, while their social policy strategies have given high priorities to empowering individual women by strengthening their access to social rights, especially in forms enabling women to attain a degree of individual economic independence. The equity strategies have been strongest in the United States and Canada and to some extent Australia, while the social policy strategies have had greatest success in Australia and to some extent Britain.

The constructions of gender in these policy regimes cannot be explained by liberal ideologies and institutional structures alone. Gender relations are central in the welfare states of virtually all countries, including those commonly identified with other types and political traditions. In contemporary history at least, all social policy regimes confront to some extent labour markets which are segregated by gender and/or marked by gender differentials in pay and conditions, and which rest on an asymmetric division of labour which assigns women the larger share of responsibility for care and other forms of unpaid work. Gender differences in vulnerability to the need for such social support as income maintenance and social services are similarly widespread, as are gender differences in needs for the affirmation and protection of rights to personal security and bodily integrity in and outside marriage, including in rights to reproductive autonomy. The gender dimensions of the four social policy regimes that we have considered share these general features as well as the particularities of their liberal type. So also, it would seem, do the social policy regimes which characterise welfare states of other types.

On this account, the terms which we have used to gender the analysis of liberal social policy regimes have application beyond the liberal type. Drawing on both mainstream and feminist approaches to social policy, this approach brings the multiple gender elements of social policy into the interpretation of capitalist society and political economy. The aim has been to understand states, markets and families through the interplay of gender with class, and to some extent also with race and ethnicity. While our own focus has been on the distinctive form of this interplay when conditioned by liberal ideology, the analysis might equally consider the influence of other political traditions. While we have chosen to frame ours as a comparison among most similar cases, there is equally an argument for comparing cases across a range of types, as Diane Sainsbury (1996) has recently done.

We would suggest that the three-fold institutional structures of state, market and family provide a critical key to the class and gender dimensions of social policy regimes, whatever their type. This triangle of relations invites the kind of comparative study attempted here of variations in the institutional contours of these sectors and the kinds of interfaces between them set up in the social policy regimes of different countries. It is particularly apt in the light of women's increasing participation in paid employment in many countries, and highlights the many and varied policy linkages between work and family life that have developed in different social policy regimes.

Comparative study has particular capacity to illuminate the part social policies play in the gender division of labour across family and economy, and in the associated inequalities in resources, power and social participation as they affect different classes and other social groups. In their turn, these class and gender inequalities are closely interwoven with the structures of the economy, occupation and employment, and with the distributions of opportunity, income and living standards. States, markets and families are implicated together in these policies and their effects. Social policy discussion must also include a concern with the regulatory dimension of state–market relations. In the case of liberal policy regimes this role has largely taken legal form in employment equity legislation and tribunals, whose benefits have generally been most accessible to professionally educated women. Some of these gains are under challenge in all four countries. While regulation in relation to employment equity and associated dimensions may be seen as positive regulation, it must be recognised that there is a negative type of social regulation which increasingly characterises liberal welfare states. This is most acutely reflected in the regulation of sole parents in the United States, not only in relation to increased labour market requirements, but also in the restricting of the duration of benefits and the denial of benefits to those who give birth while on benefits. Negative social regulation undoubtedly takes different and varying forms in the other liberal welfare states and especially in other types of social policy regimes, with differing and varying distributions of benefit. These too can be appreciated through their linkages with states, markets and families.

On the family side, social policy regimes reflect and give rise to different patterns of gender roles and family forms, with policy effects which vary according to gender, class, culture, education and life course circumstances. These patterns are reflected in women's patterns of labour force participation. Expectations about gender and family form central principles of income security and family policies, and we have found policy assumptions about when and how parents and marital partners have different roles or share the same, interchangeable responsibilities to be a fruitful point of entry for understanding their gendered character. These assumptions are important in the frameworks of social rights represented in income security provisions for old age, disability, unemployment and sole parenthood, and in the systems of social stratification which such rights underpin. We have drawn particular attention to the gendering of such rights through their capacity to insulate those who claim them from the full force of the labour market (decommodification), their capacity to support access to the labour market and employment income, and to ensure a measure of personal autonomy against forced economic dependence of oneself and one's children on the income of a marital partner. Although there has been a general trend in policy development away from gender difference towards gender neutrality, this has by no means been uniform or true of all western countries, and the orientation of policy to gender neutrality or gender difference provides a key term for comparative analysis. We have also been concerned to connect states, markets and families with social policy regulation of personal and family life, governing areas such as infant and maternal welfare, fertility control and the broader domain of biopolitics. Our specific concern with the examination of liberal welfare states led us to focus the present discussion on abortion and social policy support for women's reproductive autonomy. This is only one part of a much broader spectrum of issues about the role of the welfare state in reproductive life, whose linkages and parallels with more conventional areas of social policy inquiry invite further exploration. Here, too, we argue that the institutional frameworks of states, markets and families give a productive starting point for exploring a wider range of national regimes and policy fields.

Similarly, the perspective developed here in discussing the role of women's movements in shaping social policy regimes potentially has wider application. Our analysis has been concerned with the way in which gender equality issues have been understood and represented in four liberal polities, and in the relation between the mobilisation strategies of movement groups and the political opportunity structures they have faced, including the nature of the political alliances available to them. Examination of countries in the liberal group has drawn our attention to affinities between movement demands, especially as voiced by their liberal feminist elements, and ideological discourses of freedom and individualism. Such affinities may be less salient in other countries, where movements have made greater, lesser or different demands, or whose political environments have been differently receptive. Hence the same approach may yield quite different insights when applied to other cases.

As we noted in Chapter 1, our aim has been to identify and describe dimensions of commonality and variation in the gender structures of social policy regimes widely regarded as liberal in character. There is further work to be done – and it will be theoretically and empirically challenging – in developing a full causal account of the origins of these commonalities and the sources of variation in the inscription of gender and class in this and other welfare state types. Comparative inquiry has an important role to play in this project, and we look forward to being part of it in continuing research on welfare state formation and restructuring. In the meantime, we hope we have contributed to present understandings of gender and class as key dimensions of social policy, in and beyond the relations of state, market and family in Australia, Canada, Great Britain and the United States.

References

Abella, Rosalie 1991, 'Equality and human rights in Canada: Coping with new issues', *University Affairs*, 22: 20–4.

Abromovitz, Mimi 1988, *Regulating the Lives of Women: Social Welfare Policy from Colonial Times to the Present*, Boston, South End Press.

ABS *see* Australian Bureau of Statistics.

Acker, Joan 1989, *Doing Comparable Worth: Gender, Class, and Pay Equity*, Philadelphia, Temple University Press.

ACTU 1990, *Employer-Supported Child Care*, Melbourne, ACTU.

Adamson, Nancy, Linda Briskin and Margaret McPhail 1988, *Feminist Organizing for Change: The Contemporary Women's Movement in Canada*, Toronto, Oxford University Press.

Affirmative Action Agency 1992, *Quality and Commitment: The Next Steps: The Final Report of the Effectiveness Review of the Affirmative Action (Equal Employment Opportunity for Women) Act 1986*, Canberra, Australian Government Publishing Service.

Alcoff, Linda 1994, 'Cultural feminism versus post-structuralism: The identity crisis in feminist theory', in Nicholas Dirks, Geoff Eley and Sherry Ortner (eds), *Culture/Power/History: A Reader in Contemporary Social Theory*, Princeton, Princeton University Press: 96–122.

Allen, Judith 1990, 'Does feminism need a theory of the state?', in Sophie Watson (ed.), *Playing the State: Australian Feminist Interventions*, London, Verso: 21–38.

Altman, Jon and Will Sanders 1992, 'From exclusion to dependence: Aborigines and the welfare state in Australia', in John Dixon and Robert Scheurell (eds), *Social Welfare for Indigenous Peoples*, London, Routledge.

Amenta, Edwin 1993, 'The state of the art in welfare state research on social spending efforts in capitalist democracies since 1960', *American Journal of Sociology*, 99: 750–63.

Andrew, Caroline 1984, 'Women and the welfare state', *Canadian Journal of Political Science*, 17 (4): 667–83.

Andrews, David M. 1994, 'Capital mobility and state autonomy: Toward a structural theory of international monetary relations', *International Studies Quarterly*, 38: 193–218.

AOSW *see* Australia, Office of the Status of Women.

Australia, National Health and Medical Research Council 1996, *An Information Paper on Termination of Pregnancy in Australia*, Canberra, Australian Government Publishing Service.

Australia, Office of the Status of Women 1995, *Australian Women's Year Book, 1995*, Canberra, Australian Government Publishing Office.

Australia, Office of the Status of Women, Department of the Prime Minister and Cabinet 1991, *National Agenda for Women: Implementation Report*, Canberra, Australian Government Publishing Service.

Australian Bureau of Statistics 1991, *Underemployed Workers in Australia*, Canberra, Australian Government Publishing Service.

—— 1992, *August Labour Force Australia*, Canberra, ABS.

—— 1994, *Distribution and Composition of Employee Earnings and Hours 1993 Survey*, Canberra, Australian Bureau of Statistics.

Australian National Audit Office 1997, *Equity in Employment in the Australian Public Service PSMC and Other Agencies*, Canberra, Australian National Audit Office.

Bacchi, Carol Lee 1990, *Same Difference: Feminism and Sexual Difference*, Sydney, Allen & Unwin.

Baker, Maureen 1995, *Canadian Family Policies: Cross-National Comparisons*, Toronto, University of Toronto Press.

Bakker, Isabella (ed.) 1996, *Rethinking Restructuring: Gender and Change in Canada*, Toronto, University of Toronto Press.

Balbo, Laura 1982, 'The servicing work of women and the capitalist state', *Political Power and Social Theory*, 3: 251–70.

Baldock, Cora V. and Bettina Cass (eds) 1983, *Women, Social Welfare and the State in Australia*, Sydney, Allen & Unwin.

Baldwin, Peter 1990, *The Politics of Social Solidarity: Class Bases of the European Welfare State, 1875–1975*, Cambridge, Cambridge University Press.

Baldwin, Tom 1997, 'Blair: Single mothers must work', *UK Electronic Telegraph*, 1 June.

Bane, Mary Jo 1988, 'Politics and policies of the feminization of poverty', in Margaret Weir, Ann Shola Orloff and Theda Skocpol (eds), *The Politics of Social Policy in the United States*, Princeton, Princeton University Press: 381–96.

Barnett, Bernice McNair 1995, 'Black women's collectivist movement organizations: Their struggles during the "doldrums"', in Myra Marx Ferree and Patricia Yancey Martin (eds), *Feminist Organizations: Harvest of the New Women's Movement*, Philadelphia, Temple University Press: 199–222.

Barrett, Michele and Anne Phillips (eds) 1992, *Destabilizing Theory*, Stanford, Stanford University Press.

Barry, Norman 1990, *Welfare*, Milton Keynes, Open University Press.

Battle, Ken 1997, 'Transformations: Canadian social policy since 1985', Paper presented at the Annual Meeting of the American Sociological Association, Toronto.

Beck, Ulrich 1992, *Risk Society: Towards a New Modernity*, trans. Mark Ritter, London, Sage Publications.

Beckett, Jeremy 1987, *Torres Strait Islanders, Custom and Colonialism*, Cambridge, Cambridge University Press.

Beilharz, Peter 1994, *Transforming Labor: Labour Tradition and the Labor Decade in Australia*, Cambridge, Cambridge University Press.

Bell, Winifred 1965, *Aid to Dependent Children*, New York, Columbia University Press.

Bellingham, Bruce and Mary Pugh Mathis 1994, 'Race, citizenship, and the bio-politics of the maternalist welfare state', *Social Politics*, 1 (2): 157–89.

Bergmann, Barbara and Heidi Hartmann 1995, 'A welfare reform based on help for working parents', *Feminist Economics*, 1 (2): 85–9.

Blank, Rebecca 1997, *It Takes a Nation*, Princeton, Princeton University Press.

Blank, Rebecca and Alan Blinder 1986, 'Macroeconomics, income distribution and poverty', in Sheldon Danziger and Daniel Weinberg (eds), *Fighting Poverty: What Works and What Doesn't*, Cambridge, Harvard University Press: 180–208.

Blank, Rebecca, Gary Burtless, William Dickens, LaDonna Pavetti, and Mark Rom 1995, 'A primer on welfare reform', in Kent Weaver and William Dickens (eds), *Looking Before We Leap: Social Science and Welfare Reform*, Washington, DC, Brookings: 27–74.

Blum, Linda M. 1991, *Between Feminism and Labor: The Significance of the Comparable Worth Movement*, Berkeley, University of California Press.

Bock, Gisela and Pat Thane (eds) 1991, *Maternity and Gender Politics: Women and the Rise of the European Welfare States, 1880s–1950s*, New York, Routledge.

Bolderson, Helen and Deborah Mabbett 1991, *Social Policy and Social Security in Australia, Britain and the USA*, Aldershot, Avebury.

Borchorst, Anette 1994, 'The Scandinavian welfare states – patriarchal, gender neutral or woman-friendly?', *International Journal of Contemporary Sociology*, 31: 1–23.

—— and Birte Siim 1987, 'Women and the advanced welfare state – a new kind of patriarchal power?', in Anne Showstack Sassoon (ed.), *Women and the State*, London, Hutchinson: 128–57.

Boris, Eileen 1995, 'The racialized gendered state: Constructions of citizenship in the United States', *Social Politics*, 2 (2): 160–80.

Bradbury, Bruce 1994, 'The transformation of dependency in the Australian social security system', paper presented at the SPRC Seminar, 'Dependency, the Life Course and Social Policy', Sydney, Social Policy Research Centre, University of New South Wales.

—— 1996, *Income Support for Parents and Other Carers*, SPRC Reports and Proceedings no. 127, Sydney, Social Policy Research Centre, University of New South Wales.

Bradshaw, Jonathan, John Ditch, Hilary Holmes and Peter Whiteford 1993, 'A comparative study of child support in fifteen countries', *Journal of European Social Policy*, 3 (4): 255–71.

Brennan, Deborah 1994, *The Politics of Australian Child Care: From Philanthropy to Feminism*, Cambridge: Cambridge University Press.

Brodie, Janine 1992, 'Choice and no choice in the House', in Janine Brodie, Shelley A. M. Gavigan and Jane Jenson (eds), *The Politics of Abortion*, Toronto, Oxford University Press: 57–116.

—— (ed.) 1995, *Women and Canadian Public Policy*, Toronto, Harcourt Brace.

—— and Jane Jenson 1988, *Crisis, Challenge and Change: Party and Class in Canada Revisited*, Ottawa, Carleton University Press.

Brown, Carol 1981, 'Mothers, fathers and children: From private to public patriarchy', in Lydia Sargent (ed.), *Women and Revolution: A Discussion of the Unhappy Marriage of Marxism and Feminism*, Boston, South End Press: 239–67.

Bryden, Kenneth 1974, *Old Age Pensions and Policy-Making in Canada*, Montreal, McGill-Queen's University Press.

Bryson, Lois 1983, 'Women as welfare recipients: Women, poverty and the state', in Cora V. Baldock and Bettina Cass (eds), *Women, Social Welfare and the State in Australia*, Sydney, Allen & Unwin: 130–45.

—— 1992, *Welfare and the State*, London, Macmillan.

—— 1995, 'Two welfare states: One for women, one for men', in Anne Edwards and Susan Margarey (eds), *Women in a Restructuring Australia*, Sydney, Allen & Unwin: 60–76.

Burchell, Graham, Colin Gordon and Peter Miller (eds), 1991, *The Foucault Effect: Studies in Governmentality*, Chicago, University of Chicago Press.

Burkhauser, Richard and Karen Holden (eds) 1982, *A Challenge to Social Security: The Changing Roles of Women and Men in American Society*, New York, Academic Press.

Burt, Sandra 1990, 'Organized women's groups and the state', in William D. Coleman and Grace Skogstad (eds), *Policy Communities and Public Policy in Canada*, Mississauga, Ontario, Copp Clark Pitman Ltd: 191–211.

Burtless, Gary 1986, 'Public spending for the poor: Trends, prospects and economic limits', in Sheldon Danziger and Daniel Weinberg (eds), *Fighting Poverty: What Works and What Doesn't*, Cambridge, Harvard University Press: 18–49.

Burton, Clare 1985, *Subordination, Feminism and Social Theory*, Sydney, Allen & Unwin.

—— 1991, *The Promise and the Price: The Struggle for Equal Opportunity in Women's Employment*, Sydney, Allen & Unwin.

Bussemaker, Jet and Kees van Kersbergen 1994, 'Gender and welfare states: Some theoretical reflections', in Diane Sainsbury (ed.), *Gendering Welfare States*, London, Sage Publications: 8–25.

Butler, Judith and Joan W. Scott (eds) 1992, *Feminists Theorize the Political*, New York, Routledge.

Callendar, Claire 1992, 'Redundancy, unemployment and poverty', in Caroline Glendinning and Jane Millar (eds), *Women and Poverty in Britain in the 1990s*, London and New York, Harvester Wheatsheaf: 129–48.

Campbell, Robert M. and Leslie A. Pal 1989, *The Real Worlds of Canadian Politics*, Peterborough, Broadview Press.

Canada 1984, *Equality in Employment: A Royal Commission Report*, Ottawa, Minister of Supply and Services Canada.

Canada 1992, *The Government Response to the Report of the Standing Committee on Health and Welfare, Social Affairs, Seniors and the Status of Women*, Ottawa, Government of Canada.

Canada, House of Commons Special Committee on Social Security 1943, *Report on Social Security for Canada*, prepared by Dr L. C. Marsh for the Advisory Committee on Reconstruction, Ottawa, Edmond Cloutier.

Canada, Human Resources Development 1994, 'News release: Lloyd Axworthy Tables New Employment Equity Act', 12 December.

Canada, Special Committee on Child Care 1987, *Sharing the Responsibility*, Ottawa, Parliament of Canada.

Card, David and Richard B. Freeman (eds) 1994, *Small Differences that Matter: Labor Relations and Income Maintenance in Canada and the United States*, Chicago, University of Chicago Press.

Cass, Bettina 1983, 'Redistribution to children and mothers: A history of child endowment and family allowances', in Cora V. Baldock and Bettina Cass (eds), *Women, Social Welfare and the State in Australia*, Sydney, Allen & Unwin: 54–84.

—— 1993, 'Caring work and welfare regimes: Policies for sole parents in four countries', in Sheila Shaver (ed.), *Comparative Perspectives on Sole Parents Policy: Work and Welfare*, SPRC Reports and Proceedings no. 106, Sydney, Social Policy Research Centre, University of New South Wales: 93–106.

—— 1994, 'Citizenship, work and welfare: The dilemma for Australian women', *Social Politics*, 1 (1): 106–24.

Castles, Francis 1985, *The Working Class and Welfare*, Sydney, Allen & Unwin.

—— 1993, 'Changing course in economic policy: The English-speaking nations in the 1980s', in Francis Castles (ed.), *Families of Nations: Patterns of Public Policy in Western Democracies*, Aldershot, Dartmouth: 3–34.

—— 1994, 'The wage earner's welfare state revisited: Refurbishing the established model of Australian social protection, 1983–1993', *Australian Journal of Social Issues*, 29 (2): 120–45.

—— 1996a, 'Australian social policy: Where we are now', *Just Policies* (May): 12–15.

—— 1996b, 'Needs-based strategies of social protection in Australia and New Zealand', in Gøsta Esping-Andersen (ed.), *Welfare States in Transition: National Adaptations in Global Economies*, London, Sage Publications: 88–115.

—— and Peter Mair 1984, 'Left-right political scales: Some "expert" judgements', *European Journal of Political Research*, 12 (1): 73–88.

—— and Deborah Mitchell 1993, 'Worlds of welfare and families of nations', in Francis Castles (ed.), *Families of Nations: Patterns of Public Policy in Western Democracies*, Aldershot, Dartmouth: 93–128.

Cates, W. Jr 1981, 'The Hyde Amendment in Action', *Journal of the American Medical Association*, 246 (10): 1109–12.

Census of Canada 1991, Statistics Canada, Catalogue 93–106, in Statistics Canada, Housing, Family and Social Statistics Division, Target Groups Project, *Women in Canada: A Statistical Report 1990*, 2nd edn, Ottawa, Statistics Canada.

Centre for the American Woman and Politics 1993, *Fact Sheet*, November.

Clement, Wallace and John Myles 1994, *Relations of Ruling: Class and Gender in Postindustrial Societies*, Montreal, Quebec and Kingston, Ontario, McGill-Queen's University Press.

Cohen, Jean L. 1996, 'Democracy, difference, and the right to privacy', in Seyla Benhabib (ed.), *Democracy and Difference: Contesting the Boundaries of the Political*, Princeton, NJ, Princeton University Press: 187–217.

Cohen, Stephen S. and John Zysman 1987, *Manufacturing Matters: The Myth of Post-Industrial Economy*, New York, Basic Books.

Coleman, Karen 1988, 'The politics of abortion in Australia: Freedom, church and state', *Feminist Review*, 29: 79–97.

Collins, Patricia Hill 1990, *Black Feminist Thought: Knowledge, Consciousness, and the Politics of Empowerment*, New York, Routledge.

Commission on Social Justice 1994, *Social Justice: Strategies for National Renewal*, London, Vintage.

Commonwealth of Australia 1992a, *Government Response to 'Half Way to Equal'*, The Report of the Inquiry into Equal Opportunity and Equal Status for Women in Australia by The House of Representatives Standing Committee on Legal and Constitutional Affairs, Canberra, Australian Government Publishing Service.

—— 1992b, *Women in Australia*, Australia's Second Progress Report on Implementing the United Nations' Convention on the Elimination of All Forms of Discrimination Against Women, Canberra, Australian Government Publishing Service.

—— 1994, *Child Care Australia June 1993*, Canberra, Australian Bureau of Statistics, Cat. no. 4402.0.

Connell, R. W. 1987, *Gender and Power*, Stanford, Stanford University Press.

—— 1995, *Masculinities*, Berkeley, University of California Press.

Cooke, Kenneth 1987, 'The withdrawal from paid work of the wives of unemployed men: A review of research', *Journal of Social Policy*, 16 (3): 371–82.

Cooper, Barry, Allan Kornberg and William Mishler (eds) 1988, *The Resurgence of Conservatism in Anglo-American Democracies*, Durham, Duke University Press.

Costain, Anne N. and W. Douglas Costain 1987, 'Strategies and tactics of the women's movement in the United States: The role of political parties', in Mary Fainsod Katzenstein and Carol McClurg Mueller (eds), *The Women's Movements of the United States and Western Europe: Consciousness, Political Opportunity, and Public Policy*, Philadelphia, Temple University Press: 196–214.

Crompton, Rosemary, Linda Hantrais and Pamela Walters 1990, 'Gender relations and employment', *British Journal of Sociology*, 41 (3): 329–50.

Crompton, Susan 1991, 'Who's looking after the kids? Child care arrangements of working mothers', *Perspectives on Labour and Income*, 3 (2): 68–76.

Curthoys, Ann 1994, 'Australian feminism since 1970', in Norma Grieve and Ailsa Burns (eds), *Australian Women*, New York, Oxford University Press: 14–28.

Dale, Angela and Judith Glover 1990, *An Analysis of Women's Employment Patterns in the UK, France and the USA*, London, Department of Employment.

Dale, Jennifer and Peggy Foster 1986, *Feminists and State Welfare*, London, Routledge & Kegan Paul.

Daly, A. E. 1991, 'The impact of welfare on the economic status of Aboriginal women', Discussion Paper no. 7, Canberra, Centre for Aboriginal Economic Policy Research, Australian National University.

Daly, Mary 1994, 'Comparing welfare states: Toward a gender-friendly approach', in Diane Sainsbury (ed.), *Gendering Welfare States*, London, Sage Publications: 101–17.

Daniels, Cynthia R. 1993, *At Women's Expense: State Power and the Politics of Fetal Rights*, Cambridge, Ma., Harvard University Press.

Danziger, Sandra K. and Sheldon Danziger 1995, 'Will welfare recipients find work when welfare ends?', in Isabel V. Sawhill (ed.), *Welfare Reform: An Analysis of the Issue*, Washington, DC, Urban Institute.

Davis, Flora 1991, *Moving the Mountain: The Women's Movement in America Since 1960*, New York, Simon and Schuster.

Day, Shelagh and Stan Persky 1988, *The Supreme Court of Canada Decision on Abortion*, Vancouver, New Star Books Ltd.

Deacon, Desley 1989, *Managing Gender: The State, the New Middle Class and Women Workers, 1890–1930*, Melbourne, Oxford University Press.

DEET *see* Department of Employment, Education and Training.

DeParle, Jason 1997a, 'U.S. welfare system dies as state programs emerge', *New York Times*, 30 June: A1, 10.

—— 1997b, 'Getting Opal Caples to work', *New York Times Magazine*, 24 August: 32–7, 47, 54, 59–61.

—— 1997c, 'Welfare to work: A sequel', *New York Times*, 28 December.

—— 1997d, 'Tougher welfare limits bring surprising results', *New York Times*, 30 December.

Department of Employment, Education and Training, Women's Bureau 1988, *Australian Women's Employment Strategy*, Canberra, Australian Government Publishing Service.

Dex, Shirley 1992, 'Women's part-time work in Britain and the United States', in Barbara D. Warme, Katherina L. P. Lundy and Larry A. Lundy (eds), *Working Part-Time: Risks and Opportunities*, New York, Praeger: 161–74.

—— and Patricia Walters 1989, 'Women's occupational status in Britain, France and the USA', *Industrial Relations Journal*, 20: 203–12.

Dickey, Brian 1980, *No Charity There: A Short History of Social Welfare in Australia*, Sydney, Nelson.

Dobbin, Frank, John R. Sutton, John W. Meyer and W. Richard Scott 1993, 'Equal opportunity law and the construction of internal labor markets', *American Journal of Sociology*, 99 (2): 396–427.

Eardley, Tony and Merrin Thompson 1997, *Does Case Management Help Unemployed Job Seekers?*, SPRC Reports and Proceedings no. 132, Sydney, Social Policy Research Centre, University of New South Wales.

Eardley, Tony, Jonathan Bradshaw, John Ditch, Ian Gough and Peter Whiteford 1996, *Social Assistance in OECD Countries*, vols I and II, Department of Social Security, Research Report nos 46 and 47, London, HMSO.

Economic Council of Canada 1990, *Good Jobs, Bad Jobs: Employment in the Service Economy*, Ottawa, Economic Council of Canada.

Economist 1997, 'Tony Blair's big idea', *Economist* (US edition), 6 December: 59.

Edin, Kathryn and Laura Lein 1997, *Making Ends Meet: How Single Mothers Survive Welfare and Low-Wage Work*, New York, Russell Sage Foundation.

Edwards, Anne and Susan Margarey (eds) 1995, *Women in a Restructuring Australia*, Sydney, Allen & Unwin.

Eisenstein, Hester 1996, *Inside Agitators: Australian Femocrats and the State*, Philadelphia, Temple University Press.

Eisenstein, Zillah 1981, *The Radical Future of Liberal Feminism*, New York, Longman.

Ellingsaeter, Anne Lise 1992, *Part-time Work in European Welfare States*, Oslo, Institute for Social Research.

Ellwood, David 1988, *Poor Support: Poverty in the American Family*, New York, Basic Books.

Employment Gazette 1992, 'Results of the 1991 labour force survey', *Employment Gazette*: 153–73.

England, Paula 1992, *Comparable Worth: Theories and Evidence*, New York, Aldine de Gruyter.

Equal Opportunities Commission 1991, *Pay and Gender in Britain*, London, Industrial Relations Services.

—— 1992, *Pay and Gender in Britain: 2*, London, IRS/EOC.

Ergas, Yasmine 1990, 'Child-care policies in comparative perspective', in OECD (ed.), *Lone-Parent Families: The Economic Challenge*, Paris, OECD.

Esping-Andersen, Gøsta 1985, *Politics Against Markets: The Social Democratic Road To Power*, Princeton, Princeton University Press.

—— 1990, *The Three Worlds of Welfare Capitalism*, Cambridge, Polity Press.

—— 1996a, 'After the golden age? Welfare state dilemmas in a global economy', in Gøsta Esping-Andersen (ed.), *Welfare States in Transition: National Adaptations in Global Economies*, London, Sage Publications: 1–31.

—— (ed.) 1996b, *Welfare States in Transition: National Adaptations in Global Economies*, London, Sage Publications.

—— and Walter Korpi 1987, 'From poor relief to institutional welfare states: The development of Scandinavian social policy', in Robert Erikson, E. J. Hansen, Stein Ringen and Hannu Uusitalo (eds), *The Scandinavian Model: Welfare States and Welfare Research*, New York, M. E. Sharpe: 39–74.

European Commission Childcare Network 1990, *Childcare in the European Community 1985–1990*, Brussels, European Commission.

Eurostat, *Yearbook* 1995, Luxembourg, Office for Official Publication of the European Communities.

Evaluation and Statistical Services Branch, Department of Finance 1993, *Promotional Opportunities for Women in the APS*, Canberra, Australian Department of Finance.

Evans, Patricia 1992, 'Targeting single mothers for employment: Comparisons from the United States, Britain, and Canada', *Social Service Review*, 66: 376–98.

—— 1993, 'From workfare to the social contract: Implications for Canada of recent US welfare reforms', *Canada Public Policy*, 19: 54–67.

—— and Eilene McIntyre 1987, 'Welfare, work incentives and the single mother: An interprovincial comparison', in Jacqueline Ismael (ed.), *The Canadian Welfare State*, Calgary, University of Alberta Press: 101–25.

Ewer, Peter, Ian Hampson, Chris Lloyd, John Rainford, Stephen Rix and Meg Smith 1991, *Politics and the Accord*, Sydney, Pluto Press.

Finch, Janet and Dulcie Groves (eds) 1983, *A Labour of Love: Women, Work and Caring*, Boston, Routledge & Kegan Paul.

Findlay, Sue 1988, 'Facing the state: The politics of the women's movement reconsidered', in Heather Jon Moloney and Meg Luxton (eds), *Feminism and Political Economy*, Toronto, Methuen: 31–50.

Fineman, Martha 1995, *The Neutered Mother, the Sexual Family, and Other Twentieth Century Tragedies*, New York, Routledge.

Flora, Peter 1986, *Growth to Limits: The Western European Welfare States Since World War II*, vol. 1, Berlin, Walter de Gruyter.

—— and Jens Alber 1981, 'Modernization, democratization, and the development of welfare states in Western Europe', in Peter Flora and Arnold J. Heidenheimer (eds), *The Development of Welfare States in Europe and America*, New Brunswick, Transaction Books: 37–80.

Folbre, Nancy 1994, *Who Pays for the Kids? Gender and the Structures of Constraint*, New York, Routledge.

Foucault, Michel 1980, *The History of Sexuality*, vol. 1, New York, Vintage.

Francome, Colin 1984, *Abortion Freedom: A Worldwide Movement*, London, Allen & Unwin.

—— 1988, 'United Kingdom', in Paul Sachdev (ed.), *The International Handbook on Abortion*, New York, Greenwood Press: 458–72.

Franklin, Donna 1997, *Ensuring Inequality: The Structural Transformation of the African-American Family*, New York, Oxford University Press.

Franzway, Suzanne, Dianne Court and R. W. Connell 1989, *Staking a Claim: Feminism, Bureaucracy and the State*, Cambridge, Polity Press.

Fraser, Nancy 1989, 'Women, welfare and the politics of need', in Nancy Fraser, *Unruly Practices*, Minneapolis, University of Minnesota Press: 144–60.

—— 1994, 'After the family wage: Gender equity and the welfare state', *Political Theory*, 22: 591–618.

—— 1997, *Justice Interruptus: Critical Reflections on the 'Postsocialist' Condition*, New York, Routledge.

—— and Linda Gordon 1994, 'A genealogy of dependency: Tracing a keyword of the U.S. welfare state', *Signs*, 19(2): 309–36.

Freeden, Michael 1978, *The New Liberalism: An Ideology of Social Reform*, Oxford, Clarendon Press.

Freeman, Jo 1975, *The Politics of Women's Liberation*, New York, McKay.

—— 1987, 'Whom you know versus whom you represent: Feminist influences in the Democratic and Republican parties', in Mary Fainsod Katzenstein and Carol McClurg Mueller (eds), *The Women's Movements of the United States and Western Europe: Consciousness, Political Opportunity, and Public Policy*, Philadelphia, Temple University Press: 215–44.

Friedman, Dana E. 1991, *Linking Work–Family Issues to the Bottom Line*, New York, The Conference Board.

Friedman, Marilyn 1997, 'Autonomy and social relationships: Rethinking the feminist critique', in Diana Tietjens Meyers (ed.), *Feminists Rethink the Self*, Boulder, Westview: 40–61.

Friedman, Milton 1962, *Capitalism and Freedom*, Chicago, University of Chicago Press.

Fudge, Judy and Patricia McDermott (eds) 1991a, *Just Wages: A Feminist Assessment of Pay Equity*, Toronto, University of Toronto Press.

—— 1991b, 'Pay equity in a declining economy: The challenge ahead', in Judy Fudge and Patricia McDermott (eds), *Just Wages: A Feminist Assessment of Pay Equity*, Toronto, University of Toronto Press: 281–8.

Garfinkel, Irwin and Sara McLanahan 1986, *Single Mothers and Their Children: A New American Dilemma*, Washington, DC, Urban Institute.

Gavigan, Shelley A. M. 1992, 'Beyond *Morgentaler*: The legal regulation of reproduction', in Janine Brodie, Shelley A. M. Gavigan and Jane Jenson (eds), *The Politics of Abortion*, Toronto, Oxford University Press.

Gelb, Joyce 1987, 'Social movement "success": A comparative analysis of feminism in the United States and the United Kingdom', in Mary Fainsod Katzenstein and Carol McClurg Mueller (eds), *The Women's Movements of the United States and Western Europe: Consciousness, Political Opportunity, and Public Policy*, Philadelphia, Temple University Press.

Geller-Schwartz, Linda 1995, 'An array of agencies: Feminism and state institutions in Canada', in Dorothy McBride Stetson and Amy Mazur (eds), *Comparative State Feminism*, London, Sage Publications: 40–58.

Gilbert, Neil and Barbara Gilbert 1989, *The Enabling State*, New York, Oxford University Press.

Gilder, George 1981, *Wealth and Poverty*, New York, Basic Books.

Gillespie, Ed and Bob Schellhas (eds) 1994, *Contract with America: The Bold Plan by Rep. Newt Gingrich, Rep. Dick Armey and the House Republicans to Change the Nation*, New York, Times Books.

Gilligan, Carol 1982, *In a Different Voice: Psychological Theory and Women's Development*, Cambridge, Ma., Harvard University Press.

Ginsburg, Faye 1989, *Contested Lives*, Berkeley, University of California Press.

Glass Ceiling Commission 1995, *Good for Business: Making Full Use of the Nation's Human Capital: The Environmental Scan: A Fact-finding Report of the Federal Glass Ceiling Commission*, Washington, DC, US Department of Labor.

Glendinning, Caroline 1992, '"Community Care": The financial consequences for women', in Caroline Glendinning and Jane Millar (eds), *Women and Poverty in Britain in the 1990s*, London and New York, Harvester Wheatsheaf: 162–75.

Glendon, Mary Ann 1987, *Abortion and Divorce in Western Law*, Cambridge, Ma., Harvard University Press.

Glenn, Evelyn Nakano 1992, 'From servitude to service work: Historical continuities in the racial division of paid reproductive labor', *Signs*, 18: 1–43.

Glezer, Helen 1988, *Maternity Leave in Australia: Employer and Employee Experiences*, Melbourne, Australian Institute of Family Studies.

Gober, Patricia 1997, 'The role of access in explaining state abortion rates', *Social Science and Medicine*, 44 (7): 1003–116.

Goelman, Hillel 1992, 'Day care in Canada', in Michael E. Lamb, Kathleen J. Sternberg, Carl-Philip Hwang and Anders G. Broberg (eds), *Child Care in Context*, Hillsdale, New Jersey, L. Erlbaum: 223–66.

Goldberg, Gertrude 1990, 'Canada: Bordering on the feminization of poverty', in Gertrude Goldberg and Eleanor Kremen (eds), *The Feminization of Poverty: Only in America?*, New York, Praeger: 59–90.

—— and Eleanor Kremen (eds) 1990, *The Feminization of Poverty: Only in America?*, New York, Praeger.

Goodin, Robert, 1985, *Protecting the Vulnerable*, Chicago, University of Chicago Press.

Goodwin, Joanne, 1992, 'An American experiment in paid motherhood: The implementation of mothers' pensions in early twentieth century Chicago', *Gender and History*, 4 (3): 323–42.

Gordon, Linda 1988, 'What does welfare regulate?', *Social Research*, 55: 609–30.

—— (ed.) 1990, *Women, the State and Welfare*, Madison, University of Wisconsin Press.

—— 1994, *Pitied but not Entitled: Single Mothers and the History of Welfare*, New York, Free Press.

—— 1995, 'Putting children first: Women, maternalism, and welfare in the early twentieth century', in Linda K. Kerber, Alice Kessler-Harris and Kathryn K. Sklar (eds), *U.S. History as Women's History: New Feminist Essays*, Chapel Hill, University of North Carolina Press: 63–86.

—— and Nancy Fraser 1994, '"Dependency" demystified: Inscriptions of power in a keyword of the welfare state', *Social Politics*, 1 (1): 14–31.

Gornick, Janet 1992, 'The economic position of working age women, relative to men: A cross-national comparative study', paper presented at ISA Research Committee 19 Workshop, University of Bremen, Germany, September.

—— and Jerry A. Jacobs 1996, 'A cross-national analysis of the wages of part-time workers: Evidence from the United States, the United Kingdom, Canada and Australia', *Work, Employment and Society*, 10 (1): 1–27.

—— 1997, 'Gender, the welfare state, and public employment: A comparative study of seven industrialized countries', Luxembourg Income Study Working Paper no. 168.

——, Marcia Meyers and Katherine Ross 1997, 'Supporting the employment of mothers: Policy variation across fourteen welfare states', *Journal of European Social Policy*, 7: 45–70.

Graham, Hilary 1983, 'Caring: A labour of love', in Janet Finch and Dulcie Groves (eds), *A Labour of Love: Women, Work and Caring*, Boston, Routledge & Kegan Paul: 1–10.

Gray, John 1995, *Liberalism*, 2nd edn, Buckingham, Open University Press.

Great Britain, Inter-departmental Committee on Social Insurance and Allied Services 1942, *Social Insurance and Allied Services*, Report by Sir William Beveridge, London, HMSO.

Gregory, Jeanne 1992, 'Notes and issues, equal pay for work of equal value: The strengths and weaknesses of legislation', *Work, Employment and Society*, 6 (3): 461–73.

Gregory, Robert G. and Ronald C. Duncan 1981, 'Segregated labour market theories and the Australian experience of equal pay for women', *Journal of Post-Keynesian Economics*, 3 (3): 403–28.

Groves, Dulcie 1992, 'Occupational pension provision and women's poverty in old age', in Caroline Glendinning and Jane Millar (eds), *Women and Poverty in Britain in the 1990s*, London and New York, Harvester Wheatsheaf: 193–206.

—— and Janet Finch 1983, 'Natural selection: Perspectives on entitlement to the invalid care allowance', in Janet Finch and Dulcie Groves (eds), *A Labour of Love: Women, Work and Caring*, Boston, Routledge & Kegan Paul: 148–66.

Guest, Dennis 1980, *The Emergence of Social Security in Canada*, Vancouver, University of British Columbia Press.

—— 1997, *The Emergence of Social Security in Canada*, 3rd edn, Vancouver, University of British Columbia Press.

Gustafsson, Siv 1994, 'Childcare and types of welfare states', in Diane Sainsbury (ed.), *Gendering Welfare States*, London, Sage Publications: 45–61.

Haas, Linda 1992, *Equal Parenthood and Social Policy: A Study of Parental Leave in Sweden*, Albany, State University of New York.

Haas-Wilson, Deborah 1993, 'The economic impact of state restrictions on abortion: Parental consent and notification laws and Medicaid funding restrictions', *Journal of Policy Analysis and Management*, 12 (3): 498–511.

Hakim, Catherine 1992, 'Explaining trends in occupational segregation: The measurement, causes, and consequences of the sexual division of labour', *European Sociological Review*, 8, 127–52.

—— 1993a, 'Notes and issues: The myth of rising female employment', *Work, Employment and Society*, 7 (1): 97–120.

—— 1993b, 'Segregated and integrated occupations: A new approach to analysing social change', *European Sociological Review*, 9 (3): 289–314.

—— 1996, *Key Issues in Women's Work*, London, Athlone.

Hall, Phillipa and Di Fruin 1993, 'Gender aspects of enterprise bargaining: The good, the bad and the ugly', in D. E. Morgan (ed.), *Dimensions of Enterprise Bargaining and Organisational Relations*, University of New South Wales Studies in Australian Industrial Relations Monograph no. 36, Kensington, Industrial Relations Research Centre, University of New South Wales.

Hanratty, Maria J. and Rebecca M. Blank 1992, 'Down and out in North America: Recent trends in poverty rates in the United States and Canada', *The Quarterly Journal of Economics*, February: 233–54.

Hantrais, Linda 1993, 'Women, work and welfare in France', in Jane Lewis (ed.), *Women and Social Policies in Europe: Work, Family and the State*, Aldershot, Edward Elgar: 116–37.

Harder, Sarah 1990, 'Flourishing in the mainstream: The U.S. women's movement today', in Sara E. Rix (ed.), *The American Woman, 1990–1991*, New York, Norton.

Harris, Jose 1993, *Private Lives, Public Spirit: Britain 1879–1914*, London, Penguin.

Hartsock, Nancy 1983, *Money, Sex and Power: Toward a Feminist Historical Materialism*, Boston, Northeastern University Press.

Hartz, Louis 1955, *The Liberal Tradition in America: An Interpretation of American Political Thought Since the Revolution*, New York, Harcourt, Brace & World Inc.

—— 1964, *The Founding of New Societies*, New York, Harcourt, Brace & World Inc.

Hawke, Ann 1992, 'How do Australian part-time workers compare to their US counterparts?', Centre for Economic Policy Research, Paper no. 273, Canberra, Australian National University.

Hayek, Friedrich A. 1944, *The Road to Serfdom*, London, Routledge & Kegan Paul.

Health and Welfare Canada 1991, *Inventory of Income Security Programs in Canada, July 1990*, published by authority of the Minister of National Health and Welfare, Ottawa, Minister of Supply and Services, Canada.

Heitlinger, Alena 1993, *Women's Equality, Demography and Public Policies*, London and New York, Macmillan and St Martin's Press.

Henshaw, Stanley K. 1990, 'Induced abortion: A world review, 1990', *Family Planning Perspectives*, 22 (2): 76–89.

Hernes, Helga M. 1987, *Welfare State and Woman Power*, Oslo, Norwegian University Press.

—— 1988, 'The welfare state citizenship of Scandinavian women', in Kathleen B. Jones and Anna G. Jónasdóttir (eds), *The Political Interests of Gender: Developing Theory and Research with a Feminist Face*, London, Sage Publications: 187–213.

Hicks, Alexander and Joya Misra 1993, 'Political resources and the growth of welfare in affluent capitalist democracies, 1960–1982', *American Journal of Sociology*, 99: 668–710.

Hindess, Barry 1987, *Freedom, Equality and the Market: Arguments on Social Policy*, London, Tavistock.

Hirschman, Albert O. 1970, *Exit, Voice, and Loyalty: Responses to Decline in Firms, Organizations and States*, Cambridge, Ma., Harvard University Press.

Hirst, Paul and Grahame Thompson 1996, *Globalization in Question*, Cambridge, Polity Press.

Hobson, Barbara 1990, 'No exit, no voice: Women's economic dependency and the welfare state', *Acta Sociologica*, 33: 235–50,

—— 1993, 'Feminist strategies and gendered discourses in welfare states: Married women's right to work in the United States and Sweden', in Seth Koven and Sonya Michel (eds), *Mothers of a New World: Maternalist Politics and the Origins of Welfare States*, New York, Routledge: 396–430.

—— 1994, 'Solo mothers, social policy regimes and the logics of gender', in Diane Sainsbury (ed.), *Gendering Welfare States*, London, Sage Publications: 170–87.

Hochschild, Airlie R. 1995, 'The culture of politics: Traditional, postmodern, cold-modern, and warm-modern ideals of care', *Social Politics*, 2 (3): 331–46.

Hockin, Thomas A. 1975, *Government in Canada*, New York, W. W. Norton & Co.

Huber, Evelyn and John Stephens 1996, 'Political power and gender in the making of the social democratic service state', Paper presented at the meeting of RC19 of the International Sociological Association, Canberra, August.

——, Charles Ragin and John D. Stephens 1993, 'Social democracy, Christian democracy, constitutional structure, and the welfare state', *American Journal of Sociology*, 99: 711–49.

Huggins, Jackie 1994, 'A contemporary view of Aboriginal women's relationship to the white women's movement', in Norma Grieve and Ailsa Burns (eds), *Australian Women: Contemporary Feminist Thought*, Melbourne, Oxford University Press: 70–9.

ILO 1989, 'Protective legislation on part-time workers', *Conditions of Work Digest*, 8 (1): 58–130.

—— 1993, *Workers with Family Responsibilities*, Geneva, International Labour Office.

IRC (Australian Industrial Relations Commission) 1991, National Wage Case, Canberra, April.

Jaffe, Frederick S., Barbara L. Lindheim and Philip R. Lee 1981, *Abortion Politics, Private Morality and Public Policy*, New York, McGraw-Hill.

Jencks, Christopher and Kathryn Edin 1995, 'Do poor women have the right to bear children?', *The American Prospect*, 20 (Winter): 43–52.

Jenson, Jane 1986, 'Gender and reproduction: Or, babies and the state', *Studies in Political Economy*, 20: 9–45.

—— 1989, '"Different" but not "Exceptional": Canada's permeable fordism', *Canadian Review of Sociology and Anthropology*, 26 (1): 69–94.

—— 1990, 'Representations of gender: Policies to "protect" women workers and infants in France and the United States before 1914', in Linda Gordon (ed.), *Women, the State and Welfare*, Madison, University of Wisconsin Press: 152–77.

—— 1992, 'Getting to *Morgentaler*: From one representation to another', in Janine Brodie, Shelley A. M. Gavigan and Jane Jenson (eds), *The Politics of Abortion*, Toronto, Oxford University Press.

—— 1997a, 'Who cares? Gender and welfare regimes', *Social Politics*, 4 (2): 182–7.

—— 1997b, 'Competing representations: The politics of abortion in Canada', in Caroline Andrew and Sanda Rodgers (eds), *Women and the Canadian State*, Montreal, McGill-Queens University Press.

—— and Rianne Mahon 1993, 'Representing solidarity: Class, gender and crisis in Social-democratic Sweden', *New Left Review*, 201: 76–100.

Johnson, Vivien 1981, *The Last Resort: A Women's Refuge*, Ringwood, Victoria, Penguin.

Jónasdóttir, Anna G. 1988, 'On the concept of interest, women's interests, and the limitations of interest theory', in Kathleen B. Jones and Anna G. Jónasdóttir (eds), *The Political Interests of Gender: Developing Theory and Research with a Feminist Face*, London, Sage Publications: 33–65.

Jones, George 1997, '1m single mothers face call to seek jobs', *UK Electronic Telegraph*, 2 June.

Jones, Helen and Jane Millar (eds), 1996, *The Politics of the Family*, Aldershot, Avebury.

Jones, Kathleen 1990, 'Citizenship in a woman-friendly polity', *Signs*, 15 (4): 781–812.

Joshi, Heather 1992, 'The cost of caring', in Caroline Glendinning and Jane Millar (eds), *Women and Poverty in Britain in the 1990s*, London and New York, Harvester Wheatsheaf: 110–25.

Kahn, Peggy 1992, 'Introduction: Equal pay for work of equal value in Britain and the USA', in Peggy Kahn and Elizabeth Meehan (eds), *Equal Value/Comparable Worth in the UK and the USA*, Basingstoke, Macmillan: 1–29.

Kamerman, Sheila 1986, 'Women, children and poverty: Public policies and female-headed families in industrialized countries', in Barbara Gelpi et al. (eds), *Women and Poverty*, Chicago, University of Chicago Press: 41–63.

Kandiyoti, Deniz 1991, 'Bargaining with patriarchy', in Judith Lorber and Susan Farrell (eds), *The Social Construction of Gender*, Thousand Oaks, Sage Publications: 104–18.

Kaplan, Gisela 1992, *Contemporary Western European Feminism*, London, Allen & Unwin.

Katz, Michael B. 1986, *In the Shadow of the Poorhouse: A Social History of Welfare in America*, New York, Basic Books.

Katzenstein, Mary Fainsod 1987, 'Comparing the feminist movements of the United States and Western Europe: An overview', in Mary Fainsod Katzenstein and Carol McClurg Mueller (eds), *The Women's Movements of the United States and Western Europe: Consciousness, Political Opportunity, and Public Policy*, Philadelphia, Temple University Press: 3–22.

Katzenstein, Mary Fainsod and Carol McClurg Mueller (eds) 1987, *The Women's Movements of the United States and Western Europe: Consciousness, Political Opportunity, and Public Policy*, Philadelphia, Temple University Press.

Kaul, Hjørdis 1991, 'Who cares? Gender inequality and care leave in the Nordic countries', *Acta Sociologica*, 34: 115–25.

Keigher, Sharon M. and Robyn I. Stone 1994, 'The United States of America', in Adalbert Evers, Marja Pijl and Clare Ungerson (eds), *Payments for Care: A Comparative Overview*, Public Policy and Social Welfare no. 16, European Centre Vienna, Aldershot, Avebury: 321–46.

Kessler-Harris, Alice 1995, 'Designing women and old fools: The construction of the Social Security Amendments of 1939', in Linda K. Kerber, Alice Kessler-Harris and Kathryn K. Sklar (eds), *U.S. History as Women's History: New Feminist Essays*, Chapel Hill, University of North Carolina Press: 87–106.

Kewley, Thomas 1973, *Social Security in Australia, 1900–72*, Rev. edn, Sydney, Sydney University Press.

Keynes, John Maynard 1963, *The General Theory of Employment, Interest and Money*, London, Macmillan and Co. Ltd.

King, Anthony, Bruce Bradbury and Marilyn McHugh 1995, *Why Do the Wives of Unemployed Men Have Such Low Employment Rates?*, SPRC Reports and Proceedings no. 125, Sydney, Social Policy Research Centre, University of New South Wales.

Kittay, Eva F. 1997, 'Human dependency and Rawlsian equality', in Diane Tietjens Meyers (ed.), *Feminist Rethink the Self*, Boulder, Westview: 219–66.

Klatch, Rebecca 1990, 'The two worlds of women of the new right', in Louise Tilly and Patricia Gurin (eds), *Women, Politics and Change*, New York, Russell Sage Foundation: 529–52.

Klein, Ethel 1987, 'The diffusion of consciousness in the United States and Western Europe', in Mary Fainsod Katzenstein and Carol McClurg Mueller (eds), *The Women's Movements of the United States and Western Europe: Consciousness, Political Opportunity, and Public Policy*, Philadelphia, Temple University Press: 23–43.

Knijn, Trudie 1994, 'Fish without bikes: Revision of the Dutch welfare state and its consequences for the (in)dependence of single mothers', *Social Politics*, 1: 83–105.

Korpi, Walter 1989, 'Power, politics, and state autonomy in the development of social citizenship', *American Sociological Review*, 54: 309–28.

Korpi, Walter and Joakim Palme 1998, 'The paradox of redistribution and strategies of equality: Welfare state institutions, inequality and poverty in western countries', *American Sociological Review*.

Koven, Seth and Sonya Michel (eds) 1993, *Mothers of a New World: Maternalist Politics and the Origins of Welfare States*, New York, Routledge.

Kudrle, Robert T. and Theodore R. Marmor 1981, 'The development of welfare states in North America', in Peter Flora and Arnold J. Heidenheimer (eds), *The Development of Welfare States in Europe and America*, New Brunswick, Transaction Books: 81–123.

Labour Canada Women's Bureau 1990, *Work-related Child Care in Canada*, Ottawa, Labour Canada.

Lake, Marilyn 1992, 'Mission impossible: How men gave birth to the Australian nation – nationalism, gender and other seminal acts', *Gender and History*, 4: 305–22.

Land, Hilary 1976, 'Women: Supporters or supported?', in Diana Barker and Sheila Allen (eds), *Sexual Divisions and Society: Process and Change*, London, Tavistock: 108–32.

—— 1978, 'Who cares for the family?', *Journal of Social Policy*, 7: 257–84.

Langan, Mary and Ilona Ostner 1991, 'Gender and welfare: Toward a comparative framework', in Graham Room (ed.), *Toward a European Welfare State?*, Bristol, School for Advanced Urban Studies: 127–50.

Lee, Julie-Ann 1994, 'Women and enterprise bargaining: The corset of the 1990s?', *Australian Journal of Public Administration*, 53 (2): 189–200.

Leibfried, Stephan 1992, 'Towards a European welfare state? On integrating poverty regimes into the European Community', in Serge Ferge and J. Eivind Kolberg (eds), *Social Policy in a Changing Europe*, Boulder, Westview: 245–79.

—— and Paul Pierson (eds) 1995, *European Social Policy: Between Fragmentation And Integration*, Washington, DC, Brookings.

Leira, Arnlaug 1992, *Welfare States and Working Mothers*, Cambridge, Cambridge University Press.

Lewis, Jane 1980, *The Politics of Motherhood: Child and Maternal Welfare in England 1900–1939*, London, Croom Helm.

—— 1992, 'Gender and the Development of Welfare Regimes', *Journal of European Social Policy*, 2 (3): 159–73.

—— 1994, 'Gender, the family and women's agency in the building of "welfare states": The British case', *Social History*, 19 (1): 37–55.

—— 1997, 'Gender and welfare regimes: Further thoughts', *Social Politics*, 4: 160–77.

—— (ed.) 1993, *Women and Social Policies in Europe: Work, Family and the State*, Aldershot, Edward Elgar.

—— and Gertrude Åstrom 1992, 'Equality, difference, and state welfare: Labor market and family policies in Sweden', *Feminist Studies*, 18: 59–86.

—— and Celia Davies 1991, 'Protective legislation in Britain, 1870–1990: Equality, difference and their implications for women', *Policy and Politics*, 19 (1): 13–25.

Lieberman, Robert C. 1995, 'Race and the organization of welfare policy', in Paul E. Peterson (ed.), *Classifying by Race*, Princeton, Princeton University Press: 156–87.

Lightman, Ernie S. 1997, '"It's not a walk in the park": Workfare in Ontario', in Eric Shragge (ed.), *Workfare: Ideology for New Under-Class*, Toronto, Garamond Press Ltd: 85–108.

Liljestrand, Petra 1995, 'Legitimate state and illegitimate parents: Donor insemination politics in Sweden', *Social Politics*, 2: 270–304.

Lipset, Seymour M. 1979, *The First New Nation*, New York, W. W. Norton.

—— 1990, *Continental Divide: The Values and Institutions of the United States and Canada*, New York, Routledge.

Lister, Ruth 1990, 'Women, economic dependency and citizenship', *Journal of Social Policy*, 19: 445–67.

—— 1992, *Women's Economic Dependency and Social Security*, Manchester, Equal Opportunities Commission.

—— 1994a, 'Dilemmas in engendering citizenship', paper presented at the Conference 'Crossing Borders', Stockholm, Sweden, May.

—— 1994b, 'The Child Support Act in the United Kingdom', *Social Politics*, 1 (2): 211–22.

—— 1996, 'Back to the family: Family policies and politics under the Major government', in Helen Jones and Jane Millar (eds), *The Politics of the Family*, Aldershot, Avebury: 11–32.

Little, Margaret H. 1995, 'The blurring of boundaries: Private and public welfare for single mothers in Ontario', *Studies in Political Economy*, 47: 89–109.

Lovenduski, Joni 1986, *Women and European Politics: Contemporary Feminism and Public Policy*, Amherst, The University of Massachusetts Press.

—— 1995, 'An emerging advocate: The Equal Opportunities Commission in Great Britain', in Dorothy McBride Stetson and Amy Mazur (eds), *Comparative State Feminism*, London, Sage Publications: 114–31.

—— and Vicky Randall 1993, *Contemporary Feminist Politics: Women and Power in Britain*, Oxford, Oxford University Press.

Lucashenko, Melissa 1994, 'No other truth? Aboriginal women and Australian feminism', *Social Alternatives*, 12 (4): 21–4.

Luker, Kristin 1984, *Abortion and the Politics of Motherhood*, Berkeley, University of California Press.

McCaffery, Edward 1997, *Taxing Women*, Chicago, University of Chicago Press.

MacDonald, Martha 1995, 'Economic restructuring and gender in Canada: Feminist policy initiatives', *World Development*, 23 (11): 2005–17.

McGlen, Nancy E. and Karen O'Connor 1995, *Women, Politics, and American Society*, Englewood Cliffs, New Jersey, Prentice Hall.

McGrath, Ann 1993, '"Beneath the skin": Australian citizenship, rights and Aboriginal women', in Renate Howe (ed.), *Women and the State*, North Melbourne, La Trobe University Press: 99–114.

McHugh, Marilyn and Jane Millar 1997, 'Sole mothers in Australia: Supporting mothers to seek work', in Simon Duncan and Rosalind Edwards (eds), *Single Mothers in International Contexts: Mothers or Workers?*, London, Taylor and Francis: 149–78.

McIntosh, Mary 1978, 'The state and the oppression of women', in Annette Kuhn and Andrea Wolpe (eds), *Feminism and Materialism*, London, Routledge & Kegan Paul: 254–89.

Macintyre, Stuart 1985, *Winners and Losers: The Pursuit of Social Justice in Australia's History*, Sydney, Allen & Unwin.

MacKinnon, Catharine 1989, *Towards a Feminist Theory of the State*, Cambridge, Ma., Harvard University Press.

McLanahan, Sara, Lynne Casper, and Annemette Sørenson 1995, 'Women's roles and women's poverty in eight industrialized countries', in Karen Oppenheim Mason and An-Magritt Jensen (eds), *Gender and Family Change in Industrialized Countries*, Oxford, Oxford University Press, and New York, Clarendon Press: 258–78.

McLaughlin, Ethne and Carol Glendinning 1996, 'Paying for care in Europe: Is there a feminist approach?', in Linda Hantrais and Steen Mangen (eds), *Cross-National Research Methods in the Social Sciences*, London, Pinter.

Macnicol, John 1980, *The Movement for Family Allowances, 1918–45: A Study in Social Policy Development*, London, Heinemann.

Macpherson, C. B. 1962, *The Political Theory of Possessive Individualism*, London, Oxford University Press.

Mandel, Michael 1989, *The Charter of Rights and the Legalization of Politics in Canada*, Toronto, Wall & Thompson.

Marie Stopes International 1997, *UK Fees at Marie Stopes International, 07/03/97*, http://www.mariestopes.org.uk/

Marshall, Thomas H. 1950, *Citizenship and Social Class and Other Essays*, Cambridge, Cambridge University Press.

Mason, John Kenyon 1990, *Medico-Legal Aspects of Reproduction and Parenthood*, Aldershot, Dartmouth.

Melville, Roselyn 1993, 'Turbulent environments: women's refuges, collectivity and the state', unpublished PhD thesis, University of New South Wales.

Meyer, Madonna Harrington 1996, 'Making claims as workers or wives: The distribution of social security benefits', *American Sociological Review*, 61 (June): 449–65.

Michel, Sonya forthcoming, *Children's Interests/Mothers' Rights: The Shaping of America's Child Care Policy*, New Haven, Yale University Press.

—— and Seth Koven 1990, 'Womanly duties: Maternalist politics and the origins of welfare states in France, Germany, Great Britain and the United States, 1880–1920', *The American Historical Review*, 95(4): 1076–108.

Millar, Jane 1989, *Poverty and the Lone-Parent Family: The Challenge to Social Policy*, Brookfield, Avebury.

—— 1992, 'Lone mothers and poverty', in Caroline Glendinning and Jane Millar (eds), *Women and Poverty in Britain in the 1990s*, London and New York, Harvester Wheatsheaf: 149–61.

—— 1994, 'State, family and personal responsibility: The changing balance for lone mothers in the United Kingdom', *Feminist Review*, 48 (Autumn): 24–39.

—— 1996, 'Poor mothers and absent fathers: Support for lone parents in comparative perspective', in Helen Jones and Jane Millar (eds), *The Politics of the Family*, Aldershot, Avebury: 45–64.

—— and Peter Whiteford 1993, 'Child support in lone-parent families: Policies in Australia and the UK', *Policy and Politics*, 21: 59–72.

Mink, Gwendolyn 1994, *Wages of Motherhood: Inequality in the Welfare State, 1917–1942*, Ithaca, Cornell University Press.

—— 1995, 'Wage work, family work and welfare politics', *Feminist Economics*, 1 (2): 95–8.

Mishra, Ramesh 1990, *The Welfare State in Capitalist Society, Policies of Retrenchment and Maintenance in Europe, North America and Australia*, Toronto, University of Toronto Press.

Mitchell, Deborah 1993, 'Sole parents, work and welfare: Evidence from the Luxembourg Income Study', in Sheila Shaver (ed.), *Comparative Perspectives on Sole Parents Policy: Work and Welfare*, SPRC Reports and Proceedings no. 106, Sydney, Social Policy Research Centre, University of New South Wales: 53–89.

—— 1997, 'Family policy in Australia: A review of recent developments', Discussion Paper no. 50, Graduate Program in Public Policy, Australian National University.

—— and Geoffrey Garrett 1996, 'Women and the welfare state in the era of global markets', *Social Politics*, 3: 185–94.

—— and Ann Harding 1993, 'Changes in poverty among families during the 1980s: Poverty gap versus poverty head-count approaches', NATSEM Discussion Paper no. 2, Canberra National Centre for Social and Economic Modelling, University of Canberra.

Mitchell, Margaret 1987, *Caring for Canada's Children: A Special Report on the Crisis in Childcare*, New Democratic Minority Report on Special Committee on Child Care Report, Ottawa, Government of Canada.

Moloney, J. 1989, 'On maternity leave', *Perspectives on Labour and Income*, 1 (2): 26–42.

Molyneux, Maxine 1985, 'Mobilization without emancipation? Women's interests, the state and revolution in Nicaragua', *Feminist Studies*, 11: 227–54.

Monson, Renée A. 1997, 'State-ing sex and gender: Collecting information from mothers and fathers in paternity cases', *Gender & Society*, 11(3): 279–95.

Moore, Barrington 1967, *The Social Origins of Dictatorship and Democracy*, Boston, Beacon.

Moran, Michael and Bruce Wood 1996, 'The globalization of health care policy?', in Philip Gummett (ed.), *Globalization and Public Policy*, Cheltenham, Edward Elgar: 125–42.

Moss, Peter 1991, 'Day care for young children in the United Kingdom', in Edward Melhuish and Peter Moss (eds), *Day care for Young Children: International Perspectives*, London and New York, Routledge.

Mouffe, Chantal (ed.) 1992, *Dimensions of Radical Democracy: Pluralism, Citizenship, Community*, London and New York, Verso.

—— 1995, 'Feminism, citizenship, and radical democratic politics', in Linda Nicholson and Steven Seidman (eds), *Social Postmodernism: Beyond Identity Politics*, Cambridge, Cambridge University Press: 315–31.

Murray, Charles 1984, *Losing Ground: American Social Policy 1950–1980*, New York, Basic Books.

Myles, John 1989, *Old Age in the Welfare State*, Lawrence, University Press of Kansas.

—— 1991a, 'Post-industrialism and the service economy', in Daniel Drache and Meric S. Gertler (eds), *The New Era of Global Competition: State Policy and Market Power*, Montreal, McGill-Queen's University Press.

—— 1991b, 'Social structures and welfare policies: Perspectives for Canada and the United States', Working Paper, Ottawa, Department of Sociology and Anthropology, Carleton University.

—— 1996, 'When markets fail: Social welfare in Canada and the United States', in Gøsta Esping-Andersen (ed.), *Welfare States in Transition: National Adaptations in Global Economies*, London, Sage Publications: 116–40.

—— and Don Black 1986, 'Dependent industrialisation and the Canadian class structure: A comparative analysis', *Canadian Review of Sociology and Anthropology*, 23 (2): 157–81.

—— and Paul Pierson 1997, 'Friedman's revenge: The reform of "liberal" welfare states in Canada and the United States', *Politics and Society*, 25 (4): 443–72.

—— and Les Teichrow 1991, 'The politics of dualism: Pension policy in Canada', in John Myles and Jill Quadagno (eds), *States, Labor Markets and the Future of Old-Age Policy*, Philadelphia, Temple University Press: 84–104.

National Abortion Federation 1997, *Fact Sheet: Economics of Abortion*, 06/27/97, http://www.cais.com/naf/facts/econ.htm

National Council for One Parent Families 1997, *Lone Parents Into the Workplace: The Business Case*, London, NCOPF.

National Council of Welfare 1987, *Welfare in Canada: The Tangled Safety Net*, Ottawa, Minister of Supply and Services, Canada.

—— 1988, *Child Care – A Better Alternative*, Ottawa, Minister of Supply and Services, Canada.

—— 1989, *A Pension Primer*, Ottawa, Minister of Supply and Services, Canada.

—— 1990, *Women and Poverty Revisited*, Ottawa, Minister of Supply and Services, Canada.

—— 1992, *Poverty Profile, 1980–1990*, Ottawa, Minister of Supply and Services, Canada.

Nelson, Barbara 1984, 'Women's poverty and women's citizenship: Some political consequences of economic marginality', *Signs*, 10: 209–32.

—— 1990, 'The origins of the two-channel welfare state: Workmen's compensation and Mothers' Aid', in Linda Gordon (ed.), *Women, the State and Welfare*, Madison, University of Wisconsin Press: 123–51.

—— and Najma Chowdhury (eds) 1994, *Women and Politics Worldwide*, New Haven, Yale University Press.

NHMRC 1996 *see* Australia, National Health and Medical Research Council.

Nisbet, Robert A. 1966, *The Sociological Tradition*, London, Heinemann.

Norris, Pippa 1987, *Politics and Sexual Equality: The Comparative Position of Women in Western Democracies*, Boulder, Rienner.

O'Connor, Julia S. 1993a, 'Citizenship, class, gender and labour market participation in Canada and Australia', in Sheila Shaver (ed.), *Gender, Citizenship and the Labour Market: The Australian and Canadian Welfare States*, SPRC Reports and Proceedings no. 109, Sydney, Social Policy Research Centre, University of New South Wales: 4–37.

—— 1993b, Ownership, class and public policy', in Jim Curtis, Edward Grabb and Neil Guppy (eds) *Social Inequality in Canada: Patterns, Problems, Policies*, Scarborough, Ontario, Prentice Hall Canada: 75–88.

—— 1993c, 'Gender, class and citizenship in the comparative analysis of welfare state regimes: Theoretical and methodological issues', *British Journal of Sociology*, 44: 501–18.

—— 1996, *From women in the welfare state to gendering welfare state regimes*, *Current Sociology*, 44 (2): 1–124.

—— 1998a, 'Employment equality strategies and their representation in the political process in Canada: A story of possibilities, contradictions, and limitations', in Caroline Andrew and Manon Tremblay (eds), *Women and Political Representation in Canada/Les Femmes et la representation politique au Canada*, Ottawa, University of Ottawa Press: 85–112.

—— 1998b, 'Social justice, social citizenship and the welfare state 1965–1995: Canada in comparative context', in Rick Helmes-Hayes and James Curtis (eds), *The Vertical Mosaic Revisited*, Toronto, University of Toronto Press: 180–231.

O'Donnell, Carol and Phillipa Hall 1988, *Getting Equal*, London, Allen & Unwin.

OECD 1985, *The Integration of Women into the Economy*, Paris, OECD.

—— 1988, 'Women's activity, employment and earnings: A review of recent developments', *Employment Outlook*, Paris, September: 129–72.

—— 1989, 'The path to full employment: Structural adjustment for an active society', *Employment Outlook*, July: 7–12.

—— 1990, 'Child care in OECD countries', *Employment Outlook*, Paris, July: 123–51.

—— 1994, *Women and Structural Change: New Perspectives*, Paris, OECD.

—— 1996, 'Earnings inequality, low-paid employment and earnings mobility', *Employment Outlook*, July: 59–108.

Offe, Claus 1984, *The Contradictions of the Welfare State*, Cambridge, Ma., MIT Press.

Office of the Status of Women 1993 (2nd edn), *Women – Shaping and Sharing the Future: The New National Agenda for Women 1993–2000*, Canberra, Australian Government Publishing Service.

Okin, Susan M. 1981, 'Women and the making of the sentimental family', *Philosophy and Public Affairs*, 11 (1): 65–88.

Omi, Michael and Howard Winant 1994, *Racial Formation in the United States*, New York, Routledge.

Ontario Social Assistance Review Committee 1988, *Transitions*, Toronto, Queen's Printer.

Orloff, Ann Shola 1991, 'Gender in early U.S. social policy', *Journal of Policy History*, 3: 249–81.

—— 1993a, *The Politics of Pensions: A Comparative Analysis of Britain, Canada and the United States, 1880–1940*, Madison, University of Wisconsin Press.

—— 1993b, 'Gender and the social rights of citizenship: State policies and gender relations in comparative perspective', *American Sociological Review*, 58 (3): 303–28.

—— 1996, 'Gender and the welfare state', *Annual Review of Sociology*, 22: 51–70.

Ostner, Ilona 1993, 'Slow motion: Women, work and the family in Germany', in Jane Lewis (ed.), *Women and Social Policies in Europe: Work, Family and the State*, Aldershot, Edward Elgar: 92–115.

—— and Jane Lewis 1995, 'Gender and the evolution of European social policies', in Stephan Leibfried and Paul Pierson (eds), *European Social Policy: Between Fragmentation and Integration*, Washington, DC, Brookings: 159–93.

Paintin, David B. 1985, 'Legal abortion in England and Wales', in Ciba Foundation Symposium, *Abortion: Medical Progress and Social Implications*, London, Pitman: 4–20.

Pal, Leslie 1993, *Interests of State: The Politics of Language, Multiculturalism and Feminism in Canada*, Montreal, McGill-Queen's University Press.

Palme, Joakim 1990, 'Pension rights in welfare capitalism: The development of old-age pensions in 18 OECD Countries 1930 to 1985', Stockholm, Sweden, Swedish Institute for Social Research Dissertation Series no. 14.

—— 1997, 'The development of old-age pensions', in Walter Korpi and Joakim Palme, 'Contested citizenship: A century of social policy development in the western world', papers presented at a Conference on 'The Welfare State at the Crossroads', Sigtuna, Sweden.

Parvikko, Tuija 1991, 'Conceptions of gender equality: Similarity and difference', in Elizabeth Meehan and Selma Sevenhuijsen (eds), *Equality Politics and Gender*, London, Sage Publications: 36–51.

Pateman, Carole 1989, *The Disorder of Women*, Cambridge, Polity Press.

Pear, Robert 1997, 'Rewards and penalties vary in states' welfare programs', *New York Times*, 23 February: 16.

Pearce, Diana 1978, 'The feminization of poverty: Women, work and welfare', *Urban and Social Change Review*, 11: 28–36.

—— 1986, 'Toil and trouble: Women workers and unemployment compensation', in Barbara Gelpi et al. (eds), *Women and Poverty*, Chicago, University of Chicago Press: 141–62.

Pedersen, Susan 1993, *Family, Dependence and the Origins of the Welfare State: Britain and France, 1914–1945*, Cambridge, Cambridge University Press.

Pepin, Lucy 1987, *Choices for Childcare: Now and the Future, Liberal Minority Report on the Special Committee on Child Care Report*, Ottawa, Government of Canada.

Petchesky, Rosalind P. 1986, *Abortion and Woman's Choice*, London, Verso.

—— 1995. 'The body as property: A feminist re-vision', in Faye Ginsburg and Rayna Rapp (eds), *Conceiving the New World Order: The Global Politics of Reproduction*, Berkeley, University of California Press: 387–406.

Petersen, Kerry 1993, *Abortion Regimes*, Aldershot, Dartmouth.

—— 1996, 'Abortion laws: Comparative and feminist perspectives in Australia, England and the United States', *Medical Law International*, 2: 77–105.

Phillips, Anne 1993, *Democracy and Difference*, University Park, The Pennsylvania State University Press.

Phoenix, Ann 1996, 'Social constructions of lone motherhood: A case of competing discourses', in Elizabeth Bortolaia Silva (ed.), *Good Enough Mothering? Feminist Perspectives on Lone Motherhood*, London, Routledge: 175–90.

Pierson, Christopher 1991, *Beyond the Welfare State?*, Cambridge, Polity Press.

Pierson, Paul 1994, *Dismantling the Welfare State? Reagan, Thatcher and the Politics of Retrenchment*, Cambridge, Cambridge University Press.

—— 1996, 'The new politics of the welfare state', *World Politics*, 48: 143–79.

Piven, Frances Fox 1985, 'Women and the state: Ideology, power, and the welfare state', in Alice Rossi (ed.), *Gender and the Life Course*, New York, Aldine: 265–87.

—— and Richard A. Cloward 1993, *Regulating the Poor: The Functions of Public Welfare*, rev. 2nd edn, New York, Vintage Books.

Plant, Raymond 1991, *Modern Political Thought*, Oxford, Blackwell.

Polanyi, Karl 1957, *The Great Transformation: The Political and Economic Origins of Our Time*, Boston, Beacon Press.

Pringle, Helen 1997, 'Is abortion illegal?', *Australian Journal of Political Science*, 32 (1): 93–110.

Pringle, Rosemary and Sophie Watson 1992, '"Women's interests" and the post-structuralist state', in Michele Barrett and Anne Phillips (eds), *Destabilizing Theory*, Stanford, Stanford University Press: 53–73.

Probert, Belinda 1997, 'The social shaping of work: Struggles over new boundaries', Keynote Address, National Social Policy Conference, University of New South Wales, July.

Pusey, Michael 1991, *Economic Rationalism in Canberra*, Cambridge, Cambridge University Press.

Quadagno, Jill 1988, *The Transformation of Old Age Security*, Chicago, University of Chicago Press.

—— 1994, *The Color of Welfare: How Racism Undermined the War on Poverty*, New York, Oxford University Press.

Rainwater, Lee 1993, 'The social wage in the income package of working parents', Luxembourg Income Study Working Paper no. 89.

Randall, Vicky 1987, *Women and Politics: An International Perspective*, Chicago, University of Chicago Press.

—— 1995, 'The irresponsible state? The politics of child daycare provision in Britain', *British Journal of Political Science*, 25: 327–48.

—— 1996, 'Feminism and child daycare', *Journal of Social Policy*, 25 (4): 485–505.

Rawson, D. 1991, 'Has the old politics reached an impasse?', in Francis Castles (ed.), *Australia Compared: People, Policies and Politics*, Sydney, Allen & Unwin: 219–38.

Reiger, Kerreen 1985, *The Disenchantment of the Home*, Melbourne, Oxford University Press.

Reskin, Barbara F. and Patricia A. Roos (eds) 1990, *Job Queues, Gender Queues: Explaining Women's Inroads into Male Occupations*, Philadelphia, Temple University Press.

Rhode, Deborah 1994, 'Feminism and the state', *Harvard Law Review*, 107: 1181–208.

Rhodes, Martin 1995, 'A regulatory conundrum: Industrial relations and the "social dimension"', in Stephan Leibfried and Paul Pierson (eds), *European Social Policy: Between Fragmentation and Integration*, Washington, DC, Brookings: 78–122.

—— 1996, 'Globalization and West European welfare states: A critical review of recent debates', *Journal of European Social Policy*, 6 (4): 305–27.

Ries, P. and A. Stone 1992, *The American Woman 1992–93: A Status Report*, New York, W. W. Norton & Co.

Riley, Denise 1988, *'Am I That Name?': Feminism and the Category of 'Women' in History*, Minneapolis, University of Minnesota Press.

Rimlinger, Gaston 1971, *Welfare Policy and Industrialization in Europe, America, and Russia*, New York, John Wiley & Sons.

Roberts, Dorothy 1993, 'Racism and patriarchy in the meaning of motherhood', *Journal of Gender and the Law*, 1: 1–38.

—— 1995, 'Race, gender, and the value of mothers' work', *Social Politics*, 2: 195–207.

—— 1997, *An Excerpt from Killing the Black Body*, New York, Pantheon.

Rodman, Hyman, Betty Sarvis and Joy Walker Bonar 1987, *The Abortion Question*, Columbia University Press.

Rosenfeld, Rachel A. and Arne L. Kalleberg 1990, 'A cross-national comparison of the gender-gap in income', *American Journal of Sociology*, 96 (1): 69–106.

—— 1991, 'Gender inequality in the labour market: A cross-national perspective', *Acta Sociologica*, 34 (3): 207–15.

Ross, Loretta J. 1993, 'African-American women and abortion: 1800–1970', in Stanlie James and Abena Brisea (eds), *Theorising Black Feminisms*, New York, Routledge: 141–59.

Royal Commission on the Status of Women in Canada 1970, *Report*, Ottawa, Queen's Printer.

Rubery, Jill 1988, 'Women and recession: A comparative perspective', in Jill Rubery (ed.), *Women and Recession*, London, Routledge & Kegan Paul: 253–86.

Rubin, Eva R. 1987, *Abortion, Politics and the Courts*, rev. edn, New York, Greenwood Press.

Rubin, Gayle (with Judith Butler) 1994, 'Sexual traffic', *Differences*, 6: 62–99.

Ruggie, Mary 1984, *The State and Working Women*, Princeton, Princeton University Press.

—— 1988, 'Gender, work, and social progress: Some consequences of interest aggregation in Sweden', in Jane Jenson, Elisabeth Hagen, and Ceallaigh Reddy (eds), *Feminization of the Labour Force*, New York, Oxford University Press: 172–88.

Ryan, Edna and Anne Conlon 1975, *Gentle Invaders: Australian Women at Work, 1788–1974*, Sydney, Nelson.

Ryan, Lyndall and Margie Ripper 1993, 'Women, abortion and the state', *Journal of Australian Studies*, 37: 72–86.

Sachdev, Paul 1988a, 'Canada', in Paul Sachdev (ed.), *The International Handbook on Abortion*, New York, Greenwood Press: 66–97.

Sachdev, Paul (ed.) 1988b, *The International Handbook on Abortion*, New York, Greenwood Press.

Sainsbury, Diane 1993, 'Dual welfare and sex segregation of access to social benefits: Income maintenance policies in the UK, the US, the Netherlands and Sweden', *Journal of Social Policy*, 22: 69–98.

—— 1996, *Gender, Equality and Welfare States*, Cambridge, Cambridge University Press.

—— (ed.) 1994, *Gendering Welfare States*, London, Sage Publications.

Sapiro, Virginia 1986, 'The gender basis of American social policy', *Political Science Quarterly*, 101: 221–38.

Saraceno, Chiara 1994, 'The ambivalent familism of the Italian welfare state', *Social Politics*, 1: 60–82.

Sarvasy, Wendy 1992, 'Beyond the difference versus equality policy debate: Postsuffrage feminism, citizenship, and the quest for a feminist welfare state', *Signs*, 17: 329–62.

Sassoon, Anne Showstack (ed.) 1987, *Women and the State*, London, Hutchinson.

Saunders, Peter 1995, 'Improving work incentives in a means-tested welfare system: The 1994 Australian social security reforms', SPRC Discussion Paper no. 56, Sydney, Social Policy Research Centre, University of New South Wales.

—— and George Matheson 1991, 'Sole parent families in Australia', *International Social Security Review*, 44 (3): 51–76.

Sawer, Marian 1990, *'Sisters in Suits': Women and Public Policy in Australia*, Sydney, Allen & Unwin.

—— 1991, 'Why has the women's movement had more influence in Australia than elsewhere?', in Francis Castles (ed.), *Australia Compared: People, Policies and Politics*, Sydney, Allen & Unwin: 258–77.

—— 1995, 'Femocrats in glass towers? The Office of the Status of Women in Australia', in Dorothy McBride Stetson and Amy Mazur (eds), *Comparative State Feminism*, London, Sage Publications.

Schoer, K. 1987, 'Part-time employment: Britain and West Germany', *Cambridge Journal of Economics*, 11: 83–94.

Scott, Joan 1988, 'Gender: A useful category of historical analysis', in Joan Scott, *Gender and the Politics of History*, New York, Columbia University Press: 28–50.

Shaffer, Martha 1994, 'Foetal rights and the regulation of abortion', *McGill Law Journal*, 39 (1): 58–100.

Sharp, Rhonda 1995, 'Women and superannuation: Super bargain or raw deal?', in Anne Edwards and Susan Margarey (eds), *Women in a Restructuring Australia*, St Leonards, NSW, Allen & Unwin: 175–90.

Shaver, Sheila 1987, 'Design for a welfare state: The Joint Parliamentary Committee on Social Security', *Historical Studies*, 22 (8): 411–31.

—— 1989a, 'Social policy regimes: Gender, race and the welfare state', paper presented at the conference on 'Women in the Welfare State', University of Wisconsin, Madison.

—— 1989b, 'Sex and money in the fiscal crisis', in Richard Kennedy (ed.), *Australian Welfare: Historical Sociology*, Melbourne, Macmillan: 154–71.

—— 1990, 'Gender, social policy regimes and the welfare state', SPRC Discussion Paper no. 16, Sydney, Social Policy Research Centre, University of New South Wales.

—— 1991, '"Considerations of mere logic": The Australian age pension and the politics of means testing', in John Myles and Jill Quadagno (eds), *States, Labor Markets and the Future of Old-Age Policy*, Philadelphia, Temple University Press: 105–26.

—— 1995, 'Women, employment and social security', in Anne Edwards and Susan Magarey (eds), *Women in a Restructuring Australia*, St Leonards, NSW, Allen & Unwin: 141–57.

—— 1997, 'Sole parent poverty: How does Australia compare?', in Michael Bittman (ed.), *Poverty in Australia: Dimensions and Policies*, SPRC Reports and Proceedings no. 135, Sydney, Social Policy Research Centre, University of New South Wales: 67–82.

—— and Jonathan Bradshaw 1993, 'The recognition of wifely labour by welfare states', SPRC Discussion Paper no. 44, Sydney, Social Policy Research Centre, University of New South Wales.

Shragge, Eric 1997a, 'Workfare: An overview', in Eric Shragge (ed.), *Workfare: Ideology for New Under-Class*, Toronto, Garamond Press Ltd: 17–34.

Shragge, Eric (ed.) 1997b, *Workfare: Ideology for New Under-Class*, Toronto, Garamond Press Ltd.

Siedlecky, Stefania 1988, 'Australia', in Paul Sachdev (ed.), *The International Handbook on Abortion*, New York, Greenwood Press: 22–35.

—— and Diana Wyndham 1990, *Populate and Perish*, Sydney, Allen & Unwin.

Siim, Birte 1988, 'Towards a feminist rethinking of the welfare state', in Kathleen B. Jones and Anna G. Jónasdóttir (eds), *The Political Interests of Gender: Developing Theory and Research with a Feminist Face*, London, Sage Publications: 160–86.

—— 1990, 'Women and the welfare state: Between private and public dependence, a comparative approach to care work in Denmark and Britain', in Clare Ungerson (ed.), *Gender and Caring Work and Welfare in Britain and Scandinavia*, Toronto, Harvester Wheatsheaf: 80–109.

Sivard, Ruth 1985, *Women: A World Survey*, Washington, DC: World Priorities.

Sklar, Katherine Kish 1993, 'The historical foundations of women's power in the creation of the American welfare state, 1830–1930', in Seth Koven and Sonya Michel (eds), *Mothers of a New World: Maternalist Politics and the Origins of Welfare States*, New York, Routledge: 43–93.

Skocpol, Theda 1992, *Protecting Soldiers and Mothers*, Cambridge, Ma., Harvard University Press.

—— and Gretchen Ritter 1991, 'Gender and the origins of modern social policies in Britain and the United States', *Studies in American Political Development*, 5: 36–93.

Smart, Carol 1989, *Feminism and the Power of Law*, New York, Routledge.

Smeeding, Timothy 1997, 'Reshuffling responsibilities in old age: The United States in a comparative perspective', Luxembourg Income Study Working Paper no. 153.

——, Michael O'Higgins and Lee Rainwater 1990, *Poverty, Inequality and the Distribution of Income in an International Context*, London, Wheatsheaf Books.

——, Barbara Boyle Torrey and Lee Rainwater 1988, 'Patterns of income and poverty: The economic status of children and the elderly in eight countries', in John L. Palmer, Timothy Smeeding and Barbara Boyle Torrey (eds), *The Vulnerable*, Washington, DC, Urban Institute Press: 89–119.

—— 1993, 'Going to extremes: An international perspective on the economic status of the U.S. aged', Luxembourg Income Study Working Paper no. 87.

Smith, Dorothy 1987, *The Everyday World as Problematic*, Boston, Northeastern University Press.

Sollinger, Rickie 1993, '"A complete disaster": Abortion and the politics of hospital abortion committees, 1950–1970', *Feminist Studies*, 19 (2): 241–68.

Spalter-Roth, Roberta and Heidi Hartmann 1994, 'AFDC recipients as care-givers and workers: A feminist approach to income security policy for American women', *Social Politics*, 1 (2): 190–210.

Special Committee on the Review of the Employment Equity Act 1992, *Employment Equity*, Ottawa, Parliament of Canada.

Standing, Guy 1995, 'Labor insecurity through market regulation: Legacy of the 1980s, challenge for the 1990s', in Katherine McFate, Roger Lawson and William J. Wilson (eds), *Poverty, Inequality and the Future of Social Policy: Western States in the New World Order*, New York, Russell Sage Foundation: 153–96.

Stasiulis, Daiva and Nira Yuval-Davis 1995, *Unsettling Settler Societies: Articulations of Gender, Race, Ethnicity, and Class*, Thousand Oaks, Sage Publications.

Statistics Canada 1990, *Women in Canada: A Statistical Report*, Ottawa, Canadian Government Publishing Centre.

—— 1993, *The Labour Force Annual Averages 1991*, Ottawa, Statistics Canada.

—— 1995, *Earnings of Men and Women*, Cat. no. 13–217, Ottawa, Canadian Government Publishing Centre.

Status of Women, Canada 1979, *Towards Equality for Women*, Ottawa, Ministry of Supply and Services.

—— 1986, *Report of the Task Force on Child Care*, Ottawa, Ministry of Supply and Services.

—— 1993, 'Canada's national machinery for the advancement of women: A case study', unpublished document, Status of Women Canada.

Steinberg, Ronnie J. and Alice Cook 1988, 'Policies affecting women's employment in industrial countries', in Anne Helton Stromberg and Shirley Harkness (eds), *Women Working: Theories and Facts in Perspective*, Mountain View, California, Mayfield Publishing Company: 307–28.

Steinmetz, George 1993, *Regulating the Social: The Welfare State and Local Politics in Imperial Germany*, Princeton, Princeton University Press.

Stetson, Dorothy McBride 1995, 'The oldest women's policy agency: The Women's Bureau in the United States', in Dorothy McBride Stetson and Amy Mazur (eds), *Comparative State Feminism*, London, Sage Publications: 254–71.

Stryckman, Judith and Daphne Nahmiash 1994, 'Canada', in Adalbert Evers, Marja Pijl and Clare Ungerson (eds), *Payments for Care: A Comparative Overview*, Public Policy and Social Welfare no. 16, European Centre Vienna, Aldershot, Avebury: 307–20.

Summers, Anne 1994 (1975), *Damned Whores and God's Police* (rev. edn), Ringwood, Victoria, Penguin Australia.

Tarrow, Sidney 1983, 'Struggling to reform: Social movements and policy changes during cycles of protest', Western Societies Occasional Paper no. 15, Ithaca, Center for International Studies.

—— 1994, *Power in Movement: Social Movements, Collective Action and Politics*, Cambridge, Cambridge University Press.

Tatalovich, Raymond 1997, *The Politics of Abortion in the United States and Canada: A Comparative Study*, Armonk, New York, M. E. Sharpe.

Taylor, Charles 1989, *Sources of the Self: The Making of the Modern Identity*, Cambridge, Harvard University Press.

Taylor-Gooby, Peter 1991, 'Welfare State Regimes and Welfare Citizenship', *Journal of European Social Policy*, 1 (2): 93–105.

Thornton, Margaret 1990, *The Liberal Promise: Anti-Discrimination Legislation in Australia*, Melbourne, Oxford University Press.

Tietze, Christopher, Jacqueline D. Forrest and Stanley K. Henshaw 1988, 'United States of America', in Paul Sachdev (ed.), *The International Handbook on Abortion*, New York, Greenwood Press: 473–94.

Tilly, Chris 1991, 'Reasons for the continuing growth of part-time employment', *Monthly Labor Review*, 114 (3): 10–18.

Titmuss, Richard M. 1958, *Essays on the Welfare State*, London, Allen & Unwin.

—— 1974, *Social Policy: An Introduction*, London, Allen & Unwin.

Tronto, Joan 1993, *Moral Boundaries: A Political Argument for an Ethic of Care*, New York, Routledge.

Tuohy, Caroline 1993, 'Social Policy: Two Worlds', in Michael M. Atkinson (ed.), *Governing Canada: Institutions and Public Policy*, Toronto, Harcourt Brace Jovanovitch: 275–305.

UK DSS *see* United Kingdom, Department of Social Security.

Ungerson, Clare 1987, *Policy is Personal: Sex, Gender, and Informal Care*, London, Tavistock.

—— (ed.) 1990, *Gender and Caring, Work and Welfare in Britain and Scandinavia*, Toronto, Harvester Wheatsheaf.

—— 1997, 'The commodification of care: Current policies and future politics', in Barbara Hobson and Anne Marie Berggren (eds), *Crossing Borders: Gender and Citizenship in Transition*, Stockholm, Swedish Council for Planning and Co-ordination of Research: 201–31.

United Kingdom, Department of Social Security 1992, *Social Security Statistics 1992*, Government Statistical Service, London, HMSO.

—— 1996, *Social Security Statistics 1996*, Government Statistical Service, London, The Stationary Office.

United Nations 1995, *The World's Women, 1995: Trends and Statistics*, New York, United Nations.

United States, Bureau of the Census 1993, *Statistical Abstract of the United States: 1993*, 113th edn, Washington, DC, Government Printing Office.

United States, Committee on Ways and Means, House of Representatives 1996, *1996 Green Book: Background Material and Data on Programs Within the Jurisdiction of the Committee on Ways and Means*, Washington, DC, US Government Printing Office.

United States, Department of Health and Human Services Office of Family Assistance 1991, *Characteristics and Financial Circumstances of AFDC Recipients, FY 1991*, Washington, DC, US Department of Health and Human Services.

United States, Social Security Administration 1993, *Statistical Supplement to the Social Security Bulletin, 1992*, Washington, DC, US Department of Health and Human Services.

US CWM *see* United States, Committee on Ways and Means.

Valverde, Mariana 1991, *The Age of Light, Soap, and Water: Moral Reform in English Canada, 1885–1925*, Toronto, McClelland & Stewart.

Vickers, Jill, Patricia Rankin and Christine Appelle 1993, *Politics as if Women Mattered: A Political Analysis of the National Action Committee on the Status of Women*, Toronto, University of Toronto Press.

Vogel, Ursula 1988, 'Under permanent guardianship: Women's condition under modern civil law', in Kathleen B. Jones and Anna G. Jónasdóttir (eds), *The Political Interests of Gender: Developing Theory and Research with a Feminist Face*, London, Sage Publications: 135–59.

—— 1991, 'Is citizenship gender-specific?', in Ursula Vogel and Michael Moran (eds), *The Frontiers of Citizenship*, New York, St Martin's Press: 58–85.

Waerness, Kari 1984, 'Caring as women's work in the welfare state', in Harriet Holter (ed.), *Patriarchy in a Welfare Society*, Oslo, Universitetsforlaget: 67–87.

Wainer, Jo 1997, 'Abortion before the High Court', *Australian Feminist Law Journal*, 7: 133–8.

Walker, Alan 1992, 'The poor relation: Poverty among older women', in Caroline Glendinning and Jane Millar (eds), *Women and Poverty in Britain in the 1990s*, London and New York, Harvester Wheatsheaf: 176–92.

Wasoff, Fran and Sue Morris 1996, 'The Child Support Act: A victory for women?', in Helen Jones and Jane Millar (eds), *The Politics of the Family*, Aldershot, Avebury: 65–82.

Watson, Sophie 1990, 'The state of play: An introduction', in Sophie Watson (ed.), *Playing the State: Australian Feminist Interventions*, London, Verso: 3–20.

Watts, Martin J. 1993, 'Explaining trends in occupational segregation: Some comments', *European Sociological Review*, 9: 315–9.

—— and Judith Rich 1991, 'Equal Opportunity in Australia? The role of part-time employment in occupational sex segregation', *Australian Bulletin of Labour*, June: 155–74.

—— 1992, 'Labour market segmentation and the persistence of occupational sex segregation in Australia', *Australian Economics Papers*, 31 (58): 58–76.

Watts, Rob 1987, *Foundations of the National Welfare State*, Sydney, Allen & Unwin.

Weaver, Kent R. 1998, 'Ending welfare as we know it', in Margaret Weir (ed.), *The Social Divide: Political Parties and the Future of Activist Government*, Washington, DC, and New York, Brookings Institution Press and Russell Sage Foundation: 361–416.

Weiner, Nan and Morley Gunderson 1990, *Pay Equity Issues, Options and Experiences*, Toronto, Butterworths.

Weir, Margaret (ed.) 1998, *The Social Divide: Political Parties and the Future of Activist Government*, Washington, DC, and New York, Brookings Institution Press and Russell Sage Foundation.

——, Ann Shola Orloff and Theda Skocpol (eds) 1988, *The Politics of Social Policy in the United States*, Princeton, Princeton University Press.

Wennemo, Irene 1997, 'Family support', paper presented at a Conference on 'The Welfare State at the Crossroads', Sigtuna, Sweden.

Western, Bruce and Katherine Beckett 1997, 'How unregulated is the U.S. labor market? The dynamics of jobs and jails, 1980–1995', paper presented at the Annual Meeting of the American Sociological Association, Toronto, August.

Whiteford, Peter 1995, 'The use of replacement rates in international comparisons of benefit systems', *International Social Security Review*, 48 (2): 3–30.

Whitehouse, Gillian 1992, 'Legislation and labour market gender inequality: An analysis of OECD countries', *Work, Employment and Society*, 6 (1): 65–8.

Widerberg, Karen 1991, 'Reforms for women – on male terms – the example of the Swedish legislation on parental leave', *International Journal of Sociology of Law*, 19: 27–44.

Williams, Fiona 1989, *Social Policy: A Critical Introduction: Issues of Race, Gender, and Class*, Cambridge, Polity Press.

—— 1995, 'Race/ethnicity, gender and class in welfare states: A framework for comparative analysis', *Social Politics*, 2: 127–59.

Williamson, John and Fred Pampel 1993, *Old-Age Security in Comparative Perspective*, New York, Oxford University Press.

Wilson, Elizabeth 1977, *Women and the Welfare State*, London, Tavistock.

Wilson, William Julius 1997, *When Work Disappears: The World of the New Urban Poor*, New York, Alfred Knopf.

Windebank, Jan 1996, 'To what extent can social policy challenge the dominant ideology of mothering?', *Journal of European Social Policy*, 6: 147–61.

Withorn, Ann 1981, *To Serve the People: An Enquiry Into the Success of Service Delivery as a Social Movement Strategy*, Ann Arbor, University Microfilms.

Wolin, Sheldon S. 1961, *Politics and Vision: Continuity and Innovation in Western Political Thought*, London, Allen & Unwin.

World Health Organization 1995, *World Health Statistics Annual*, Geneva, World Health Organization.

Wright, Erik Olin and Janeen Baxter, with Gunn Elisabeth Birkelund 1995, 'The gender gap in workplace authority in seven nations', *American Sociological Review*, 60 (3): 407–35.

Yeatman, Anna 1990, *Bureaucrats, Technocrats, Femocrats*, Sydney, Allen & Unwin.

—— 1994, *Postmodern Revisionings of the Political*, London, Routledge.

—— 1996, 'Interpreting contemporary contractualism', *Australian Journal of Social Issues*, 31 (1): 39–54.

Young, Iris Marion 1990, *Justice and the Politics of Difference*, Princeton, Princeton University Press.

—— 1994, 'Gender as seriality: Thinking about women as a social collective', *Signs*, 19 (3): 713–38.

Index

266